THE GREATEST SEASON

THE GREATEST SEASON

Warwickshire in the summer of 1994

Patrick Murphy

photographs by Graham Morris

foreword by Ian Bell

FAIRFIELD BOOKS

Fairfield Books
17 George's Road, Bath BA1 6EY
tel: 01225-335813
www.fairfieldbooks.org.uk

PHOTOGRAPHS
The photographs that appear in this book are © Graham Morris

with the exception of the following:

Page 6 © PA Images
Pages 11, 17, 50, 116 © Getty Images
Pages 28, 52, 160, 166 © Roger Wootton
Pages 56, 105, 107, 113, 114, 187, 189 by kind permission of the club

First published 2019

ISBN: 978 1 9996558 6 0

Printed and bound in Great Britain by
CPI Group, Croydon, Surrey

Contents

Jubilant Warwickshire supporters mob Roger Twose and Dermot Reeve at the end of the NatWest final at Lord's in 1993
Somewhere further back on the outfield is the 11-year-old Ian Bell

Foreword by Ian Bell

That 1994 season made me want to become a Warwickshire cricketer. Even now, I get a little nervous seeing some of them, though they became friends – simply because they were heroes to me. I was just twelve that year, at an age when I needed sporting heroes to look up to.

Those three seasons when the Bears won six trophies have been an inspiration for the next generation of Warwickshire players. You look at the quality of overseas players we signed then – Brian Lara, Allan Donald and Shaun Pollock in three successive seasons. You just don't get quality like that for a whole county season anymore. When you factor in such class with the drive, inspiration, hunger and desire to win that the rest of the squad showed, then you have a tremendous group of players.

Clearly they were brilliantly led and coached by Dermot Reeve and Bob Woolmer. Bob had that ability to spot things that made a difference to your game. He was Pakistan coach when I went there with England in 2005. I was just 23, trying to sort out a Test match technique and mental approach. Bob didn't want to be seen coaching an opposition player but he sidled up to me and said quietly, 'Don't grip the bat handle so tightly, relax a little with your bottom hand.' It worked, and I finished England's top scorer in that series. I had worked with him at Warwickshire and knew his special gift of making a player better. He did that for so many at Edgbaston in those great years of the '90s.

My family was steeped in Warwickshire CCC during that period. My dad was a member, and I was a Junior Bear, playing on the Colts Ground then rushing over to watch Brian Lara bat. The year before, I had raced onto the Lord's outfield to celebrate our fantastic victory against all the odds in the NatWest Trophy Final. It was the day that fired my desire to go back there one day as a Warwickshire player.

For some reason our tickets that day saw us sat alongside the Sussex supporters, and they were full of it for most of the match. Once they had gone past 300 we all thought 'game over' and I can still hear the strains of 'Sussex by the Sea', their supporters' song. But then, as it got darker and darker, Asif Din played that amazing innings. When Roger Twose hit the winning run, I was off, jumping around on the grass with my dad, as Dermot Reeve had his bat and helmet nicked!

After that day, it was a major ambition of mine to make a hundred at Lord's in a one-day final for Warwickshire and be Man of the Match. I managed both. From supporter to player at Lord's, it doesn't get much better than that. Whenever I go to Lord's I think of those finals but also the ones in '89 and '93 that inspired me as a boy.

Will Warwickshire's 1994 season be matched by another club? I doubt it. There are only three competitions up for grabs now, rather than four. The game has changed so much in the past twenty years. T20 batting is very different from the four-day approach, and I'm not sure if any one county can be as dominant as Warwickshire in '94 and '95.

In those days only Warwickshire played the reverse sweep whereas now it's an accepted shot. Back then, many felt it was poor cricket. But it was known as the Warwickshire way, encouraged by Bob and Dermot, and became the catalyst for change. Soon many other counties were embracing it. When I was making my way later as a young batsman on the staff, it was just accepted that we had to learn how to reverse sweep.

Dermot was clearly the perfect captain at that time, always pushing his players to be positive. There were a few big characters in that dressing room, but Dermot got them to raise their game. Just five defeats from 43 matches in the '94 season is fantastic. Those players found a way most of the time.

To do justice to such a great achievement is a challenge to a writer, but Pat Murphy has got it spot on. Pat's been around at Edgbaston for more than forty years, I've known him all my career, and he's trusted by both current and former players. He's seen the Bears in good times and bad but always wanted us to do well. Pat's managed to tease some great tales out of the '94 heroes and has brought that historic summer to life.

I hope all Bears supporters find room for this epic story on their bookshelves.

Acknowledgements

This book owes so much to Brian Halford, that excellent Midlands sports reporter, who provided the initial impetus to the project and then some invaluable source material. When Brian handed over the reins to me in sad personal circumstances, he continued to help and encourage selflessly. Any factual errors and/or misplaced conclusions must be laid at my door, while Brian should be suitably garlanded.

The same latitude should be applied to my publisher, Stephen Chalke of Fairfield Books. An exemplary support and sounding-board, Stephen has been a first-class publisher for so many cricket writers down the years, and I know I speak for them also in wishing him a relaxed, yet fulfilling retirement from the trade he has served so singularly.

I am delighted that so many of the photographs in this book have never seen the light of day until now. Graham Morris, one of the best cricket photographers over the past four decades, always seemed to be at the same Warwickshire games as me in 1994, pointing his lens at both the action on the pitch and chronicling the quirky events off it. He has trawled painstakingly through his archives to bring fresh insights from the '94 season. Any gaps have been filled by Roger Wootton, splendid photographer and a cheerful part of the Edgbaston furniture for many years.

Working at the BBC Pebble Mill studios for so many years, it was never a hardship to stroll down the Pershore Road to catch some county cricket and get to know the Warwickshire players. From the start, the likes of David Brown, Neal Abberley, Dennis Amiss, MJK Smith, Steve Rouse, John Jameson and Bob Willis could not have been more helpful or sociable. Enjoyable stints with them in the Extra Cover Bar at close of play cemented friendships that have lasted to this day.

By the time the 1994 season came around, with Warwickshire on the cusp of cricket history, I had happily become part of the scenery at Edgbaston, no doubt outstaying my welcome in the dressing room far too often, happily drinking in the wisdom dispensed by so many fine players. As a reporter for BBC Radio Five Live Sport that summer, it was hardly a chore to divide my time covering England games and the rise and rise of Warwickshire.

Revisiting those deeds of 1994 has been a delight. The Bears' players of that era have been as cheerfully accommodating as ever, while the current administrative staff – led by chief executive Neil Snowball, chairman Norman Gascoigne, cricket operations manager Keith Cook and head of media relations Tom Rawlings – have embraced this celebration of a great achievement by a special group of players.

I thought it a worthwhile exercise to enlist the views of not only those at Edgbaston in 1994, but also the professionals at the other counties. I didn't want the book to appear too 'in house', too hagiographic, so broadening out the assessments of such an achievement needed input from those at the sharp end – who could judge, a quarter of a century on, just what made that Warwickshire side so special. Clearly, the Bears weren't the most popular squad of their time – serial winners often aren't – but not one opposition player from this period cared to minimise the scale of their triumphs. When you win six trophies in 24 months (September 1993 – September 1995), caveats tend to fade swiftly among hard-nosed professionals from other counties.

So this book is dedicated to county cricket and the countless fine people who have played it. Many years ago, my broadcasting hero John Arlott told me the best way to try improving as a cricket reporter was to get to know the players, as he did at Hampshire in the 1940s. I end the analogy with John there, because he was a genius at his trade, the nonpareil – but that pearl of advice proved invaluable for me. The support, co-operation and friendships I have received from county cricketers up and down the land have been a constant pleasure for me in over forty years of cricket broadcasting.

With the health and future of county championship cricket yet again under scrutiny, this is as good a time as any to extol the virtues of this grand old competition. And Warwickshire's historic 1994 season stands out as the benchmark. They weren't too shabby the following season either!

Patrick Murphy
March 2019

Simply the best?

Dermot Reeve never knowingly undersold himself or any of his team-mates in a career that confounded many a sceptic, but surely he's allowed a dose of hyperbole in claiming that Warwickshire's historic 1994 season was 'probably the greatest season any side has ever had in any sport'.

Warwickshire's chairman, MJK Smith, in the past a fine batsman and England captain, a wise old sage and not given to outlandish claims, contents himself with this summary: 'I'm not saying we were the greatest ever that year. I played against some excellent county sides in my time. But I will say that no one threatened to win all four trophies in the same season. So it's the greatest performance by any county team in the history of the game.'

We are no doubt on safer ground confining historic comparisons to cricket, because there are just too many variables when assessing the respective merits of great sides in other sports. You might have thought there were no contenders other than Warwickshire in naming the Team of the Year in the BBC Sports Personality Awards in December 1994 – but Wigan Warriors, the pride of rugby league that year, carried off the bauble.

So best not to attempt grandiose claims – although there are similarities with Warwickshire '94 and the Leicester City team that burgled the 2015/16 Premier League trophy from under the noses of the fancied, gilded thoroughbreds who appeared to doze off for a few months and then couldn't catch a side that put such a premium on the collective, with star players given licence to thrill.

Like Leicester City, Warwickshire went top at the business end of the season – 1 August, to be precise – and never looked like yielding to anyone. That amused and delighted their coach Bob Woolmer: 'I don't believe others realised how well we were playing and how good we were until it was too late. They didn't take us seriously until it was too late. Under the radar was just fine for us.'

Winning championships entails physical and mental stamina, plus match-winning qualities, especially in the long haul of an English summer, with clogged motorways to endure, and varying pitches up and down the land, with little time to practise skills.

Travel, play, recover. Be lucky with injuries, also. At the start of July, Warwickshire played four games in different competitions in the space of seven days and won three of them, including the Benson & Hedges Cup Final at Lord's, with all its accompanying tensions. Warwickshire kept winning. Tim Munton summed up the prolonged challenge: 'After a time, every match felt like a cup final. It was fantastic. Pressure, what pressure?'

If you can scoop two trophies out of the four on offer in recent decades, then you've had an excellent season. Warwickshire won, in effect, two championships – the blue riband and the Sunday League – losing just four games out of 34. A season that began on 28 April was still vital for Warwickshire until 18 September, when the AXA Equity & Law League was won on a dank, cheerless Sunday in Bristol. In between, they won the Benson & Hedges Cup and were thwarted by the toss of the coin in losing the NatWest Final.

Three trophies and one second. Unprecedented in the English game. Since 1972, four trophies had been there for the taking every season and only six other sides had landed the double of championship and a knock-out trophy in the same summer. None managed the championship and two other trophies. Other than Warwickshire in 1994, only Gloucestershire in 2000 have secured three trophies in one summer, but their three did not include the championship – they finished fourth in Division Two. And no one in the English game would deny that the championship title remains the most coveted, the true test of enduring quality. Gloucestershire never got close to it during their golden run of seven knockout trophies in six seasons from 1999 to 2004.

Of course, MJK Smith is right to extol great county sides from other eras. Surrey won the county championship for seven successive seasons in the 1950s, while Yorkshire twice won four titles in a row in the 1920s and 1930s. They also won seven titles in ten years from 1959 onwards, while the best sustained performance of the modern age is that of Essex, with five in ten years from 1983.

But we keep returning to the facts. In 1994 Warwickshire played 43 competitive games, won

32 of them, lost just five, drew five, and there was one no-result. The winning championship margin of 42 points was the largest since Essex in 1979. Their run rate per 100 balls was 61.11, far superior to their nearest rivals for the title, Leicestershire (52.74) and Nottinghamshire (49.52). There were some mutterings around the shires that year about the Edgbaston pitches favouring Warwickshire, yet of their 11 championship victories, six were away from home and in the County Pitches Table of Merit, they finished fourth out of 18.

So many of the cognoscenti failed to spot Warwickshire's potential at the start of that season (16/1 to win the title) that some hasty revisionism was in order when the juggernaut started to roll ominously on. The tag of 'Larashire' stuck for a time. Warwickshire had been amazingly lucky to land the services of Brian Lara just a few days before he posted the world record Test score of 375 in Antigua against England. Within 11 days Lara had played the first of many ravishing hundreds for Warwickshire, whose players and supporters could not believe their good fortune.

Lara's contract was worth £40,000, which was grand larceny when you consider what he achieved from Antigua onwards. His salary was paid three times over by the huge spike in new members at Edgbaston, and his arrival and achievements simply galvanised all at the club.

MJK Smith, who played alongside the great West Indian Rohan Kanhai at Edgbaston, tried and failed as England captain to dismiss Garry Sobers cheaply and watched Viv Richards decimate many attacks while summarising for BBC TV, weighs his words carefully when assessing Lara's first careless rapture in April/May 1994: 'I haven't seen anyone bat better than Brian in those first six weeks with us. He certainly gave value for money!'

Lara did not just intimidate opposition bowlers, entrance spectators and thrill the club's marketing department. He inspired his new team-mates, making them believe anything was possible. He scored at a phenomenal rate, his championship runs accruing at five and a half per over, giving Warwickshire so much more time to bowl out the opposition twice, always the most satisfactory way to win championship games. Soon the word on the county grapevine was

loud and unanimous: 'Don't set Warwickshire targets in a run chase. With Lara, anything's possible.'

But it was ridiculous to brand them as a one-man team. Yes, they had the world's best batsman, an authentic genius. But they had the championship's best wicket-keeper in Keith Piper, a balanced bowling attack suitable for all surfaces, the best captain in Dermot Reeve with a tremendous deputy in Tim Munton, an outstanding slip cordon who seemed equipped with fly-paper hands, and in Trevor Penney and Dominic Ostler the finest fielders in the land.

Penney's expertise in the backward point area, his dazzling speed and footwork, his knack of invariably hitting the stumps while seemingly off-balance was now acknowledged on the county circuit. Yet batsmen, brains frazzled by his presence, still took him on. Ostler, prehensile in the slips and athletic in the outfield, with a remarkably powerful throwing arm, wins this accolade from MJK Smith: 'I haven't seen a better all-round fielder in my sixty years at the club than Dominic Ostler.'

Time and again that season a moment of fielding brilliance rescued Warwickshire. Yeomen characters like Gladstone Small, Tim Munton, Andy Moles and Neil Smith – none of them greyhounds in the field – raised their standards, inspired by the brilliance of the younger players around them, tapping into the pre-season demands of Woolmer and Reeve that every player could improve his fielding.

So many personal challenges drove on Lara's unheralded team-mates in 1994. Paul Smith, that mercurial all-rounder and match-winner when the planets were favourably aligned, had been in many mediocre Warwickshire sides in the 1980s and was desperate to make a statement before a deteriorating knee finished his career. 'I was just fed up with us losing so often and playing poorly. We weren't stretched enough in the '80s, too many were happy just to score a thousand runs or take a few wickets and hope for a benefit. I wanted to be excited. And win things.'

Keith Piper, a superb, natural wicket-keeper but lacking concentration in previous seasons, soon knuckled down in 1994, when he found a supportive, helpful soul-mate in Lara. Piper, a young man with a lively social life and relaxed attitude to time-keeping, took to getting to the ground an hour early to help

standing: MJK Smith, Bob Woolmer, Trevor Penney, Keith Piper, Neil Smith, Dominic Ostler, Dickie Davis, Michael Bell, Roger Twose, Asif Din, Dennis Amiss

sitting: Paul Smith, Tim Munton, Dermot Reeve, Gladstone Small, Brian Lara

Absent but playing key roles later: Andy Moles, Dougie Brown, Graeme Welch

others. 'The guys couldn't believe it. I was giving throw-downs to Brian, he was helping me with my practice, and everyone was mucking in. The fielding practice was sharp and competitive. That paid off when we walked onto the park.'

Neil Smith remembers the times when the team was in trouble and someone had to bail his mates out. 'It always panned out, where someone dug us out of a hole. Time and again, someone stepped up to the plate. Our team spirit was incredible. You simply trusted your mates totally.'

Gladstone Small, a first-team regular since 1980, an Ashes winner with England, knows the elements necessary to forge an excellent team spirit. 'Ours wasn't a factional dressing room, everyone trusted each other as cricketers. We were the best-coached team in England, with all of us encouraged to work at our skills and try them out in the middle, with no recriminations if you failed.' Small didn't even mind

when the younger players mischievously pinched his bottom in the showers, joking he had the best buttocks on the circuit!

It still seems amazing that, of the 34 cricketers chosen by England's selectors for two tours in the winter of 1994/95, only Keith Piper from the county team of the year got on the 'A' tour to India. Around that time, the supremo of England Raymond Illingworth opined that Warwickshire's season was just a fluke, that the old order would soon be restored. That probably explains his unimaginative selections. Illingworth's reaction to Warwickshire winning the title and the NatWest Trophy in 1995 is not recorded. That made six trophies in 24 months for the Bears. Larashire, anyone?

By the time Warwickshire had wrapped up the title on 2 September, beating Hampshire by an innings, the accolades from within the county game had started to rain down on them. Mark Nicholas, Hampshire's captain that day, was a massive fan. 'They just hung on in there. You often think in professional sport – can this go on? Self-doubt starts to creep in because of success, but they had the momentum and key contributions seemed to come from everyone. Never in seventeen years of professional cricket have I come across less self-centred play. Never have I seen cricketers more tickled by each other's success – or so bent on cameos that mean nothing in averages but mean everything in victory.'

Matthew Fleming was a key figure in Kent's team that year. He had been an army officer in the Royal Green Jackets before county cricket, later captained Kent and played one-day cricket for England. He has since forged a successful business career. His take on Warwickshire 1994 is interesting. 'I consider them now as a business model and a hugely successful one at that. They had a mixture of noisy, irritating players, led by the annoying Reeve and really sound, likeable guys. But they had an aura, the sum of the disparate parts. What comes first, the dynamic leader/chief executive or the committed, talented workforce who then inspire the leader? I'm not sure, but Warwickshire certainly got it right.'

Certainly no one shied away from making tough decisions at the club. When it looked as if Manoj Prabhakar's ankle injury would prevent him playing at the start of the season, the new chief executive Dennis Amiss thanked him for his pains and immediately focused on landing Lara. Later in the summer, Amiss had no qualms in telling the captain Reeve that his form didn't warrant a place in the championship side, that Munton would lead the team and Reeve should concentrate on skippering the one-day unit. Amiss was also determined to hold the ring on the deteriorating relationship midsummer between Lara and Reeve, intent on steering a diplomatic course, banking on the rest of the squad to stick together. 'I basically said we were winning everything, that Brian was central

to all that and we had to understand the pressures he was under. Keep winning and you'd pick up enough bonuses and glory to make it all worthwhile.'

There was stability and continuity off the field, to help the hothouse atmosphere of the dressing room when matters inevitably got a tad heated over the course of a long season. As well as MJK Smith and Dennis Amiss in key roles, there was another former Warwickshire player as head groundsman in Steve Rouse. Rouse had played in the side that won the championship in 1972 and, underneath the gruff exterior, Rouse wanted the Bears to prosper. He enjoyed an excellent working relationship with coach Woolmer and captain Reeve.

Mark Nicholas believes the presence of those former Bears players was important. 'Good fellowship, blokes who really cared about the club and could do something tangible about it. Perhaps other counties should do the same. Look at Amiss – a gentle, kind person but as a player he was as tough as they come and he was the same as chief exec when he had to be.'

Amiss's most significant decision came in 1991, as chairman of cricket, when he persuaded the club to plump for Bob Woolmer as the new coach. Without Woolmer, there would have been no treble three years later. He was that influential, that creative, so far ahead of his time. The Warwickshire players of that period still rhapsodise about Woolmer's enthusiasm, knowledge, tactical innovation, boldness, his unerring knack of finding a nugget that would add an extra one per cent to the team dynamic.

Genius is the infinite capacity for taking pains, it was once said, and Woolmer and Reeve undoubtedly deserved all the accolades coming their way in September 1994 for their vision, dynamism, attention to detail and quirkiness.

But the path to history at Edgbaston had already been mapped out by another captain/coach combination a couple of years earlier.

Warwickshire in 1994

Chairman	MJK Smith
Chief Executive	Dennis Amiss
Director of Coaching	Bob Woolmer
Head Groundsman	Steve Rouse
Scorer	Alex Davis

	place of birth	born	f/c debut for Warks
Dermot Reeve *(captain)*	Hong Kong	1963	1988
Tim Munton *(vice-captain)*	Melton Mowbray	1965	1985
Asif Din	Uganda	1960	1981
Michael Bell	Birmingham	1966	1992
Dougie Brown	Stirling	1969	1992
Michael Burns	Barrow	1969	1992
Richard Davis	Margate	1966	1994
Brian Lara	Trinidad	1969	1994
Andy Moles	Solihull	1961	1986
Dominic Ostler	Solihull	1970	1990
Trevor Penney	Rhodesia	1968	1992
Keith Piper	Leicester	1969	1989
Jason Ratcliffe	Solihull	1969	1988
Gladstone Small	Barbados	1961	1980
Neil Smith	Birmingham	1967	1987
Paul Smith	Gosforth	1964	1982
Roger Twose	Torquay	1968	1989
Graeme Welch	Durham	1972	1994

Dermot Reeve played for Sussex from 1983 to 1987
Dickie Davis played for Kent from 1986 to 1993

Before the Season

Installing the building blocks

Warwickshire did not suddenly rock up at Edgbaston in April 1994 and start playing outstanding cricket. It had taken years to get to that special place where the players were so confident of their worth, the collective will, awareness of their own individual games, with total trust in their captain and coach. Even before all the hooplah associated with Brian Lara's arrival, there was a serenity about the team, who were happily approaching the season under the radar.

The gestation period had taken six years. It started when a new captain/coach combination joined forces in 1988. Warwickshire were in a trough, a slough of despond. In 12 of the previous 15 seasons, they had finished in the bottom half of the championship. Apart from a solitary triumph in winning the John Player League in 1980, their one-day record was dismal. Too often Edgbaston resembled a concrete mausoleum, resounding to jeers of 'Roobish! Take him off!' as the disconsolate players shrivelled at the derision.

Andy Lloyd and Bob Cottam were determined to change all that. Lloyd had been a first-team batsman for a decade, and briefly an England opener before he ducked into a short ball from Malcolm Marshall and retired hurt in his first and only Test innings. Cottam, a fine seam bowler who played four times for England, was a superb bowling coach who later performed that role on England tours. He came with a reputation of being happy to apply the boot to the posterior in any dressing room he inhabited.

'I told the players that it was time they stood up to be counted, to start earning a new two-year contract,' says Cottam. 'Too many of them were just coasting, they had soft underbellies.' Andy Moles, by then an established opening batsman, remembers some harsh strictures: 'Bob used to say we were all too comfortable, nice and comfy in our fur-lined jockstraps. The easy life had to stop. Bob and Andy challenged us, put the blueprint down, and then Bob Woolmer and Dermot kept the ball rolling.'

That gentle soul Asif Din summed it up pithily: 'Bob and Andy hardened up our bellies.'

Cottam also had a sharp eye for a youngster's potential. In his three years at Edgbaston he signed Keith Piper, Roger Twose, Trevor Penney, Dougie Brown and Graeme Welch as well as approving the capture of Dominic Ostler on the recommendation of one of the other coaches, Neal Abberley. 'I looked for character in a young player, someone who wouldn't go into his shell over a bollocking but fight back, determined to prove me wrong.' The comfort zone at Edgbaston was now being blown apart.

Cottam's expertise in coaching bowlers was obvious. He transformed Tim Munton from being a steady fast-medium bowler into an England player inside a couple of years. 'Tim was never going to be a better fast bowler so we worked on developing an awkward length, learning the rudiments of swing, with various grips, releasing the ball at the right moment with subtle variations in pace. He was a joy to work with.'

Munton returns the compliment: 'Bob Cottam was the major influence in my career. In the 1989/90 season, day after day in the Edgbaston nets, he transformed my bowling.' In the process Munton became a vital, cherished member of a hugely successful Warwickshire team.

The Cottam/Lloyd combo did not get off to a particularly harmonious start when the coach suggested, with his usual tact, that the captain might consider dropping himself from the hurly-burly of the Sunday League. That advice was summarily ignored by Lloyd, and Cottam settled down to a congenial enough working pattern: 'I did the background stuff and left Andy to do all the necessary on the pitch. I wasn't one of those coaches who send out messages to the captain every five minutes or so. It worked well enough.'

It seemed to do so. From 1988, for the next five seasons, Warwickshire stayed in the championship's top six (second in 1991), won the NatWest Trophy in 1989 and reached the semi-finals in '91 and '92. There were encouraging signs that the new crop of young players was tougher, braver and less disposed to chugging along in the hope of a benefit. The emergence of a young fast bowler in the South African Allan Donald gave the side an overdue cutting edge.

Donald was excellently handled by Andy Lloyd, who wisely realised that his precious cargo must not be overburdened. 'Ease and grace, AD, ease and grace,' the captain used to counsel his strike bowler, and he responded magnificently season after season.

Lloyd remembers the defeatist mindset of those early days only too well. 'I took over a team that was only too happy to draw games. That had to stop.' He pinpoints a championship match at Edgbaston in the '88 season when he felt he made an important breakthrough with his players. Against the reigning county champions, Nottinghamshire, the match was dawdling along on a slow pitch. Lloyd told Tim Robinson, his opposite number, that he would make a sporting declaration if some easy runs were offered in the next few overs. That transpired, but then Lloyd astonished his players by declaring on 111/4, setting Nottinghamshire just 206 to win in 49 overs. Lloyd had to face some apoplectic bowlers in his dressing room but, after winning them round, they bowled out their opponents for 44.

'I went from villain to hero in just a couple of hours. Afterwards I closed the dressing-room door and said we had to start looking at ourselves, be more positive, because we had one of the best seam attacks in the country and a lot of promise in that squad. From then on, we changed our attitude, going for victories. We also played the games at a quicker pace, didn't let things stagnate, waiting for something to turn up. The young players picked up on that and started to believe we really could win more often.'

One of those young players was Dominic Ostler, who loved being at the heart of Lloyd's thought processes. Lloyd nicknamed him 'Parker' after Lady Penelope's chauffeur in the TV series *Thunderbirds*, as Ostler drove his captain to the away matches, drinking in the knowledge. 'Andy was a great guy, really funny, and I loved those conversations. At the start of the '91 season he mapped out how our championship would pan out, homing in on the matches he was certain we could win and where the opposition teams were vulnerable. He was right in so many of his forecasts.'

It was Lloyd who turned Ostler into such a tremendous slip fielder, to add to his gathering prowess as an out-fielder. 'I had never practised slip fielding, and one day against Sussex I was grazing down at third man. The captain was getting very annoyed at catches getting dropped in the slips. Suddenly he shouted, "Parker! Get up here in the slips now!" I slipped in, caught a couple and loved it – diving full length, showing off, telling Piper to bend his back. That was typical Andy Lloyd, backing a hunch.'

Lloyd, a devotee of National Hunt racing and a regular, genial presence on Midlands racetracks, was always happy to take a punt as Warwickshire's captain, and his countless hunches appealed to his team as he slowly gained respect. A bibulous, gregarious character, Lloyd was a popular figure on the county circuit, but his bonhomie was kept at bay when he stepped onto the pitch, leading his players. The game face was truly donned, as his good friend Mark Nicholas remembers from the days when he captained Hampshire.

'We were playing at Portsmouth, and Allan Donald was now a serious, genuinely fast bowler. I opened the batting with Paul Terry and prepared to take strike from Donald. I looked back and saw Piper, yards away. I later found out it was a distance of 29 paces – miles back! I said to Paul, "Are they taking the piss out of me? We'll have to run if it's on the way to Piper – how else are we going to score?" I took first ball, and there was my mate Andy Lloyd right under my nose at silly point. I asked him why he was so quiet, and he just looked straight through me, stony-faced. That morning I was his enemy, not his friend; he wouldn't engage with me. It summed up how Andy was intent on transforming Warwickshire.'

After three seasons Bob Cottam left Warwickshire, tired of committee influence, frustrated that they wouldn't back him in trying to sign the Gloucestershire all-rounder Kevin Curran. 'I was just worn down by all the politics. But I was absolutely delighted by all the players' success a few years later.'

In the winter of 1990/91 Andy Lloyd played another crucial part in the rise and rise of the Bears. Dennis Amiss, now the chairman of cricket after his distinguished playing career had ended three years earlier, wanted Bob Woolmer to be Cottam's successor. Woolmer had played in the same England team as Amiss, they had both been banned by England for playing for Kerry Packer and South African Breweries. They were firm friends.

First trophy for Warwickshire for nine years
Left to right: Neal Abberley (assistant coach), Gladstone Small, Paul Smith, Allan Donald, Geoff Humpage, Bob Cottam (cricket manager/coach), Andy Lloyd (captain), Tim Munton, Alvin Kallicharran, Neil Smith, Asif Din, Andy Moles

Amiss lobbied hard for Woolmer, arguing that his blend of innovation and expertise made him the ideal candidate. But he was smart enough to acknowledge that the captain had to be on board in the decision on such a vital role. Their working relationship was central to the appointment. So Lloyd visited Woolmer in his home at Cape Town. After a congenial barbecue they sat in Woolmer's study and talked for three hours about Warwickshire. 'I told Bob all I knew about my players and where they could improve. Within a few days he had sent me a detailed summary, with stacks of ideas. Very impressive.'

Lloyd recommended Woolmer fulsomely, and his appointment was swiftly confirmed.

Woolmer arrived fizzing with ideas, and on the 1991 pre-season tour to Trinidad he swamped the players with innovative ideas. He demanded an improvement in the way they played the spinners; he said they had to learn how to sweep and also to reverse sweep. No more playing defensively against the spinners with a straight bat, because it may get you out and you're also not getting many runs because you're defending. Woolmer said they didn't work the ball around enough, they were too content to wait for the loose ball which rarely comes from a good spinner. They must look to dominate the spinners from the first ball; maidens were no longer allowed.

Andy Lloyd was fully in agreement, and in his mid-30s he started to play the sweep, which Woolmer appreciated. 'The younger players would see a senior batsman change his approach to playing spinners, and hopefully they would tap into this dynamic, new approach.' They did. All Woolmer asked is that they practised the sweep and reverse sweep diligently in the nets before trying it out in the middle. Then, if they failed by playing it, there would be no recriminations.

Dermot Reeve was enthusiastically on board, having his misgivings confirmed about his side's conformity against spinners. Reeve was a daring batsman against spin in one-day games, yet he reckoned he was only dismissed three times in his career playing the reverse sweep. For him it was a business stroke, simple common sense, designed to upset the spinners. Premeditate the shot, be ready to extemporise. And practise it zealously.

Reeve maintains Warwickshire's daring against spin was the single most important factor in their 1994 triumphs, with the genesis that Cape Town meeting in 1991. The facts support him. Against spinners in the Sunday League and NatWest competitions in 1994 they scored 44 runs for each wicket they lost at a rate of 5.5 runs an over – where their opponents scored 16 runs per wicket at a rate of 3.8 an over.

Woolmer, Lloyd and Reeve saw the sweep and the reverse sweep as personal crusades over the next few years, winning over not just the players but also some influential people at the club. Dennis Amiss walked into the dressing room one day and told young Dominic Ostler he didn't like to see him playing the reverse sweep, that the best way to hit the off-spinner was to get down the pitch and hit him inside out over extra cover. Woolmer told Amiss not to interfere, which impressed those present. They knew that Woolmer and Amiss were such good friends and that Woolmer owed his position at the club to Amiss. But Woolmer would not be swayed.

Surrey's off-spinner James Boiling unwittingly landed two young batsmen in some strife, after they had failed against him in two Sunday League matches. Jason Ratcliffe just could not get going against Boiling, and the asking rate soared to 10 an over. He then got out to Boiling, bowled playing the reverse sweep. Boiling finished with 2/40 in his eight

overs, and Surrey won by 18 runs. Ratcliffe was told he had been guilty of poor cricket because he had not practised the reverse sweep enough. Later he did work hard at it and became an accomplished player of the shot.

Trevor Penney also floundered against Boiling, allowing him to bowl a maiden, with six men on the legside and three on the off. He was told to report to Edgbaston at eight o'clock the following morning 'where I got the biggest bollocking of my career.' Penney soon saw the sense of extemporisation and blossomed into a very dangerous, dextrous one-day batsman.

After two years working with Woolmer as a trusted lieutenant, Reeve was clearly the captain-in-waiting. Lloyd's form had started to taper away and he was no longer an automatic choice for the first XI, despite his unselfish, positive batting. Reeve replaced him as captain, with the procedure unravelling messily, as the news leaked out with a couple of championship games of the 1992 season still to go. Nothing, though, should detract from the part that Andy Lloyd played in Warwickshire's later years of plenty.

For the next two years Woolmer and Reeve were an outstanding combination. They would talk cricket for hours, often in Birmingham's restaurants where the cutlery would be utilised for fielders as Reeve munched on his pasta and Woolmer calmly demolished a rack of lamb and savoured a glass or two of his favourite South African Pinotage. Reeve respected Woolmer's knowledge of the scientific aspects of cricket, the greater need for stamina and better fielding. 'Bob was a great one for finding that extra one per cent that made us better – even down to eyesight tests. He'd bring in experts from Birmingham University on all sorts of topics that didn't appear related. Bob was shrewd enough to realise the players would eventually get bored by his voice alone so the experts would automatically get their attention.'

Neil Smith was always a positive all-rounder, even when his career was on the line in the late 1980s, but he was rapt in admiration for Woolmer's ethos. 'We were given freedom to go and play the way we wanted to play. You were allowed to hit the ball in the air or hit your first ball for four. In any successful side, if players are given responsibility and freedom to express themselves, then they flourish.'

Reeve says Woolmer was years ahead of his time. 'I remember him saying to me once that we should try to score at ten runs an over that day. Nobody was thinking like that then. A couple of decades later, everyone's doing it. He had a saying that every ball's an event. You couldn't afford to bowl a loosener, wides or no balls. When we won the championship in 1994 we conceded the least amount of extras in the country.'

Reeve and Woolmer were adamant that Warwickshire could prosper via the power of positive thinking. They wanted a challenging environment, but encouragement to try something different was their mantra. Reeve recalls: 'We were lucky to have a bunch of guys who were very good cricketers but also bought totally into what we were trying to do. If someone drops a catch, he doesn't mean to drop it. There's no point in getting angry or blaming anyone. Go the other way and become super-encouraging. If you get out, don't sit around, moaning and groaning. Stay upbeat, it's infectious. You play your best cricket when you're relaxed and enjoying it. Fear is such a strong emotion but, instead of feeling pressure, we just thought of it as a challenge and relished that challenge. The way to do that is to be confident and visualise yourself being successful and going out there and winning.'

Such a Panglossian outlook was certainly needed towards the end of the 1993 season, the first of the Woolmer/Reeve axis. There was a whiff of anti-climax in the air, as the Bears flunked out of the Benson & Hedges Cup at the first time of asking, finished 10th in the Sunday League and 16th in the championship. There were extenuating factors: the absence of Allan Donald for the last six weeks, due to international duties, a daunting injury list, the inevitable troughs younger players experience and the challenges of a transitional period. But Woolmer and Reeve, while stressing the green shoots of optimism, needed some breathing space to get some of the committee and a few supporters off their backs, to be able to continue the encouraging progress of recent seasons.

It was to be provided, momentously, by a charming Ugandan Asian in the latter stages of his career at Edgbaston. Asif Din's Match entered Warwickshire folklore almost as soon as it was over – for the stunning victory itself and for its significance the following summer.

The NatWest Final of 1993

Just a couple of days before the match that defined his career, Asif Din spent a blissful day in the Shropshire countryside with his old mentor David Brown, who had signed him when head coach at Warwickshire. After a day's fishing and shooting, Asif said before he left: 'Are you a betting man, Browny? Then put some money on me being top scorer on Saturday.'

It was a big call from Asif, known to all as 'Gunga'. Injuries and loss of form had restricted him to just six championship games and, with his contract up at the end of the season, he faced an uncertain future at the age of 32. But in the last six weeks he had recaptured some of his old fluency in the Sunday League games, and the management had told him he was playing at Lord's.

'Gunga' was a flair player, who hit the ball into unconventional areas. Not a technically orthodox batsman, but gifted and the type you'd back when he was on a hot streak of form. Bob Cottam, his old coach at Edgbaston, used to be concerned about his lack of confidence: 'If he'd been involved in a run-out, he'd sit alone in the dressing room, very worried about what his team-mates were saying about him. He was definitely one you'd put an arm around his shoulder.'

But 'Gunga' breezed into Lord's that Saturday, full of optimism. It wasn't even dented when Sussex scored 321, off the back of Martin Speight's élan and David Smith's rugged hundred. Gladstone Small and Tim Munton, an opening pair usually relied upon for parsimony and early wickets, were routed and Sussex posted the highest total in 31 years of Lord's finals. At the halfway stage they were overwhelming favourites.

At least two of the Warwickshire XI didn't see it that way. When Jason Ratcliffe was caught behind, it was 18/2 and it appeared a forlorn hope for Warwickshire. But Ratcliffe told his team-mates, 'Lads, that's the best wicket I've ever batted on, it's a lovely day out there – come on, we can win this!' Ratcliffe may have been deliberately thumping the hyperbolic tub, reflecting the prevailing optimism of the Reeve/Woolmer regime, but he struck just the right defiant note. Asif Din saw it the same way: 'I was stretched out on the couch in my corner of the dressing room, watching us bat on TV and felt fine about our chances. I was down to bat at number seven and Dermot suddenly said to me, "Gunga, bat five, ok?" I don't know if he was backing a hunch or not – he often did – but I was so relaxed that I thought no more about it.'

At 93/3 Asif walked out to join Paul Smith, another mercurial flair player who relished the big occasion. Smith told his new partner, 'Let's just get to tea, then we'll assess it.' Mission accomplished. Smith batted splendidly, unfurling some classy off-drives and Asif squirted the ball wristily into untenanted areas. They got to 164 in the 36th over, still a long way adrift, needing a run a ball from then on. These days such an asking rate, with six wickets in hand, is gettable, but in 1993 one-day batsmanship had yet to reach the heady expansiveness and invention of the current game. Sussex were still in charge of the final.

When Smith was out, Dermot Reeve sauntered in, breathing defiance. Reeve kept saying, 'We just need one good over, Gunga – about fifteen or so – and we've got them.' It never did happen, but the fielding started to wobble. Asif Din remembers a key stage in the revival. 'We got to forty overs, and it was the same score as theirs. They started to get a bit twitchy in the field and all I could hear was our supporters chanting, "You Bears! You Bears!" and that made me believe we could do it. It was a great pitch, the bounce was consistent and we started to play our shots.'

Reeve and Asif added 142 in 23 overs with some outrageous improvisation – Asif stepping back, smacking the ball over cover point, Reeve working the ball expertly off his pads, the pair of them burgling some hair-raising singles.

Twenty were needed in the last two overs, the light fading fast. Reeve had kept shouting encouragement to Asif, who kept touching the little bag he carried around his neck, reflecting his Muslim faith, for inspiration. The adrenalin was overwhelming them.

Then Asif was caught in the covers for 104 off 106 balls – the innings of his life, but surely now in a lost cause. Ed Giddins bowled a superb 59th over, going for just five runs as well as taking the vital wicket of Asif Din. Giddins celebrated wildly at the end of the over and, with 15 now needed off six balls, you couldn't cavil at that. Reeve, shoulders slumped in

Asif Din congratulates Sussex's David Smith on his hundred. Neil Lenham and Dickie Bird look on.

Asif Din on the way to a hundred of his own. Peter Moores behind the stumps.

dejection, looked spent for a few moments. But at least he had squeezed out a single to keep the strike for the final over.

Reeve knew the onus was on him, because you couldn't expect the new batsman to pick up the tempo immediately against the crafty West Indian Franklyn Stephenson, an experienced, reliable fast bowler, with the best-disguised slower ball on the county circuit. He would bowl it in this final, climactic over – but when?

The fearless Roger Twose judged the situation perfectly as he marched out to join his captain. He spotted Reeve's uncharacteristic dejection, shook him by the shoulders and roared, 'Come on, Skip – we can do it!' Easier said than done, with the scoreboard lights standing out in the crepuscular gloom and both sets of supporters baying.

Reeve later admitted that he had no idea what to do as Stephenson ran up for the first ball. 'Would I even see it?' He did, clubbing it straight past the bowler for four. Good start. He played the next one out to long-on for a couple and would have been run out if wicket-keeper Peter Moores had thrown more accurately. The next, a yorker, was smeared out to long off, courtesy of a misfield, bringing two more.

Before the fourth ball, Twose strode down the pitch to his captain and shouted: 'Wherever you hit it, we're coming back for two!' He was right – Reeve, adrenalin overflowing, had to be the hero now, not the new batsman squinting in the gloom. Reeve proceeded to play the sweetest of cover drives for four, a shot he rarely played. 'To this day I don't know where that shot came from.'

Four balls gone and still no sign of the formidable Stephenson's slower delivery. He duly bowled it, and Reeve saw it late, got an inside edge and it squirted down to fine leg for a scampered single.

One to win off the last ball, provided Warwickshire didn't lose a wicket. Sussex had lost six and Warwickshire five at this stage. Two runs would be even better, making it a clearcut victory.

Reeve and Twose met for a crucial decision. The captain said, 'Peter Moores is standing up, so I think he'll bowl the slower ball because he won't risk byes or leg-byes by bowling the quicker one. If he bowls you the quicker one, get the bat on it and we'll get a run. But look for the slower ball.'

Stephenson opted for the slower ball, Twose slowed down his bat swing, waiting for it, then squirted it in the air through the offside. The batsmen sprinted the first, ran the second just to make sure, all the while yelling out their euphoria. An ecstatic fan ripped off Reeve's helmet for a souvenir. The crestfallen bowler grabbed Reeve's bat and raced off the field, brandishing it at any other intruders. Afterwards, Stephenson confessed to Reeve in the hotel bar that he was astonished at his cover-drive for four in the final over. So was Reeve!

It was a miraculous victory, given the way that one-day cricket was played in 1993. Warwickshire didn't have the peerless Donald, their two fast-bowling bankers Small and Munton went for more than six an over and Twose had to fill in, his bustling medium-pace swingers getting through eight admirably cheap overs. Neil Smith's intelligent off-breaks cost just three an over. The fielding was superb, and the aggression and spirit of the batting underlined that style was no longer important in the one-day game. Finding the gaps by whatever means was the key. And Twose stood up to the pressure of the most important delivery he faced in his career.

In any other final, Reeve would have scooped the Gold Award, not just for his heroic innings but for bowling his allotted 12 overs craftily, while ensuring the roof didn't fall in out on the field, under the Sussex onslaught. The team remained defiant, and the captain must get the plaudits for that.

But Asif Din had to be the ultimate hero. He always had a magnificent eye, and the gift of timing when the muse of inspiration sat on his shoulder. It was a remarkable hundred, full of clever placements, resounding biffs through the offside, and the simple exercise of playing the ball where there was no fielder. The management had gambled on him for the final, believing his recent form and experience justified a tough call. He ended up scoring more than 500 runs in limited-overs cricket that season.

He agrees that it was the best innings of his career: 'I got an 80 against Michael Holding on a really fast Chesterfield wicket and a hundred against a Middlesex attack of Daniel, Selvey, Edmonds and Emburey – but, in the context of the match, it has to be Lord's 1993. It was a match-winning innings. I will never forget the love from the Bears' fans that day.'

Franklyn Stephenson fails to get his hand to a return catch from Dermot Reeve

In the gloom Roger Twose, facing his first ball, hits the winning runs past fielder David Smith

Nor have those raucuous supporters. They coined a little ditty to the tune of Manfred Mann's 1968 hit 'Mighty Quinn', and whenever a group of them spot the modest 'Gunga' at Edgbaston, he is regaled with:

> Come on without, come on within,
> You've not seen nothing like the Asif Din.

'Gunga' got another couple of years in whites, hearing the Bears' fans chant his name. That one innings at a packed, breathless Lord's breathed life into a career that had appeared to run its natural course. There would have been uproar among the members if Asif hadn't got a new contract after his wonderful performance and, a few weeks later, he was awarded one for two years. Happily it qualified him for a benefit and the Birmingham public responded in gratitude to a hugely popular figure, always gracious and modest. His benefit game the following summer amused 'Gunga': 10,000 thronged Edgbaston for the Sunday League match against Worcestershire, ready to pay tribute when he batted, only for him to be run out for nought, without facing a ball, courtesy of one BC Lara. 'Gunga' whimsically observed that the crowd would prefer watching Lara bat, but surely not in that special game for him.

Asif Din never again reached the heights of Lord's 1993. He injured his shoulder in the field during the '94 season and quietly faded away. But he remains a familiar, genial presence at Edgbaston, and his vital role in that one historic match is justly venerated by supporters of a certain vintage.

The importance of the NatWest victory cannot be over-estimated in the context of the next 24 months. It was not only the first of six trophies but a vindication of the aggression, high morale and competitiveness that Woolmer, Lloyd and now Reeve had been espousing for several years. It allowed Reeve to continue justifying the positive way he captained the side, bringing self-belief to the younger players and galvanising the older ones.

'We came to believe that no game was ever lost by us until the facts said otherwise. If we could beat Sussex in those circumstances, we could take on anybody. Only those who don't play modern first-class cricket under-estimate the importance of self-confidence. It comes and goes, but the crucial thing is to hang onto it as long as you can and, if it's waning in an individual, you need supportive team-mates to revive it. I felt we were getting there at Edgbaston by the end of the 1993 season.'

Warwickshire built on that historic Lord's victory during the winter. With the superb Donald due to be absent for the '94 season, touring with South Africa, at least 80 championship wickets had to be found from somewhere to compensate. Richard Davis, a left-arm spinner, was signed from Kent and, with the developing Neil Smith alongside, the two spinners took exactly 80 wickets in the championship. Tim Munton, aware that he had to be more aggressive at the crease in Donald's absence, worked hard on his use of the bouncer in the winter nets. Roger Twose honed his technique against the short ball and returned from New Zealand full of confidence. The players continued finessing their use of the reverse sweep. Fitness levels were encouragingly high, a reassuring boost for Woolmer, who had hammered on about this for a couple of years now.

The pre-season tour to Zimbabwe was perfect on several levels. That dedicated social animal Paul Smith recalls some great practice facilities but also some splendid nights out. 'It was Trevor Penney's home turf, and the cost of living was so cheap you could buy the penthouse for ten quid. We had a great time, played some terrific cricket and came back buzzing. Team spirit was fantastic; we couldn't wait for the start of the summer.'

Bob Woolmer was a satisfied coach, and not just because the food suited his demanding palate. 'Zimbawe was ideal. Fantastic wickets, great hospitality – nothing was too much trouble. The wickets were magnificent and all the players found form.'

As the players crowded into the Old Hararians Cricket Club to watch Brian Lara's record innings on TV, they had no inkling of the remarkable effect he would have on the team's fortunes a few weeks later.

Woolmer and Reeve were quietly confident about their prospects for '94, still savouring that remarkable Lord's victory. But they concealed cannily their bullishness in April, mouthing platitudes about hoping to play attractive cricket, playing down their coup in signing Lara. Yet all the foundations were in place, and they knew it. Staying under the radar would be an option for only so long once the cricket started.

Captain Dermot Reeve with Man of the Match Asif Din

Sussex v Warwickshire, Lord's, 4 September 1993

Warwickshire won by five wickets

Umpires: H.D. Bird & M.J. Kitchen

Sussex

D.M. Smith	run out		124
C.W.J. Athey	c Piper	b Munton	0
M.P. Speight	c Piper	b Reeve	50
A.P. Wells *		b N Smith	33
F.D. Stephenson	c N Smith	b Twose	3
N.J. Lenham	lbw	b Reeve	58
K. Greenfield	*not out*		8
P. Moores +			
I.D.K. Salisbury			
A.C.S. Pigott			
E.S.H. Giddins			
	lb 11, w 18, nb 16		45
60 overs	(for 6 wickets)		**321**

1/4, 2/107, 3/183, 4/190, 5/309, 6/321

Small	12	0	71	0
Munton	9	0	67	1
Smith (PA)	7	0	45	0
Reeve	12	1	60	2
Smith (NMK)	12	1	37	1
Twose	8	1	30	1

Warwickshire

A.J. Moles	c Moores	b Pigott	2
J.D. Ratcliffe		b Stephenson	13
D.P. Ostler	c Smith	b Salisbury	25
P.A. Smith	c Moores	b Stephenson	60
Asif Din	c Speight	b Giddins	104
D.A. Reeve *	*not out*		81
R.G. Twose	*not out*		2
N.M.K. Smith			
K.J. Piper +			
G.C. Small			
T.A. Munton			
	b 3, lb 13, w 13, nb 6		35
60 overs	(for 5 wickets)		**322**

1/18, 2/18, 3/93, 4/164, 5/306

Giddins	12	0	57	1
Stephenson	12	2	51	2
Pigott	11	0	74	1
Salisbury	11	0	59	1
Greenfield	7	0	31	0
Lenham	7	0	34	0

Manoj Prabhakar

'Give me lucky generals,' Napoleon once said. The same applies to sport. Never under-estimate its importance when you analyse a successful team. Just ask Dennis Amiss and Manoj Prabhakar.

If Prabhakar had turned up fully fit to Edgbaston early in April, there would never have been a historic season such as 1994. Brian Lara would not have arrived before the month was out, taking the team to a totally new dimension. The players were more than capable of winning a one-day trophy (as they had shown the previous September at Lord's, without an overseas star in their eleven), but Lara's presence, speed of scoring and sheer inspiration meant Warwickshire could now compete on all four fronts.

Quite simply, they swapped a worthy Indian all-rounder for the best player in the world, who cost them a comparative pittance. Lara's contract was secured at a sum that was paid more than three times over by the spectacular rise that April in new members, leading to the largest membership total since the 1960s.

And it was all due to an injury picked up in a match in Dunedin, New Zealand in the second week of March which led to Prabhakar being paid off with due despatch once they knew that Lara's genius was available.

At the time Prabhakar was acknowledged as an all-rounder of international class, a doughty opening batsman and clever swing bowler, who performed the roles for India in Tests and one-day internationals. He wasn't out of place among galacticos like Azharuddin, Kumble, Srinath, Tendulkar and Kapil Dev. He had toured England twice with India, and was good enough to take 5/35 in a one-day international at Hyderabad early in '94. At the age of 31, Prabhakar was at his peak. He would surely be worth a punt by some English county.

Warwickshire's captain Dermot Reeve wanted to sign him. Not so the trio of former England players occupying key roles in cricket management at Edgbaston – Dennis Amiss, MJK Smith and Bob Woolmer. They felt strength in batting was needed and were keen on the Australian David Boon, with a nod in the direction of the West Indian Phil Simmons. The younger batsmen would benefit from the tutelage a committed overseas batter would offer.

Reeve felt an all-rounder was needed, even though Prabhakar's medium-pace was not vastly superior to what Reeve, Roger Twose and the faster Paul Smith could offer. It would surely mean that one of those three would drop out to accommodate Prabhakar.

Commendably the three wise men backed the captain, despite their misgivings. Prabhakar was signed. In his pre-season missive to the Warwickshire members, Woolmer wrote, 'I am sure that this pocket dynamo cricketer will bring enthusiasm, competitiveness and skill to the Warwickshire side.'

If Woolmer et al had prevailed, Boon would have been contracted and Lara would not have been picked up for a comparative song in mid-April, as they scrambled around for a replacement for Prabhakar.

Enter one Keith Cook to the developing plot. At the time, Cook – twenty years service done at Edgbaston – was a valued member of the club's marketing department, who willingly performed duties beyond his usual remit. Anything for his beloved Bears. He was deputed to pick up Prabhakar at Heathrow Airport one morning early in April and bring him up to Edgbaston to start his new season with the club.

The conversation on the way up the motorway was amiable enough, but then Cook noticed something disturbing. 'He was wearing those high-zipped Chelsea boots that were fashionable at the time. He undid the zip, rolled up his trouser leg and asked me what he thought of a scar. It was a recent scar on his ankle, it looked red, raw and fresh. I started wondering when he'd had that operated on. A few alarm bells started to ring because I was certain none of us at Edgbaston had known about a recent ankle operation. As soon as we got to the ground I mentioned it to Dennis Amiss.'

Very wise. It appeared that Prabhakar had flown home from India's New Zealand tour in the second week of March, after scoring 147 and bowling just 12 overs in the opening match of the tour. To Cook's untutored eye, he would struggle to be fit for the start of the county season, just three weeks later. That opinion was soon confirmed by the club's medical experts.

Manoj Prabhakar bowling for India

In 39 Tests he scored 1,600 runs, with one century, and took 96 wickets

Meanwhile Bob Woolmer had enlisted Wasim Khan to make Prabhakar feel at home, while discreet enquiries were being made. Wasim, a young, promising batsman, would take him several times to a health club in the centre of Birmingham and watched keenly as Prabhakar tried to prove his fitness. 'I noticed in the gym he was continually wiggling his ankle. I thought he's either got a very strange habit or a real problem there. Every few moments he'd wiggle his foot around as though he was trying to keep his ankle loose. He'd rented a house just a mile or so from our ground and he was telling me all about the Bollywood stars who'd be coming to see him. But I couldn't see how he was going to get on the field if he was in that much discomfort.'

Now it was time for Dennis Amiss to show some swift decision-making. He had just started in the role of chief executive, aware that there was much to learn. But underneath the genial exterior, Amiss was always a ruthless, clear-sighted character when necessary, as he showed in 1977 by signing for Kerry Packer, to the dismay of Lord's and his Warwickshire team-mates. He incurred short-term opprobrium but wouldn't be deflected from his planned course. The same applied when he signed for South African Breweries in 1982, to more displeasure from Lord's.

In his new role Amiss acted promptly. 'We couldn't have this situation. He hadn't told us about the ankle operation and there was no way he was going to be fit for the start of the season. We had to part company quickly. Our next urgent question was – who was out there?'

Brian Charles Lara, that's who. Woolmer had noted approvingly Lara's wondrous first Test hundred 15 months earlier – a dazzling 277 in Sydney. He had kept an eye on him, dreaming his dreams of working one day with a batsman who simply entranced him. By April 1994, Lara – one month shy of his 25th birthday – was toying with England's bowlers in the Caribbean, establishing himself as the supreme batsman in world cricket. Surely Warwickshire couldn't land him at short notice?

They could – and did. Lara had toured England with the West Indies in 1991 and his tour ended unluckily at, of all places, Edgbaston – where he was struck on the ankle by a fiercely driven ball in the practice nets. So he knew about Edgbaston, and there were enough top West Indies players in the Test side who could extol the virtues of county cricket to such a developing talent, who would use the experience of English conditions to further a career that appeared destined for immortality.

Lara was receptive. Luckily for Warwickshire, MJK Smith was already at the Test matches in the Caribbean, managing the England tour. With his sensible, low-key manner, Smith made a good impression on Lara, while the razzamatazz of the sales pitch was conducted by Tony Cross, vice-chairman of Warwickshire, who just happened to be out there on business.

In between the Barbados and Antigua Tests, Lara duly signed for Warwickshire at a sum – around

£40,000 – that still seems a major heist. He had already hammered England for 167 and a couple of fifties in the Test series, transcending all others with the luminous quality of his strokeplay. MJK Smith had played many years at Edgbaston with the great West Indian batsman Rohan Kanhai, and this perceptive, understated former England captain knew a gem when he saw one close up. To Smith, Lara was an absolute bargain at £40,000.

Woolmer and Amiss, awash with knowledge of the art of batting, needed no persuading to sign Lara. And within a week, they were rubbing their eyes in disbelief at their good fortune. Whoever was writing Warwickshire's scripts that April month had a deft turn for the dramatic. With the ink barely dried on his Bears contract, Lara compiled 375 in the Antigua Test, the highest individual score in Test cricket. In front of Sir Garry Sobers, who had scored 365*, 36 years previously.

Ten days after Lara was dismissed for 375 in Antigua, he took the field for Warwickshire at Edgbaston, on the first day of the county season. In the intervening few days, the phones at the club were in meltdown, the marketing department were in raptures, nearly 2,000 extra members signed up and, in the words of Keith Cook, 'On the first day he turned up for his press conference, it was just a frenzy. Almost as if David Beckham had bowled into the car park. I've never seen anything like it at Edgbaston.'

But Cook had one more vital service to provide for his club before he could enjoy such challenges. They had to ensure the reluctant Prabhakar sloped off quietly. A ticklish encounter lay in store at Prabhakar's family home. Dennis Amiss and Cook had to hand over the loaded revolver. 'Dennis said to me, "Cooky, we've got to get that company car back off Manoj." So we rocked up, had an awkward cuppa tea with quite a few people and got the car keys. So I drove the Warwickshire car back to the ground. Manoj knew the contract had to be terminated, and he was given a sweetener just to show there were no hard feelings.'

There was one consolation for Prabhakar. He did get a season in county cricket the following year, with Durham, after his ankle injury cleared up. The wickets in the north-east were a good deal more tricky than

A car on arrival
The DVLA later withdrew his special number plate

at Edgbaston, but in a weak side Prabhakar acquitted himself well enough, taking 51 championship wickets at 28.21 and scoring 896 runs at 32.00. Geoff Cook, Durham's director of cricket, who signed him, recalls a fine player: 'He was a high-class all-rounder when we signed him. A talented first-change bowler – about the pace of Hansie Cronje or Paul Collingwood – with clever variations and a surprise bouncer. As a batsman, he got stuck in on those sporting pitches. I can see why Dermot Reeve wanted to sign Prabhakar the year before.'

But, despite his obvious ability, he wasn't a Brian Lara. Who else was in April 1994?

The Characters

Dermot Reeve

The quintessential Marmite cricketer of his era, Dermot Reeve. No one was neutral about him. He was either an inspirational captain, progressive thinker ahead of his time, under-rated all-rounder – or a supreme bluffer, with a smart mouth that ran away from his brain too often. If he was a chocolate soldier, he would eat himself, many believed.

What cannot be contested is the effect he had on Warwickshire in his nine seasons at the club. His was a genuinely creative contribution, helping to transform the tactical and philosophical approach, in the process outstripping all other opponents for a halcyon period of 24 months.

There was a long list of contemporary cricketers who would happily have gripped Reeve warmly by the throat in his career – and some of them, at times, were among his Warwickshire team-mates. But they willingly followed him, buying into his blueprint, parking their reservations about his personality quirks, because the journey under Reeve was predominantly fun and exciting. And they kept winning trophies and picking up handsome bonuses. Professionals in sport invariably put winning at the top of their priority list.

To be fair to Reeve, laughter usually echoed around the Warwickshire dressing room under his captaincy. An expansive, witty, streetwise character, Reeve liked an audience and to make people laugh. With his gift for mimicry and articulate, irrelevant take on life, he could usually mine a comic seam at the daily coalface, ensuring a diverse group of players and support staff rubbed along harmoniously enough over a five-month period in the summer, day after day.

Gladstone Small had been part of the first-team furniture since 1980 and he warmed to Reeve's style of man management. 'He was very democratic, encouraging the young players to express their views openly. When I first started, we young upstarts had to change in another dressing room and wait to be asked into the first-team one. Dermot got that wall knocked down, removing an important psychological barrier. We then had freedom of expression with each other, with Dermot and Bob Woolmer demanding everyone pitched in with their opinions. It led to a lot of laughs.'

The indestructible team spirit was obvious when they struggled at times on the field. Reeve was a great believer in using humour to release tension. If a dangerous partnership was building Reeve would suddenly shout, 'Gee, fellahs, these two have put on a hundred!' and then laugh loudly and maniacally. The rest of the team would follow suit, except Small, who would only smile. That amused his team-mates even more. Sometimes, between overs, Reeve would kick around an imaginary football. It would end up with Small in the outfield who would unceremoniously kick it into the crowd, then chuckle, those distinctive shoulders heaving. Or Reeve would shout to Roger Twose, 'Akabusi Roger!' and he'd then emulate that outstanding hurdler Kriss Akabusi as he sped to his place in the field.

All this may sound childish and trivial, but Reeve believed the sheer grind of county cricket had to be alleviated somehow. 'There was a real belief in what we were doing and we ended up with a really happy bunch of guys who bought into the culture that what you do affects everybody, so you always have to encourage each other a hundred per cent. You play your best cricket when you're relaxed and enjoying it.'

It does help if you are a successful team, though. Neil Smith had played in a few poor sides for the Bears before the Woolmer/Reeve axis and enjoyed the release of tension, courtesy of the new regime. 'Dermot was invariably at the heart of all the high spirits and you laughed along with him, whether or not you liked him. Perhaps it was Dermot's way of covering up his nerves. He might have become annoying, though, if we had been losing during our great seasons.'

There was a defiant, anti-establishment aura about that 1994 Warwickshire side. Reeve admitted he was brash and seemingly over-confident to the point of cockiness, but he reasoned that he was employed to get the best out of his players and that he enjoyed his cricket more if he was aggressive on the field. When the county captains met the umpires on the eve of the '94 season, he was told that Warwickshire were the noisiest and most vocal in the middle. Reeve replied that English cricket was in danger of being too soft, that players were too friendly to the opposition on the field.

A rain break in the dressing room at Canterbury before going out to seal the 1995 championship title

Tim Curtis, Worcestershire's captain at the time, was certainly no fan of the Bears' brashness. A classy, civilised person, who valued friendships in the game as well as achievements, he got so fed up with the noise generated by the local rivals when he was batting that he stepped back from the crease and remarked, 'It's like a zoo out here.' Reeve responded with an impersonation of a sea-lion, almost all his players joined in and for the next half-hour regaled the exasperated Curtis with sundry animal noises.

Curtis has a pithy take on batting amid the usual Warwickshire cacophony. 'You know the parts played by Robert Redford and Paul Newman in *The Sting*? Well, the annoying Reeve and Twose were like them – successful but lacking their class. Bumptious is the word I would use to describe many of them. Keith Piper used to annoy me, calling me "Sir" and being overly deferential when standing up to me at the crease. I taught at Worcester Royal Grammar in the off-season and Pipes knew that.

The ones who were noisy all followed Dermot's lead. He had undoubted chutzpah, and he led them very well. They liked his cheekiness, his huge sense of self-belief.'

Unsurprisingly Dominic Cork, another professional irritant, was a huge fan of Reeve. 'My type of cricketer. In your face – standing at the crease, directing the fielders loudly, while you're trying to sort out your guard. An under-rated player, because he didn't look all that special, but he got runs and wickets at vital times. Fantastic self-belief. In the World Cup in 1996, we were due to play Pakistan in Karachi the next day when the subject of the excellent leggie Mushtaq Ahmed came up in our team meeting. Dermot piped up, "I can pick Mushy's googly – send me in early if he's bowling." He wasn't fazed at all by the others looking at the ceiling when he said that. Nor was he next day when Mushy bowled him for nought with the googly! I loved Dermot's nerve.'

Matthew Fleming begs to differ. The Kent and England all-rounder was, like Reeve, a cricketer who defied convention, confounded his critics and got the very best out of himself as a player. But the Eton-educated former army officer, and city businessman sees leadership in different terms from Reeve. 'I accept Warwickshire had a hold on us at that time and they had a definite aura about them, which stemmed from Dermot's restless, innovative dynamism. I also agree it was a great achievement for Dermot and Bob Woolmer to turn the club around. But Dermot was just annoying. He wasn't a great captain in my eyes because you also have to possess admirable personal qualities off the field to deserve that accolade.'

Tim Munton, vice-captain throughout Dermot's term as captain, has an interesting take on Reeve. They had been team-mates for six years when they shared the captaincy for championship games in the '94 season – partly due to Reeve's recurring injuries and indifferent form that meant he could not justify his place in the championship XI. If you ever wanted a sane, rational, unbiased opinion on cricketing matters around that period, Munton was the natural port of call. A quarter of a century on, he says this: 'Dermot did change as his career blossomed. The England calls came, and I guess, not surprisingly, his ego grew and we drifted apart. We were great friends for most of our careers, but our relationship suffered on a personal level in the latter years, which was a real shame. Ninety-five per cent of the time he was great company with a brilliant cricket brain – but the other five per cent was sometimes so challenging it drove us apart. But, in professional terms, he was a fantastic competitor, unparallelled and ahead of his time as a one-day captain. On reflection the fond memories definitely outstrip the negative ones.'

Mark Nicholas admired the way a Reeve side would rarely bow the knee when he was his counterpart at Hampshire. 'When you thought you had them down, they would spring back up. They had such energy in the field and when they batted. Dermot's charisma contributed strongly to that, and the team understood his flaws but followed him all the way. He could be very aggravating but he wasn't a bad person. He appeared more selfish than in fact he was. They kept winning and eventually we were rather in awe of them.

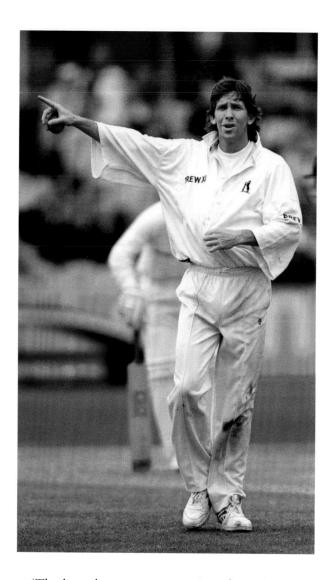

'The best three county captains of my time were Mike Brearley, Adam Hollioake and Dermot Reeve. Dermot wasn't universally liked but he should have captained England in the 1996 World Cup. Dermot not only understood deeply one-day cricket, but he re-thought the approach to it, with pinch-hitters, reverse sweeps, opening the bowling with a spinner or setting the field cleverly. He was an outsider, with England coaches of that period wary of his invention. Dermot was the Martin Peters of his generation – ahead of his time.'

Neil Smith was in that '96 England World Cup squad, under the authority of Michael Atherton and Raymond Illingworth, and the contrast was graphic with the open policy he enjoyed at Edgbaston. 'I was used to thorough, open, honest discussions under Dermot and Bob Woolmer, but we lacked that under

Athers and Illy. We just weren't prepared enough and the team unity was lacking. In two months – first in South Africa, then in India/Pakistan – I had two conversations with Illy. One about holiday homes in Spain and the other when he told me what good fielders Brian Statham and Fred Trueman were. Compare that to the cricket-based discussion at Edgbaston, where everyone was expected to voice their opinions, no matter how inexperienced they were. In the right environment and with proper backing, Dermot would have been good enough for the job in '96. He was so restless and hyperactive on the field, he wouldn't let the game drift. We pushed the boundaries in terms of speeding up the game, and his bowling changes were so intuitive. The opposition batters rarely settled; Dermot was brilliant at upsetting their rhythm.'

Gladstone Small agrees. Having been part of England's 1992 World Cup squad, he remains adamant that Reeve should have led the side four years later. 'He was the best one-day captain I ever played under. Ideas coming out of his head all the time, he made every ball seem vital. And he was good enough to be in the side as a player. But ... he rubbed a few up the wrong way.'

Graham Cowdrey was an integral part of the Kent side that invariably came off second-best when up against Warwickshire, and he credits Reeve's brilliance at mind games for some of that. Cowdrey was an acknowledged devotee of the Irish blues singer Van Morrison, travelling thousands of miles to see him. Reeve was aware of that. He also knew about Cowdrey's famous father, Colin, a man with as many cricketing theories as Reeve.

'So, whenever I came into bat, Dermot would stand in front of me, asking how my dad was and to be sure I sent back his best wishes. Then he'd get onto Van Morrison. "Have you seen him in concert lately? What's his new album like? I must catch him live soon. When are you seeing him next?" All this while I'm trying to get ready to face my first ball. It was brilliant sledging in a clever way. If you examined the two sides, player for player, there was little between us. We were a very good one-day side then – but Warwickshire always got over the line against us. Dermot had a lot to do with that.'

When I collaborated with Dermot Reeve in writing his autobiography, I found him enthralling, engaging and fascinating. A natural iconoclast, he was not your archetypal English cricketer temperamentally. Brave with his opinions, possessing an excellent memory, his eyes lit up mischievously when I suggested a chapter entitled 'Getting Up Noses', as he wryly suggested to me that he could pick a handy eleven from those he had upset in his career. Brian Lara, of course. Curtly Ambrose, who bowled three beamers at him while en route to a double hundred against Northants. Winston Benjamin managed a couple against him when playing for Leicestershire. He once had the last word over Ian Botham, someone Reeve revered and admired. Botham got Reeve out with a spot of gamesmanship and, when Reeve reluctantly dragged himself from the crease, he copped a volley of abuse from the great man, then in the twilight of his marvellous career. A more sensitive soul than Reeve would have crept back to the pavilion, ears stinging. Not Reeve. 'Pick your dummy up and put it back in your mouth. You've had your day, mate.' Not even legends could browbeat Dermot Reeve.

The chemistry between Lancashire and Warwickshire in the mid-1990s was invariably stormy and tetchy, partly due to rivalry between two fine sides. Misunderstandings were allowed to fester at times, incidents on the field began to stack up, and it appeared that Lancashire's coach David Lloyd had little time for Reeve. It all came to a head one evening in the Old Trafford committee room when both sets of players had been invited for a drink. According to Reeve, he was met by a warning from Lloyd. 'I don't like you, Reeve. You get up my nose and, if you come anywhere near me, I'll rearrange yours.' Gladstone Small saw the incident and laughs at it now: 'I think one or two of our boys were hoping Dermot would get lamped, because he could be annoying. It wasn't the usual close-of-play banter, that's for sure.' It took a meeting the following day between Reeve, Lloyd and Lancashire chairman Bob Bennett to sort out the differences. 'I had naively thought that David and I had got on well, so I was surprised at the volley of abuse,' recalls Reeve, with an amusing attempt at wide-eyed sincerity.

Reeve wasn't bothered about such spats. He never cared about being liked, preferring the respect of his team-mates and opponents. 'I've seen a few sides full of so-called nice chaps that never won anything.' He treasured Allan Donald's assessment of him: 'I'd hate to play against Dermot Reeve, he must be a pain in the neck, but he's great to have in our side.' Robin Smith, that charming man and fine batsman, first toured with Reeve on the England trip to Australia and New Zealand, and after a fortnight he told him: 'I have to apologise to you, Dermot. For years, I thought you were the biggest shit in county cricket but, now I've got to know you, you're ok.' Reeve was typically pragmatic about Smith's comment: 'It's nice to know that I had got under the skin of such a nice guy when we were in opposition, because I didn't see it as my function to be nice to the opposition.'

He had learned his trade in two hard schools – Sussex CCC and nine seasons of grade cricket in Australia – before reaching sunnier uplands at Edgbaston. By then Reeve had toughened up, he would never turn the other cheek to any cricketer, or back down. Always physically brave against the quick bowlers, never shy of a provocative quip back at them just to wind them up, Reeve soon got used to being under-estimated and denigrated as a cricketer. At Sussex, Imran Khan was the glamorous, charismatic all-rounder, not the Tiggerish Reeve, who was so eager to please and fit in. The patrician Imran clearly didn't rate Reeve as a cricketer. He once drawled to the Sussex captain, John Barclay, 'I told you, Johnny – Dermot can't bat.' Reeve wished he had stood up to Imran. 'I was almost in tears. His behaviour was something I would never do to a team-mate and a lesson I took with me when I became Warwickshire's captain – never belittle a colleague over his cricketing ability, or lack of it.'

Imran just couldn't help himself with Reeve. After the 1992 World Cup Final, Reeve went into the victorious Pakistan dressing room to congratulate Imran, who had inspired a famous victory. In his regal manner Imran said: 'Dermot, I must tell you, I'm very happy for you, you've done so well to get so far in the game' ... pause for the killer finale ... 'for someone of your limited ability.' Reeve is philosophical about the slight. 'He had never rated me on talent, but he liked the way I had made a career for myself on application and character. I suppose I ought to have been flattered.'

He certainly wasn't flattered one day in the Sussex dressing room when the batsman Alan Wells told Reeve his fortune in no uncertain terms. Reeve had been interviewed by local radio and, in his customary enthusiastic fashion, had laid out his hopes and dreams for his nascent career. He said what every young pro must think privately – that he would absolutely love to play for England, given luck, etc etc.

Wells heard about the interview and gave Reeve an unvarnished assessment of his prospects for further advancement in the game. 'You ought to just concentrate on staying in the first team, getting your cap, hoping for a benefit at the end of it all. You'll never play for England.' Reeve felt crushed. 'You have to aspire to a goal, even if you fall short for lack of talent. I knew I didn't look all that special on the cricket field. When I first saw myself on video as a Sussex player, I wasn't at all impressed – but it was the best I could manage and I was more concerned with effectiveness than style.'

The elegant Wells gained his solitary Test cap three years after Reeve. Wells made nought on debut, Reeve 59, and he won two more Test caps, played in a World Cup Final and picked up three Man of the Match awards in Lord's finals. 'When I captained Warwickshire I tried to use incidents like that one with Alan Wells to get the guys properly motivated. Make it happen for you.'

Reeve took the cheerful, supportive attitude of his Sussex captain with him when he became the Bears' captain. Reeve loved Barclay's decency and thoughtfulness. 'If you'd had a bad day in the field, you'd apologise to Johnny, and he'd find something positive. He'd praise an outswinger I'd bowled in one over and that at least I'd done my best. He had a lovely way of dealing with his players.'

The younger Warwickshire players certainly responded to Reeve's effervescence. They weren't corralled into conformity, told to shut up when spoken to. In 1994 it was significant how readily Dougie Brown and Graeme Welch stepped up to the plate so positively when Reeve's lack of form and injuries created a vacancy. The two all-rounders were brimful of confidence when arriving in the first team because the positivity engendered by Reeve and Woolmer had permeated into the second XI. Reeve was thrilled to see his tyros playing the reverse sweep as soon as they played in the first team.

Welch remembers how Reeve made him feel important, so quickly. 'He was brilliant, a great encourager to young players. He may have been a bit selfish at times but I didn't care; he wasn't there to make friends, he was a winner. Always ahead of the game, he had so many innovations, like his slower ball out of the back of the hand that baffled some good batsmen. He was full of himself and would pick fights out in the middle if nothing was happening – for example, getting under the skin of Worcestershire's Richard Illingworth, who Dermot knew had a short fuse. He'd get batsmen caught on the drive with clever field placings. He was brilliant at identifying key stages of an innings early on.'

Brown relished Reeve's enthusiasm and confidence in an emerging youngster. 'He'd pump your tyres up so well. He'd tell you that he backed you a hundred per cent because you were a good player. You never left a conversation with Dermot feeling down, he got the very best out of you. Dermot encouraged us to play in a free way, to back our judgement, provided we had practised the shots or a particular delivery long and hard. Then there would be no recriminations if it didn't work out.'

Reeve admits there were times when he just had to bluff as he spoke to his team, trying to find fresh ways of motivating them, getting that crucial half per cent that makes the difference. And many of his detractors dismiss him as an average cricketer, a bluffer. Well, a first-class career batting average of almost 35 and a bowling one of 26.82 is not that shabby, in addition to having a great pair of hands in the field. I recall Graham Gooch being very impressed by Reeve's sharpness as a fielder and general demeanour when he called him up for England duties in the summer of 1991. Gooch was well aware that substance is more relevant than style at the highest level.

Someone as hyperactive and idiosyncratic as Reeve was easy to under-estimate. But not his big-match temperament. For a time he was the best 'finisher' with the bat in the closing stages of tense one-day games and, as a bowler, his boldness and readiness to

Reverse sweeping during the NatWest semi-final against Kent in 1994

try something different set him apart from others of greater natural talent, who would just conform. Paul Nixon, a brilliant one-day player for Leicestershire around the same time, believes Reeve was the ideal 20/20 player before the term was coined a decade later. 'Dermot was absolutely outstanding as a one-day cricketer, never mind his innovative captaincy. Never shy to try anything with bat or ball, absolutely fearless and proactive. He'd be a godsend now in 20/20 cricket. His temperament would thrive on those pressures. Dermot never backed down.'

Reeve uncluttered the minds of the Warwickshire players, eradicating the fear of failure. 'I've known players who work really hard at their game in practice, but all they do is get better at batting in practice. Then, when a match comes along, they are in a different place because it's a match and they have heightened anxiety. It's about coaching confidence and ability. Play a movie in your head of yourself taking wickets or scoring runs. Do those visualisations really well.'

But even Reeve's formidable powers of self-confidence and resilience were tested midway through that historic '94 season when he was dropped from the championship side, playing only two more games after 20 June.

He was kept fresh for the one-day matches, in which he continued to excel, but his body was beginning to rebel against fighting on all four fronts and his form was suffering in the longer game. The official line from the club was that Reeve's absence was a fitness issue but the chief executive Dennis Amiss had suggested to Reeve that he should drop himself and concentrate on the shorter games. Reeve was initially taken aback by Amiss's suggestion, but by now he was becoming a trifle disillusioned. He felt he could have been supported more positively over the Lara imbroglio and resented the implicit bribe of keeping his head down as a benefit season was likely to be in the offing for him.

Even such an ebullient character as Dermot Reeve was growing weary, and he resolved to keep out of Lara's way for as much as possible, keeping his own counsel about how the boil had not been satisfactorily lanced, in his opinion. Trevor Penney noticed that Lara had fundamental tactical disagreements with the captain at times. 'I remember

Dermot Reeve going on about everyone trying to play the reverse sweep, and Brian interrupted: "You can't make everyone play it, that's rubbish." I sensed the problems between them hadn't gone away.' Lara was a big supporter of Tim Munton, who led Warwickshire to eight wins out of nine championship games, bowling brilliantly. Reeve was aware that some were now whispering that at least Munton was emphatically worth his place in the championship eleven, a point made with some force to Woolmer and Amiss by a deputation of senior players. Young Turks like Brown and Welch – fit, confident, bursting with aggression – only made the team stronger in Reeve's absence.

Dennis Amiss has no regrets about breaking the news to Reeve that he should be dropped from the next few championship matches in mid-season. 'It was just common sense. Dermot seemed to be losing confidence through poor form and niggling injuries. I know professional sport involves a lot of egos, but the young lads coming in made the championship eleven stronger for the rest of that season. As for Lara, I told Dermot that if I had been in his shoes as the captain, I'd want him in my side because he'd be winning me matches. I was backed up by Bob Woolmer and the senior players.'

Reeve obligingly posed with Munton for the happy photographs with all the trophies in September, making generous comments to the media about Munton's successful stint as captain – but several decisions by the management that summer had given him pause for thought amid all the celebratory hoopla. He resolved to get his head down for the winter of 1994/95, develop his burgeoning after-dinner speaking career – highlights: his hilarious impersonations of Imran Khan and Geoffrey Boycott – and get as fit as he could for the 1995 season. He wondered if, in fact, it would be his last.

It did prove to be his last full season, but it was a triumphant one for Reeve, both as player and captain. He missed just two championship games, averaged 33 with the bat and 17 with the ball. Warwickshire stormed to the title, with Reeve making many significant contributions, and his nerveless batting in the Lord's final sealed another NatWest Trophy victory. It was a happier season for Reeve in many ways, not least because he had no Lara to contend with. That outstanding team man and great fast bowler Allan Donald made Reeve's job so much easier.

England selection for one-day internationals and the World Cup in the winter of 1995/96 suggested there were still a few productive seasons left in Reeve. But the end was nasty, brutish and short. In June 1996, he was forced to retire immediately, due to an accumulation of arthritis in a hip joint. He was philosophical. 'I had exceeded my expectations as a county cricketer and had a great deal of fun along the way.'

Life for Reeve after his retirement had many peaks and troughs. He would have appeared a natural for a coaching career, combined with media work – at which he had begun to excel, unsurprisingly – but he battled against drugs issues and lost his way at times. He returned from Australia to Edgbaston in the summer of 2017 at the request of his old team-mate Ashley Giles, to do some coaching with the Warwickshire players. 'It was wonderful and very emotional to be back. I got quite tearful getting off the train at New Street and hearing all the Birmingham accents. Edgbaston is fantastic now, a complete stadium, with a wonderful viewing area and players' facilities that are state-of-the-art. The old pavilion, though it was a bit ramshackle, had so many happy memories for me as well.'

The sound of laughter, for a start. No one surely brought more laughs into that old dressing room than Dermot Reeve. At his best, he was a great lightning conductor for a positive, happy, confident group of players. Who cares that if he'd ever been invited onto TV's *Mastermind*, his specialist subject

*Winning captain and Man of the Match
NatWest Trophy 1995*

would have been The Life and Times of Dermot Reeve? Born and reared in Hong Kong, both parents schoolteachers, three elder brothers high achievers professionally, attending a school where 38 different languages were spoken – Dermot Reeve marched to a different drum from the bulk of contemporary cricketers. Having been written off by so many in his career, Reeve saw no reason to be shy about his achievements. Not the English way, but why should that concern Reeve?

He remains the most successful captain in Warwickshire's history, and one of the key architects of a remarkable haul of trophies in just 24 months. Popularity contests are way down the priority list in the hard-nosed world of professional sport.

Brian Lara

When you're knee-deep in eulogies for one of the greatest entertainers in cricket history, it's best to offer a human assessment first. It comes from Gladstone Small, a friend of Brian Lara, yet not blind to his behavioural defects that, at times, bedevilled his time at Edgbaston. Small had bowled at some great batsmen in his time, but only Viv Richards is just ahead of Lara in his personal pantheon.

Anyone who knows the genial, laidback Small would appreciate this testimony about Lara: 'I used to stay awake to watch BC bat for us.' No higher praise from a cricketer nicknamed 'Tetsie' by his captain Graham Gooch on an England tour to Australia. Gooch discovered that if you get bitten by the tsetse fly, then immediate drowsiness is the reaction. Small seemed to kip a lot on that tour, so the whimsical Gooch felt it was the perfect appellation for his opening bowler.

A few years later, when Lara arrived at Edgbaston, Small was the proud father of three children under the age of five, and sleep was scarce in the Small household. So he needed no second bidding to catch a few zzzzs in the physio's room when Warwickshire were batting. His perfect day when not bowling was to relax on the couch when someone obdurate like Andy Moles or Roger Twose was occupying the crease.

But not when Lara was batting for the Bears. 'That physio's bed was my sanctuary after lively nights at home with the kids. That room was known as Smally's Lounge. But there's no higher praise that I couldn't get enough of watching Brian bat. He was a total maverick. I loved how he got after the bowlers with that high backlift. His first instinct was to hit the ball.'

Fairness dictates that any assessment of Lara's stint at Edgbaston begins with his impact on the side and how he inspired his new team-mates to greatness. He certainly said all the right things when he first appeared at Edgbaston, telling the players that he expected to be part of a winning unit, that what the team achieves is greater to him than personal records, such as the recent 375 in the Antigua Test.

At the end of that season, with the players almost bored by champagne, he said: 'I came here not for the money, but to be in a winning team. I didn't want to be in a team that was bottom of the table for five months. It wasn't ever a one-man show.'

Within a month of the season, Lara's batting had consistently astonished seasoned observers inside the game. He scored six championship hundreds in seven innings, culminating with an epic 501* against Durham. So he had posted the highest Test, then highest first-class score inside six weeks. Lara had done so in varying conditions, from the heat of Antigua to the gloom of Edgbaston in his first match, then the steady rain of Taunton, orchestrating a successful run chase. He did so with style and brio that were simply entrancing. No Bradmanesque accumulator, he – his championship runs were scored at almost a run a ball.

His county captain, Dermot Reeve, with whom he endured an uneasy relationship that summer, is in no doubt that Lara is the greatest batsman he ever saw. 'I would sit there, watching him in the middle, excited like a spectator. I'd be thinking, "How did he get the ball there? Crumbs, we've got to bat after this bloke – what will the crowd think?" I felt privileged.'

Neil Smith, not a man to lavish undue praise, is adamant: 'I cannot imagine anyone batting better than Brian over that six-week period from Antigua to the Durham game. He was in a different league from anyone I'd seen before – or since. Phenomenal. His ability to manipulate the ball was astonishing.'

Tim Munton has no doubts about Lara's importance in 1994. 'We were good and getting better, a decent bet for a one-day trophy. But we'd never have won three trophies without Brian. Not only was he a global superstar who brought us great publicity, but his rate of scoring gave us bowlers more time to take 20 wickets and win the championship.'

Dennis Amiss, always a keen student of the art of batting, had just taken up the post of chief executive, but he admits that the fan took over sometimes from the boss in those early, heady days. 'I would watch from my desk, entranced. Then I'd move closer to the window, just to appreciate his genius. Brian loved to bat and never seemed to break sweat. He knew about taking a fresh guard and cashing in when he got to his hundred. So flamboyant, so West Indian. He was even better than I thought. Another West Indian, Rohan Kanhai, runs him close in my time at Edgbaston, because he was superb on all types of wickets – but I can't separate those two.'

At the end of a long summer – during the title-winning match against Hampshire at Edgbaston

Lara in '94 was an absolute nightmare for opposition captains, first to try containing him, then getting him out. The Hampshire captain Mark Nicholas, a great one for a theory, shared his latest one about Lara on the eve of the match at Edgbaston which clinched the title. He told his players, 'Lara doesn't hit well down the ground, so we'll keep the ball well up to him, straight, and not bother with a mid-off or mid-on. We'll have an extra guy in the gully and for that shot off his hip, we'll have a deep squarish leg-gully.'

The plan worked well enough early on, as Lara surveyed the options serenely. Nicholas warmly encouraged his opening bowler, Cardigan Connor, as Lara blocked the straight deliveries or left the ball outside off-stump. Next over, two straight deliveries were crashed straight back past Connor, who got his feet out of the way just in time. He inquired of Nicholas, 'How's the plan going, Skip?', only to be reassured, 'Stick with it, Cardy, it's going ok.'

The next ball, again gun-barrel straight, was hit like a shell past Connor before he had followed through. Connor said to his captain, 'How about a different plan?', to be told by a resigned Nicholas, 'I haven't got one!' Lara made a dazzling 191 off 222 balls, his usual rate of scoring that summer in the championship.

Nicholas remains in awe of Lara's craft, his ability seemingly to hit the ball almost in a 360 degree arc – a talent rarely given to batsmen. 'Whenever you moved a fielder, Brian would hit it in that gap. He gave Warwickshire a dimension that no other batsman in the world could give at that time, and he did it consistently because he wanted that – not because he was being well paid to do it. It was ridiculous the way he hit balls where there was no fielder. That is a serious skill. He gave the impression that he never found the game remotely hard.'

Gladstone Small offers an interesting insight into how Lara thought about his batting, even though he made it look so easy. 'Brian had a little drill to stop him playing too far away from his body on the offside. In the nets he'd take the leg stump and place it about eight inches outside his off-stump. Every ball that was in that area, he'd leave alone. Anything else that was straighter, he laced it. He instinctively knew what to play and what to leave. No bowler likes a batsman like that!'

Small recalls how Lara tried to play golf left-handed, only to give it up after one attempt at it, when he went round 18 holes in under a hundred strokes. 'Brian really got the golf bug that year and played right-handed very well. He was sent a fabulous set of clubs for a left-hander but tried them for one round and gave them to a very grateful Roger Twose. Brian said playing left-handed would mess up his batting. That's how dedicated he was.'

Paul Smith was cut from a similar cloth to Lara, enjoying a full social life, and they got on well during that summer, on and off the field. Lara was very helpful with technical tips, especially with the younger players, who rightly hung on his every word. By now, Smith had been a first-team player for a decade, but he was astonished at Lara's attention to detail when he joined him in the middle at Taunton. Lara was playing with breathtaking assurance in difficult, rainy conditions when Smith joined him, with two wickets down and much still to do. Lara then proceeded to tell him in detail about all the fielders and where he could steal extra runs.

'Brian said there were two to one guy's right hand and one to his left, and who had a good arm and which fielders you could take on when he was going to throw from the deep. He went through all the fielders and though I appreciated his support, I had to say, "Brian, I don't care about cover point's left hand, I'm more bothered about the bowlers and whether it's swinging or not." I was amazed how observant he was. Many thought he just fizzed it all about, that he was just a natural. He certainly was that, but he also thought deeply about batting.

'When you were as good as Brian, it was just a matter of how long he could bat. He'd see the ball a split second before anyone else. And hit it so hard, even though his bat was like a toothpick to me. Brian was always in control at the crease that summer. You gave him the strike and stood at the other end, in awe of his talent.'

Lara was obsessed about gaps in the field, rather than the fielders. He wouldn't play the reverse sweep, which was by now the signature shot of most of the Warwickshire batsmen. Lara didn't need to, because his quickness at the crease and kestrel's eye created enough opportunities for him to demolish attacks. In team meetings, as Dermot Reeve extolled the virtues of reverse sweeping to disconcert the fielders, Lara would get exasperated and interrupt the captain. 'You keep talking about the fielders but, if you just concentrate on the gaps, then the fielders don't matter.'

More than one player noticed the frisson between Lara and Reeve during those team meetings. By midsummer, they had taken up antagonistic positions, and at times the relationship boiled over into enmity. It needed some intense diplomatic work from Dennis Amiss and Bob Woolmer to keep the ship sailing away from choppy waters.

This is the point where sonorous remarks about 'there's no I in team' and the importance of team spirit get aired. In that context, it's worth recalling the perceptive comment of Steve Archibald (or his artful journalist/collaborator) about team spirit. Archibald, a fine Scottish footballer with an independent mind, once opined, 'Team spirit is an illusion, glimpsed in the immediate aftermath of victory.'

Undoubtedly, team spirit is easier to maintain when you are winning. Pragmatism enters the equation and many just hunker down, hoping a damaging atmosphere will blow over. Yet Dermot Reeve and Bob Wooolmer had worked assiduously over the past two years to develop the ideal, constructive, supportive atmosphere in the Warwickshire dressing room. Was it going to be undermined by a great player, who was also a serial match-winner?

How do you square the circle of expecting conformity from the rest of the players in time-keeping and training with treating someone distinctively different like Lara, who was cut from a different cloth?

By June, this was becoming an issue for Warwickshire's cricket management. Lara had started to complain about a surfeit of cricket, he appeared to prefer golf to net practice, he often turned up late on match days, missing the warm-ups, and he made no secret of the fact that he found the Sunday League a chore. Lara asked to be excused from the NatWest Trophy tie against Bedfordshire, because his girl-friend was arriving that day from Trinidad and he wanted to pick her up at Heathrow Airport. Reeve refused to sanction this, but Lara drove to Heathrow and was 90 minutes late for the start. He was due to bat at three, and luckily Warwickshire batted first and a substantial opening partnership meant the press didn't know what was happening. Reeve was not impressed, and he wondered how much support he would get from the cricket management if he pursued some of these issues that were perturbing him.

Full disclosure here – I collaborated with Dermot Reeve for his autobiography after he retired in 1996. In it Reeve talked frankly about his uneasy relationship with Lara, throwing much light on flashpoints that had been either glossed over or never made the public domain. It was Reeve's book, so time for him to put his side of the story, and I therefore summarise here the gist of his feelings towards Lara. Such an influential figure in Warwickshire's impressive success is entitled to be heard, without any subjectivity from this quarter.

Reeve maintains that Lara regularly complained about a knee injury and general fatigue associated with such a long season, something he had never experienced before. He often tried to dip out of Sunday League matches, saying he didn't care for them. It became almost a weekly ritual for Dennis Amiss in persuading Lara to play, especially when the TV cameras were there. Too many questions would be asked if Lara was absent.

Reeve quoted the physiotherapist Stuart Nottingham, who could find little wrong with Lara's knee, pointing out that his fascination for playing golf would have been a problem if his knee was troubling him. Lara's impressive turn of speed between the wickets and agile work in the field also indicated there was no cause for alarm.

A nasty spat in the middle at Northampton between Reeve and Lara brought extra focus on a deteriorating relationship between captain and star player. Lara swore at Reeve as the other players congregated around at the fall of a wicket, and Reeve said calmly, 'Brian, you're turning into a prima donna.' A meeting attended at the ground one evening by Reeve, Woolmer, Amiss, Munton and Lara brought an uneasy truce, which was never really going to hold. A few weeks later, there was another bust-up in the dressing room when Lara and Reeve clashed over how they had both batted against the spin of Worcestershire's Richard Illingworth, leading to a needless, annoying defeat. By now, Reeve couldn't wait for the season to end, because he felt he wasn't getting enough support. He believed the

A joyful team celebrate his record-breaking 501

prospect of being awarded a benefit in the near future was intimidating him into keeping his mouth shut – not normally the default stance of Dermot Reeve.

The captain was pleasantly surprised on the morning of the Benson & Hedges Final when Lara asked Bob Woolmer for permission to address the players in the dressing room. Reeve says that Lara apologised for his recent behaviour and that he was fully committed to the team. He shook hands with all the players and even entered into an awkward hug with Reeve.

Amiss justifies his policy of realpolitik simply. 'We were winning, the players were looking at some handsome bonuses and Brian was only there for one season. He wasn't easy to handle, that's for sure. I had a round of golf with him at the Belfry, trying to get over to him that he could get a little closer to the players, have a beer with them at close of play, rather than rushing off to play golf. Brian's agent, Jonathan Barnett, knew we'd got him for a song so he was determined to get some big deals that summer. That meant Brian was under pressure to make personal appearances.

'I kept hearing from Bobby Woolmer and Dermot that Brian was being difficult, and I had to tell them they just had to make it work, because we were going so well. Nothing was to disrupt our progress. I don't think I could've handled it differently, but it was tough on Dermot and Bob, keeping it on an even keel. In the end, we were justified. Look at our record in '94.'

In truth, the players, other than Reeve, didn't see it as such a big deal. He felt his authority was being eroded by what he saw as a craven approach towards Lara. 'I didn't like the way it seemed he wasn't enjoying county cricket after his early dazzling performances. He'd sit in the dressing room, moaning about fatigue, the demands on his time, the many autographs he had to sign. Then if Dennis Amiss asked him to pop next door to do a press conference, he'd put on that angelic smile and tell the media how important it was for him to see the team do well. A genius isn't necessarily a great team man.'

The other players were understandably less exercised. The word filtered down from the senior players that standards mustn't drop – and they didn't. They kept winning, always an effective antidote to discontent when cricketers are living in each other's pockets for months on end. Gladstone Small thinks it was simply a clash of egos between Lara and Reeve,

with the captain now used to prevailing verbally over others in meetings. Shrewdly, Small thinks Lara had been forewarned about Reeve's style of leadership. 'I reckon someone in the Caribbean put Brian on watch – he was told to keep an eye on Dermot. We didn't care. As players we knew what Brian was bringing to the table. It was a special time of his career. We had to make allowances for him, he was just passing through at Edgbaston – unlike Allan Donald, who was a true Bear. But that didn't make Brian less popular.'

Paul Smith also thinks too much has been made of the Lara/Reeve issue. 'In order to play professional sport, you have to have strong opinions. You'd probably get sacked in other walks of life if you said what's aired in a sports dressing room. Dermot was used to ruling the roost, but Brian was the star – and we knew it. I felt like I'd been asked to accompany Beethoven after twanging a guitar for years. He was a genius.'

Smith would admit to partiality towards Lara, having forged a friendship with him on the Trinidad tour before the 1991 season, but he offers an interesting insight into the commercial pressures Lara faced in 1994. The morning after his historic 501* at Edgbaston, Lara was in London with the rest of the team, preparing to face Surrey in a Benson & Hedges Cup semi-final. He had already been on Radio 4's Today programme that morning when he rang Paul Smith in his hotel room. 'Smithy, where's Tower Bridge?' 'It's that big piece of metal outside your hotel window, Brian.' Lara explained he had to have his photo taken, in a suit and bowler hat, on Tower Bridge. 'His agent had done a massive deal overnight off the back of his 501*, and the photo opportunity was essential. He was completely shattered after his innings the day before. What a way to prepare for such a big game at The Oval.'

Tim Munton recalls with affection Lara supporting a charity six-a-side event at Stratford-Upon-Avon CC, for Birmingham-based cancer charity The Get A-Head Appeal. Lara wasn't able to participate because of a prior commitment to a photo shoot for Joe Bloggs Jeans, a new sponsor of his. But he did tell Munton he would do his best to get back before the end of the event. He did, and more than made amends for not being able to play in the event, something Munton really appreciated, demonstrating the great respect between the two of them. 'He arrived wearing

Still in demand – ten years later

his blue Brew XI Warwickshire polo shirt and, once he found out the fund-raising hadn't quite gone to plan, he took to the microphone, apologised that he hadn't been able to join us earlier and auctioned the shirt on his back, signed and personalised to the lucky bidder, who appropriately paid £501 – a major contribution to the fund-raising.'

Neil Smith, poles apart temperamentally from Lara, nevertheless admired him hugely and thought the management compromises were worth it. 'I didn't have a problem with Brian getting extra freedom. If the club had not allowed him his time to relax, I think the intensity of everyone wanting a piece of him would have got too much. It's difficult to spend so many days in the field when you're scoring so many runs and then fielding both of the opposition innings. Brian delivered for us, and that's the key issue.'

It may be that Dermot Reeve felt more than anyone else that Lara was cut too much slack. There was also the nagging feeling that Lara didn't rate his captaincy as much as the majority at Edgbaston, judging by a few whispers that came back to Reeve. Amiss's emollient attitude to Lara was eventually justified and, in his first year as chief executive, determined to rid Warwickshire of the defeatist, conformist attitude of much of his playing days, he was ruthlessly pursuing victory in all competitions. In that he was hugely successful.

No doubt there were some players who at times felt as strongly as Reeve about Lara's transgressions, but such animus did not last that long. It doesn't when you are not the captain and more concerned with team victories and individual success. For his part, Reeve can point to Lara having a disciplinary problem the following year when West Indies toured and he went missing for a week. A hefty fine followed, and the same applied in 1998, when Lara ill-advisedly returned for a season as Warwickshire's captain. It was not a success, and another fine for lateness was incurred. He was worn out by commercial considerations, carrying the weak West Indies batting order and engaging in various wrangles with their board. He should have passed on that second season with Warwickshire.

But such controversies are a sideshow when you consider the remarkable batting of Brian Lara in 1994. Ask any Bears fan from that period about Lara and they won't bother with nit-picking over his one-day record (highest score 81 that season), nor his relaxed attitude to net practice or punctuality. Most of the players from that year would agree.

If he had a weakness as a batsman, it was probably only an early jitteriness against extreme pace. Certainly Devon Malcolm, at his peak in 1994, caused him some problems for both England and Derbyshire. Glenn McGrath in his pomp used to trouble him around off-stump. But no batsman in the history of the game has an infallible technique. Few could enchant like Brian Lara.

When he said farewell to international cricket in April 2007, he asked the crowd at the end of a TV interview, 'Have I entertained you?' The roars of acclamation that day were the most convincing summary of an extraordinary career.

Bob Woolmer – Director of Coaching

When Bob Woolmer was just two days old, his father pressed a cricket bat and ball into his tiny hand as he slept in his crib. 'Son, I hope this will be your life,' he said. They proved prophetic words. Apart from his family, cricket absorbed Bob Woolmer for all of his 58 years, in the course enriching and inspiring thousands of cricketers who lacked his stature as a player but were sensible enough to tap into his generosity of spirit and his restless, creative intelligence.

Statistically, Bob Woolmer was Warwickshire's greatest coach, guiding the team to five trophies in two spells as well as leaving a legacy that hoovered up two other trophies in the year after he first left the club.

Woolmer's importance lay in his imaginative methods of coaching, his willingness to challenge the orthodoxies, encouraging his players to free the spirit, dealing with failures without recrimination or fear. In his first spell of four years at Edgbaston, he was simply a one-man tutorial on the art of the possible, adopting input from other sports, introducing scientific experts, persuading his players there were other ways to win cricket matches than the conventional methods he had followed as a Kent and England batsman twenty years earlier.

'We were the best coached side in England,' says Gladstone Small. 'Bob was by far the best England coach in 1994, light years ahead.' Tim Munton agrees. 'That season was the culmination of the Bob Woolmer Finishing School that started in 1991. Dermot, of course, was highly influential, but Bob was the planner, the creative genius who believed in us.'

It took some time for other counties to grasp what was going on at Edgbaston in the '94 season. John Emburey was hugely impressed by them in May, after they almost beat Middlesex in a championship game at Lord's. 'Dermot as captain was allowed to tinker and do as he pleased, he had a well-balanced bowling attack, but Bob Woolmer's influence from the dressing room was clear, in the positive way they played. Bob was comfortably the best coach in the world at the time.'

Hugh Morris, then the Glamorgan captain, was a huge fan of Duncan Fletcher when he joined the Welsh club in 1997 and sees comparisons with Woolmer. 'For us, Duncan was a wonderful coach,

providing the cement that bound us together – and Bob Woolmer had that same aura in 1994. One of the original coaching gurus, with a great CV, Bob always thought outside the box, very intuitive. I remember soon after Bob joined Warwickshire we were out with them in Zimbabwe on a pre-season tour, and Bob was organising range hitting in a stadium. He was instructing his batsmen to hit balls into the stand, as far as possible. Nowadays, that's a standard practice for 20/20 batters but, all those years ago, we were wondering why Bob was practising it so hard. He was ahead of any other coach.'

As I write this assessment of Woolmer, I have his last book in front of me. It was published a year after his tragic death in 2007 on World Cup duty, coaching Pakistan. The proofs were checked by Woolmer just six weeks before his death, and Professor Tim Noakes and Helen Moffett finessed the tome as they came to terms with their shock and grief. I was deeply touched to be on the book's distribution list for the media, hopefully because I had always enjoyed a convivial, confiding relationship with Woolmer since he first played for England in 1975. One of his most endearing characteristics was the open, cheerful way he dealt with cricket reporters. Woolmer's 'modus operandi' was to hide nothing, preferring to trust his media contacts, using them sensibly to disseminate his thoughts more widely, and assume that all the scribes shared his love of cricket. He was rarely let down.

This final book, *Bob Woolmer's Art and Science of Cricket*, is a remarkable tract. It took ten years for him to assemble the necessary facts and opinions before publication. Typically, he was still updating his opinions a decade on, after finding new source material that made him think again. He was always open to a change of mind.

The book runs to 655 pages and, to my mind, it's the definitive insight into cricket coaching. Those better qualified than me pore over it regularly. Allan Donald, who enjoyed such a fruitful relationship with Woolmer at Warwickshire, then with South Africa, is making his way now as a coach in county cricket, having seen service on the international circuit, and Woolmer's book is his constant companion. 'I've read it many times, I've made so many notes from it. Bob

The first of many triumphs – Bob Woolmer (right) celebrates the winning of the NatWest Trophy in 1993

stretched us so much, I can hear him speaking as I read it. I remember him telling us what we was going to do when he arrived at Edgbaston in 1991, telling us how far we would be in three years' time. He was spot on.'

Dennis Amiss may have scored more first-class runs and hundreds for Warwickshire than any other player, but arguably his greatest achievement for the club was recommending Woolmer to be the new Director of Cricket in 1991. Amiss knew all about his friend's deep love and respect for the game from their times as England players, and Amiss believed strongly that the club should take a chance on someone whose CV was perhaps less impressive than older, more experienced contenders.

'Bob told our batters they needed to mess the fielders and bowlers about more, that they needed more options, like the reverse and the slog sweep. He was into computers as well, very unusual in those days in cricket, and he'd show the boys on the screen what they were doing right and wrong out in the middle. Bob gave them confidence in themselves. He was excellent at having one-to-ones, getting to know about the players' families and personal lives, as well as their cricket ambitions.

'His relationship with Dermot was excellent, until Dermot lost form in '94. They'd spark each other off with so many positive suggestions, but Bob always made it clear that the captain was in charge. Bob would say "Stay with it" if a batsman got out playing a particular shot and the coach was happy he'd practised hard at it. If ever the side had a bad day, he'd get them out that night for a meal to sort it out. Everybody was encouraged to discuss things, he believed in having arguments to get it out in the open.'

Tim Munton remembers Reeve and Woolmer having the occasional bickering spat in the dressing room, but Reeve would invariably defuse the situation with a well-timed quip. 'Dermot was excellent at lifting the mood, telling Bob to slope off, shut up and sit on the exercise bike next door. But they had a massive mutual respect for each other. The combo worked spectacularly.'

Reeve loved working with Woolmer, never feeling threatened by him. 'Bob had the knack of being apart from the players at the right times, giving them their space, but he was accessible and ready to laugh at himself. No one ever spent more time with the hairdryer in our dressing room than Bob, and the amount of work he put in at the gym did nothing for his splendid paunch – all he managed was a very strong pair of legs! Bob took all the ribbing in good part, and he helped foster a great team spirit, where the young players weren't talked down to by the elders.'

When they first met at Edgbaston, Reeve told Woolmer that it was the cricket management's job to ensure the players were the best prepared in the country. He was impressed by Woolmer stating openly that he was still learning as a coach. Woolmer showed his breadth of mind by bringing in psychologists, nutritionists and sports scientists to improve fitness and demystifying the laptop. It became a trusted tool for the players. 'He fed the science of cricket into us, even getting our eyes tested,' recalls Tim Munton. 'Bob was always looking for another half a per cent advantage.'

He got the players talking more about cricket, both in their dressing room and in the bar at close of play, instead of sloping off early in search of social indulgences. 'The young players became deep thinkers,' says Reeve, 'and they were ready to challenge the views of the senior players. That was good for team spirit.'

Woolmer was determined to improve the squad's fielding, and he did so with a tennis racket. He knew a tennis ball is harder to catch than a cricket ball, when working close up, that taking a tennis ball cleanly teaches you how to give with the ball at the moment of impact. He reasoned that constant catching practice with a cricket ball gives you sore hands so, when a chance arrives out in the middle, you might subconsciously not go for it. Woolmer would hit fifty catches to a fielder's left hand with a tennis ball, then fifty to the right hand. He would tell them to go for a catch out in the middle with both hands, but try for them one-handed in practice, because that was harder. So, after gaining confidence with one-handed takes in practice, the fielder would then be more relaxed going for chances with both hands in a match situation.

Reeve says that Woolmer's catching practice methods were totally justified. 'Our close catching became of a very high standard, giving us a head start over other counties. When I saw the Lancashire coach David Lloyd using the tennis racket in the 1995 season, I felt proud that Warwickshire had been ahead of them by several years.'

Running between the wickets had to improve, especially in one-day cricket. For Jason Ratcliffe, Woolmer's rationale was an eye-opener. 'Bob told us to be bold in our calling for singles and to trust our partner implicitly. Running between the wickets had always been relatively relaxed, but in practice we worked out that, if you nurdled a good ball round the corner and the non-striker called and went straight away, there was a run, even when it went straight to a fielder. We kept moving the field around, frustrating them with reverse sweeps, and we were taking teams for forty more runs per game on average. It took some time before other sides caught up with us.'

Woolmer would talk to every player at the end of the season, asking them where they felt they had shown a weakness. He would then tell them to go away and work on it and return for next season, with that weakness turned into a strength. It worked spectacularly for Roger Twose in the 1993/94 close season. Twose had struggled against the short ball in 1993, and Woolmer suggested a different technique. Twose worked hard in New Zealand that winter and returned a more confident, secure batsmen. Imaginative coaching had transformed his technique, and Twose enjoyed two more productive seasons before emigrating to New Zealand and becoming an international player.

The success of the reverse sweep sets Woolmer apart from the rest of the coaches at that time. When he first took over, he was amazed that Reeve was the only Warwickshire player who tried the shot. He patiently explained how productive it was, how it seriously irritated bowlers, opening up the field enticingly. He told the players that hard practice in the nets, self-confidence to try it out in the middle and support from the rest of the team would pay dividends. 'I was so pleased that so many of the guys took responsibility to work at it, then play it in a match. We had many converts.'

Woolmer loved to hear old sweats like Andy Moles, Neil Smith and Gladstone Small say 'that's great cricket' in the viewing area when the likes of Twose,

Reeve and Penney would reverse sweep. They had to be convinced by Woolmer about the shot's merits but were won round by his articulate enthusiasm. Entering his 30s, after a decade as a solid opener, Moles started to reverse sweep with gusto. Meanwhile, other county coaches looked on with scepticism while Woolmer's batsmen kept outscoring them. 'Many didn't take us seriously enough until it was too late,' he told me once. 'We were called an average side, full of journeymen and just one great player. Yet we lost only five games in five months. Is that average?'

The ultimate compliment to Woolmer's advocacy of the reverse sweep came in the match when Warwickshire clinched the 1994 championship at Edgbaston. In the course of establishing a massive first innings lead, the Bears went for occupation of the crease, wearing Hampshire's bowlers down. With the score past 500, the last man loped in for a knock. Now Tim Munton had steadfastly refrained from playing the reverse sweep all summer, but this time he decided to indulge himself. First ball from the off-spinner Shaun Udal was right in the screws and reverse swept perfectly for four by Munton. That was too much for the exasperated Hampshire captain, Mark Nicholas, who bellowed: 'That's it! I've had enough! Even f...ing Munton's reverse sweeping now. It's official – Woolmer's a f...ing genius!'

That was certainly the view of Woolmer's players, some of whom had a totally different approach to preparing for a match. Paul Smith, for example. In his time, he was a legendary boulevardier, with Ian Botham unsurprisingly his hero. Woolmer did his best to rein in Smith's excesses while recognising his mercurial all-rounder was very serious about his cricket. 'I would have breakfast regularly with Bob around 7am, just a couple of hours after coming in from an energetic session and we'd talk cricket in great depth. I wanted to win just as much as Bob, and he knew that. I'd tell him to judge me on match days, not how I prepared myself. Bob had our ears, he kept us keen by challenging us every day. He was exceptional at that. He spoke a different language from other coaches.'

Tim Munton agrees that Woolmer had an uncanny knack of moulding disparate personalities effortlessly. 'He had a way of keeping us together, challenging us to be the best we could, demanding we improved.

Blokes like Gladys, Moler, Neil Smith and myself – not the most agile movers in the field – improved because of Bob's brilliance at pushing senior pros, appealing to their pride in performance.'

He could be simplistic when necessary, eschewing the laptop approach when dealing with a player of great natural talent who was not doing himself justice. In 1994, Dominic Ostler was one of the most exciting young batsmen in the country, a punishing player who lacked self-belief at times, getting into troughs of poor form. Woolmer knew what to say. 'Get me a hundred. Just go and hit the bloody ball – use your talent. You're batting number four all season. Now get out there!'

It remains astonishing that Woolmer was never pursued by England at the height of his Edgbaston achievements. He was lured away by South Africa, hardly surprising given he lived in Cape Town, where he was rightly lauded for his unstinting coaching work in townships. At a time when England's one-day cricket was depressingly constipated, with Michael Atherton struggling to attune to its hectic demands on the field, the intuitive, smart approach of Woolmer would have been a godsend. Sri Lanka showed the way in the 1996 World Cup, with brilliant, fearless players adopting the blueprint of spinners opening the bowling, the use of pinch-hitters and subjugating spinners with reverse sweeps and slog sweeps. The Warwickshire way.

Yet the neolithic approach remained the default procedure, and Bob Woolmer never even got to coach on an England A tour. Neil Smith played for England in that 1996 World Cup and is still aghast at the neglect of Woolmer. 'Sri Lanka showed how quickly the one-day game was progressing, as we did at county level. It's taken England twenty years to get to grips with how to play it under Eoin Morgan. We wouldn't have been behind the eight ball so long under Bob – or with Dermot as captain in 1996.'

International cricket was the logical progression for Woolmer after his dazzling success with Warwickshire. He came back, though, six years later for three more seasons at Edgbaston, but the lustre had dimmed. Noticing that few played the reverse sweep anymore, he found it hard to rediscover that special alchemy that set him apart. Three troubled seasons saw him secure just one trophy, the Benson & Hedges Cup in

Back for his second spell in 2000

2002 and, unsure about his support in the dressing room or at committee level, Woolmer resigned before he was pushed out. Yet another example of the durable sporting adage 'Never Go Back'.

After that, Woolmer clocked up prodigious amounts of air-miles in the service of cricket. When he died, in March 2007, he had coached cricketers on four continents and played in the fifth for Kerry Packer in Australia. Canada, Namibia, Kenya, Holland, Ireland, High Performance Manager for the ICC – he was the Phileas Fogg of cricket coaches, forever enthused by his latest project. I bumped into him in the Caribbean a week or so before he died. Always content when seated in front of a menu with a glass of red to hand, Bob rhapsodised about the level of natural talent in the Pakistan side he was now coaching.

Tragically, his ambitions for Pakistan cricket were unfulfilled. He died in his hotel room, just hours after Pakistan lost a World Cup match to Ireland. Woolmer took the defeat in his customary urbane,

sporting manner, but it hurt him. We will never know exactly what happened in Room 374 of the Pegasus Hotel, Kingson. The rumours were disturbing, wild and ultimately unsubstantiated. Eight months later, an inquest jury returned an open verdict. The jury foreman remarked there were a number of inconsistencies, so that a more precise verdict was impossible.

Bob's widow, Gill and her two sons remain satisfied that he died of natural causes. Out of respect to the Woolmer family, the matter should rest. Bob once said to me in an interview, 'It's only a game. Nobody has died.' It was one of his favourite sayings, testimony to his equable, sincere nature. How sad that Bob did die in the service of the sport that meant so much to him and brought him so much joy.

I wonder if Bob Woolmer has been appreciated enough at Edgbaston for what he achieved. A pity he returned in 2000 for those three frustrating seasons, instead of leaving for good on a high after 1994. Tim Munton believes it is high time Woolmer was lionised more at Edgbaston. 'As a club, we need to recognise Bob's massive contribution, from the time he arrived in 1991, transformed the players and brought us to history three years later. It's almost as if he has been forgotten. Players tend to get the accolades, rather than coaches – but ask anyone from that dressing room in 1994 what he gave us.'

A statue for Woolmer then at Edgbaston? One of the stands named after him? It is true that, during the West Indies Test match in August 2017, one of the Aylesford executive boxes was named after Woolmer. Another 18 have also been named after members of that 1994 squad. So Woolmer's stature is not exactly venerated. He is in there with the others, some of whom did not make as vital a contribution as their good-natured, modest coach.

He would be highly amused by the reaction of Gladstone Small to some sort of memorial in his honour. 'If it was for me, they should put a plaque on a bar stool in the Members' Bar, for spending so much time there. For Bob? Well, he liked his food, so how about the Bob Woolmer Kitchen? Or, bearing in mind how much he loved his laptop ... what about the Bob Woolmer IT Room?

'Doesn't matter. The players won't forget Bob. We don't need any memorial to the great man.'

MJK Smith – Chairman

It is always instructive to see who Geoffrey Boycott respects and admires in the world of cricket. And why. You would not have thought a public schoolboy and then Oxford University graduate would linger long in the affections of the Sage of Fitzwilliam. But Boycott makes an exception for MJK Smith.

More than 50 years after Mike Smith led England on tours to South Africa, Australia and New Zealand, Boycott still hails him as 'Captain' whenever they bump into each other. This from a vastly experienced cricketer with Olympian standards who was also skippered by Ray Illingworth and Mike Brearley. He doesn't call them 'captain'.

The hallmark of Smith's captaincy that so impressed Boycott permeated all the aspects of his hugely impressive career in cricket over 60 years. MJK Smith knew how to run a happy ship, with no ego.

Smith was a very popular captain for England in 25 of his 50 Tests and in the 11 years he led Warwickshire. Unselfish, thoughtful, sensible, his hand on the tiller was invariably light. A side led by Smith was usually a happy one. He believed in treating his players like adults, relying on a quiet word if necessary and insisting on loyalty to them in public. In the field one of the bravest and most prehensile short-leg fielders of his age, he set a wonderful example. Mike Smith's players followed him, without questioning his natural, understated authority.

Smith's cricketing CV is outstanding:

- 39,832 first-class runs in a 25-year career
- 595 catches in 637 first-class matches, 53 in 50 Tests
- Averaged 50 for Warwickshire in 1972 – at the age of 39 – when they won the county championship
- 2,000 first-class runs in six successive seasons
- 3,249 runs in the 1959 season, the highest total since the 1940s
- Nine trophies won by Warwickshire during his years as chairman 1991 to 2003
- England manager on the tours of the West Indies in 1993/94 and Australia in 1994/95
- ICC match referee from 1991 to 1996
- The last 'double international' for England at rugby union and cricket, playing fly-half against Wales in 1956

You would never get MJK Smith talking about any of it unless the proverbial wild horses were corralled to drag it out of him. After he became club chairman, a few current players may have been gulled by his vague, absent-minded professor schtick behind the steel-rimmed glasses but after a few minutes talking cricket with him, they realised he was a serious brain. The club was very fortunate to have someone of his stature orchestrating its rise and rise.

Ashley Giles was one of those young players who soon came to respect Smith massively. 'I really used to look forward to talking cricket with MJK. I learned so much about the history of the game and the club. But you had to ask him the questions; he understood players didn't want an earbashing. Once he knew you were interested, he was fascinating.'

Tim Munton agrees. 'If he spoke cricket to you, it was always part of a conversation instead of a former player being dictatorial or strident. Having been to Oxford, he was obviously more clever than most of us, but he never imposed himself. We were incredibly lucky to have him as our chairman, in the wings, but always there with constructive support.'

Typically, Smith deflects the praise for his stewardship of the club during its most successful period in its history. He took over in 1991, at a time of internecine strife, with the members very vocal about many issues. Smith defused the tension in his customarily astute manner. 'I was pitchforked into it, but a good team runs itself and we were on the way with Andy Lloyd and Bob Woolmer on the cricket side. And administratively I had some excellent people around me.'

That is as far as he will pitch his contribution. He had already impressed by keeping a low-profile when his son Neil progressed into regular first-team action after his crucial cameo in the NatWest Trophy Final of 1989. The chairman took no part in his son's subsequent career, contenting himself with 'he's a good player, he's got a chance.' As Tim Munton recalls, 'We never thought of Neil as "the son of". MJK treated him just like any other player. It's a measure of their integrity that none of us saw anything unusual. Neil played in England one-dayers, so that means he was a good cricketer.'

Father and son with the 1989 NatWest Trophy – in the final Neil hit the winning runs with two balls to spare

In fact, father's undemonstrative support for his son was splendidly demonstrated in that final over at Lord's in '89 when, in effect, Neil won the NatWest Trophy with a straight six in the gloaming. While the rest of those in the Warwickshire CCC box indulged in euphoric, backslapping celebrations as the six was signalled, Smith père contented himself with a contented grin. He's never been one for the histrionic gesture.

Five years later, Mike Smith had a key role in a historic signing by Warwickshire CCC, and even he allowed himself a satisfied smile. He had enjoyed first-hand experience of Brian Lara's brilliance, as manager of the touring England team to the Caribbean, early in '94. Someone with Smith's awareness of the art of batsmanship fully sanctioned Warwickshire's daring pursuit of Lara for the summer and, when Smith finally supervised the signing of the contract, he was delighted.

The sequel to the deal was classic MJK Smith. Always slightly disorganised, despite his keen mind, Smith mislaid the signed contract in his Barbados hotel. For a time, the spectre loomed of going back to Lara to get him to sign on a new dotted line. That's if his management had not had second thoughts, on realising what a bargain Lara was to prove for his new employers.

'I've never been the tidiest of blokes,' admits Smith. 'Nor was a mate of mine who had come over to watch the cricket, who I gave a bed to in my hotel room. The contract was delivered to me, and I lost it. We searched high and low but had to leave it to the hotel staff eventually to find it. I'm glad that didn't happen after his 375 in Antigua a few days later. He was an even bigger asset then!'

By 1994, Mike Smith had seen and played enough cricket to be unsurprised by much. But he was beguiled by Lara in the summer of '94. He had always been fascinated by the complexity of batting, but Lara was of a different dimension. 'Only Rohan Kanhai among Warwickshire players comes close for me. I can't split them. I rarely use the word 'great' but Lara has to be. Apart from Lara, only Bradman has scored more than 350 three times – and Lara did it twice in Test matches.

'It must have been marvellous for our blokes to bat with him in '94 because you can learn so much at close quarters. At Oxford, I was privileged to bat alongside Colin Cowdrey, who was technically as good as anyone I've seen. Half the exercise of batting is to mess the bowlers about, and Lara and Kanhai were superb at that. You just couldn't bowl at them at their best – and that's the definition of a great batsman.'

Smith is too sharp just to attribute Warwickshire's great season to one genius. 'We had a splendidly varied attack and all-rounders who could bat. Often, from seven downwards, we added 150-odd runs. That turned a lot of matches. We had a group of very fine players and one great batsman, and we didn't suffer from England calls. We were also the best fielding side in the country. There were no weaknesses.'

It is typical of Smith's forensic cricket brain that he picks out Dominic Ostler's all-round brilliance in the field. Most of the focus on fielding that season was on the spectacular Trevor Penney, for his lightning work across the field and success in hitting the stumps for run-outs. But for Smith, the work of Ostler in the deep and his wonderful catching at slip was paramount. Decades earlier, when Smith was catching superbly at short leg, there were no helmets or shin guards to protect the close fielders, and he knows enough about the art of close catching to stress Ostler's importance in the slips.

Fundamentally, Mike Smith missed very little in assessing cricket and cricketers. He reduced so many tactical challenges to simplicities. He once told me the fundamental secret to successful batting was 'you hit the ball away from the fielder and it doesn't really matter where you hit it, as long as you get away with it consistently.' He's always been a great debunker of theories, MJK. To him, cricket remains a simple game but, if you want to prosper at it, it has to be approached with a clear mind.

In 1994, it appeared a perfect storm for Warwickshire, with all the component parts working harmoniously for most of the time. But stability off the field was vital. The group of former players in key positions at the club – Dennis Amiss, Steve Rouse, Neal Abberley – were a positive, supportive influence but their former captain, at the helm, was an unflappable leader. Just as he was as captain.

Mike and Neil Smith have clocked up over a hundred years' involvement with Warwickshire, and they are still popular figures at Edgbaston. Any current player who wants clear guidance about what it means to play for Warwickshire should slip into the chairman's lounge on match day and sit alongside a spry octogenarian; it will be instructive. Few words will be wasted, the odd pause will precede thoughtful sentences, and kindly advice will be generously offered – but only if Mike Smith's advice is sought. He has never been one to dominate a conversation.

At least one player from Warwickshire's Golden Age still values talking cricket with MJK. 'I still call him "Chairman", nearly twenty years after I left the club as a player,' Tim Munton says. 'I can't offer higher praise than that. I'm hugely fond of MJK.'

I can think of countless folk who would second that sentiment.

Dennis Amiss – Chief Executive

One of the smartest moves Dennis Amiss made as soon as he got the job of Warwickshire's chief executive was to throw open the doors of his home and treat his new staff to a barbie and a few bevvies.

It was April 1994, and Amiss had been an illustrious ex-player for seven years. As chairman of the cricket committee for the past three years, he was well versed in some of the Edgbaston politics, aware of various bouts of bloodletting. He was savvy enough to know that, without the full support of his players, the new job could be a bed of nails, while the key administrative staff had to be kept on-side as well.

So Dennis and Jill Amiss decided to launch the new season by hosting a convivial Sunday. Amiss stood up at one stage, to tell the players' wives and partners how important they were, while he pledged support to the players, as long as their hearts were with the club. They would be expected to appear more often at close of play in the Extra Cover Bar to mingle with the members for at least one drink.

Having endured many an earbashing over a pint from the members down the years, Amiss knew what he was asking of the 1994 intake. Some of them took to the new social order more readily than others, but Amiss's initiative brought the players closer to their supporters. 'Bob Woolmer and I thought it was very important to be in the Extra Cover Bar with our members. That increased the affection they felt for the club and for the players. There were some very happy times there. Everything seemed to come together for a magical time for all of us in 1994.'

Yet Amiss would not have been the new man in charge that historic summer if his predecessor's health hadn't failed. David Heath had been first secretary, then chief executive since 1986 but had to retire prematurely and sadly died in June 1994, aged just 62. He had presided over some fractious times on and off the field in the previous eight years and must be accorded due credit for overseeing the gradual improvement in the club's fortunes pre-'94.

So not for the first time at Edgbaston, Dennis Amiss was in the right place at the right time to continue a love affair with the club that began as a 15-year-old in 1958, the youngest to be taken onto the Warwickshire playing staff. As he eased himself

into the chief executive's chair, he could count himself lucky that his old county captain, MJK Smith, was presiding benignly as club chairman, on hand to mark his card while settling into his new role. Two months after Amiss started, Smith – touring the Caribbean as England's manager – delivered him the prize of Brian Lara's signature, and things started to fall into place.

It was the blistering start that Amiss had demanded. After 28 years as a player and three as cricket chairman, he had become frustrated at the club not punching its weight. He felt one championship, one Sunday League title and two NatWest Trophies since 1972 was a poor return, given the quality of players available. 'We had to set the bar higher. I always thought we should have won more when I was a player and then, when we had poor sides, we were being taken to the cleaners too often. I didn't like that, even though I was scoring a lot of runs.'

Eight trophies on Amiss's watch as the CEO would suggest Warwickshire got his appointment right. A modest, unassuming man, Amiss has been underestimated by many down the years. At least five times in his outstanding career, he was at a personal and professional crossroads, yet he came through them all with a clear-eyed determination and understated drive. In his early days, his tendency to run out senior batsmen led to a few encounters up against the dressing-room wall, with a menacing bat nearby. In the 1973 Trent Bridge Test, he ran out Geoffrey Boycott (no stranger to such a situation) and the opening pair didn't speak till the next Test, when the captain Raymond Illingworth had to bang their heads together. Amiss was not for backing down in the face of the legendary Boycottian ire.

At the age of 29 Amiss was dropped by Warwickshire. With a young family to support, he had to face reality. He knuckled down in the second team, suggested he might open and, on his return to the first XI, he scored 151* at the first time of asking.

In 1976 he lost his nerve for a time against quick bowling after being hit on the back of the head by Michael Holding. His travails were painful to watch as self-confidence simply oozed away, but he worked out a two-eyed stance to combat the fearsome West Indies fast bowlers to make 203 in the final Test at the Oval.

During the 1978 season the majority of Warwickshire's players barely spoke to Amiss after he signed for Kerry Packer's World Series, a development which threatened to destabilise English cricket. Amiss's response was to keep his head down and score 2,000 first-class runs, the only player to do so that summer. He found it more congenial staying out in the middle, clocking up the runs, rather than getting the cold shoulder. Eventually peace broke out, and Amiss was offered another contract by Warwickshire in 1979, but he had been prepared to end his time at Edgbaston due to his involvement with Packer.

All this has to be factored in when assessing the tough decisions Amiss had to make after he donned the chief executive's suit. His time as a player had equipped him with the necessary mental toughness to make hard decisions. You don't graduate to being one of only 25 batsmen to score a hundred first-class centuries without the requisite amount of resilience to buttress great natural ability. He hadn't scored a championship century before his England debut, batting at number five. Early in his England career, he 'bagged a pair' against the Australians in the 1968 Old Trafford Test. For a long time he felt unworthy of being seen as an England batsman. Yet Amiss also scored 11 Test centuries – and eight of those were 150 and over. He was no soft touch under his affable, approachable persona. He brought that steely determination into his new job in 1994.

'I knew that Warwickshire was a big club, and that expectations were justifiably high when I started as chief exec. When AC Smith, my old team-mate, was chief exec he used to say, "We're a big club, but we've got to be careful because the smaller clubs resent the bigger ones." But I thought that shouldn't stop us winning things. I reckoned it was my job to change that mentality and bring good players to Warwickshire. MJK bought into us being ruthless without going over the top, and we were driving us forward.'

Having a few former Warwickshire players in key roles helped Amiss come to terms with his new challenge. 'As well as MJK, we had two former team-mates in Steve Rouse as head groundsman and John Whitehouse doing my old job as cricket committee chairman. We would argue about things, as you'd expect, but come to a consensus, keeping John informed, while MJK and I dealt with things day-to-day. Bobby Woolmer and Dermot Reeve were happy to listen to what we had to offer. There was a large fulcrum of knowledge and a great deal of mutual respect, but no doubt at all that Bobby and Dermot were in charge of cricket ultimately.'

The cricket management had to be on top of its game, as the games piled on top of each other as the '94 season wore on. Initially the aim was to win at least a one-day trophy but, once the championship victories piled up off the back of Lara's prodigious feats, the strategy was re-assessed. The championship was feasible by midsummer, but the Lara/Reeve nettle had to be grasped, otherwise the season would end in rancorous anti-climax, with team spirit ebbing away.

There was more good fortune for Amiss, as Reeve's form in the championship dipped and he started to pick up some niggling injuries. Amiss was conscious that Reeve – and to a certain extent, Woolmer – was dismayed at Lara's attitude to various aspects of the season's long, hard slog. Ever the pragmatist, Amiss told captain and coach that he sympathised, but they had to make it work. Amiss tried to reason with Lara over a round of golf at the Belfry, and Lara resolved to try harder to integrate with all his team-mates, other than those he socialised with at night, but they were mostly honeyed words. Peaceful co-existence from a distance was the best Amiss could hope for with Reeve and Lara, even down to persuading Lara to play in a Sunday League match at Northampton, because the TV cameras were covering the game and questions would be asked if the star was absent. Reeve couldn't persuade Lara to get changed and ready, and it took all of Amiss's advocacy to get him on the park that day.

'It was tough for Dermot at times. He felt Brian should have stayed around for a beer with his team-mates more often, and I sympathised with that. But we had landed him for an absolute bargain just before he scored that 375, and his agent Jonathan Barnett was clearly determined to make a lot of money out of his client that summer. The promotional pressure on Brian was intense. We managed to keep him in the right frame of mind most of the time.

'Dermot rightly got frustrated occasionally. Once he was due to toss up and Brian was nowhere to be seen at the ground. He wouldn't answer Dermot's calls, and I finally got through to him on my mobile. He told me he was just leaving, and he'd be there in a few minutes. He was over two hours' drive away and I told him, "Brian, there are a lot more cars over here on the road than in Trinidad." Obviously, this would have needed to get sorted out if Brian had signed for three years, but I took the view that trying to keep things on an even keel gave us a better chance of winning trophies. I think the end product by September vindicated me.'

'Keep calm and carry on winning' was the Amiss mantra that summer, even when taking the decision to drop the captain. Reeve was surprised when Amiss broached the subject, but the chief executive faced him down. 'I told him every player had to perform to stay in the side. The young lads like Dougie Brown and Graeme Welch were snapping at Dermot's heels in the championship games; they were fresh, confident and vigorous, fitting in straight away. I know it hurt Dermot and we did our best to dress it up, telling the media he was being rested to get some niggles cleared up – but eventually it was obvious we were stronger

as a four-day unit in the second half of the season without Dermot and with the young lads thriving. Most players get dropped some time, including me when I was a regular with Warwickshire. It was up to Dermot to deal with it. After all, he was still a fantastic leader for us in the one-day games.'

As the '94 season progressed, and the likelihood of a remarkable season became feasible, the cricket management met more regularly, with Tim Munton (now the stand-in championship captain) joining Amiss, Reeve and Woolmer. The coach thought it was vital to plan the strategy for the final month of the season. 'The realisation that all four was now a distinct possibility started creating a new pressure. How long could we maintain the challenge? So we decided to meet more often and discuss at length plans for the final part of the season. We sat the players down to plan physically and mentally. Focus on the game in hand, don't let the external pressures get to you.'

Amiss's natural inclination throughout his cricket career has been to make a decision eventually, then to hunker down and see it through. Tough it out. Fight your corner. The man who ran out Frank Hayes and Alan Knott in the 1974 Test at Sabina Park ('both of them my fault'), yet batted on for 262* to save the game, was not going to be deflected in his 1994 vision by taking undue notice of Dermot Reeve's bruised ego. The captain may have got used to dominating the dressing room by force of personality, humour and shrewd man-management, but Amiss knew that Reeve's power base wasn't set in stone. You have to keep delivering as a player to keep your players' respect, and Amiss kept an ear close to the ground, assessing the vibes. Having occupied various Warwickshire dressing rooms down the years containing some difficult characters, Amiss was used to the occasional turbulence. It wasn't a case of siding with Lara instead of Reeve; it was more to do with the interests of Warwickshire CCC, as Dennis Amiss saw them.

He was equally clear-sighted in the 1994/95 winter when he rang Reeve to tell him that Lara had been preferred to Allan Donald as the club's overseas professional for 1996. So Donald would only have one more season with the Bears, in 1995, then he would probably have called time with them by the time Lara had finished his proposed three-year contract at Edgbaston. A personal view is that the preference for Lara – and his subsequent ill-starred spell as club captain in 1998 – was a disastrous decision, influenced more by marketing motives than by maintaining a harmonious dressing room. Donald had already proved himself the perfect overseas pro, the Bloemfontein Brummie, more at home in the Warwickshire dressing room than back home in Free State's.

After all this time, it still appears a poor decision on cricketing grounds. Reeve was aghast. He asked Amiss, 'Does AD know about this?' and, after he confirmed this, Amiss told Reeve, 'It's up to you and Bob to get him motivated for next summer.' From this corner, it appears unfair to have expected Reeve to do the hard yards of motivation on Donald, when the club captain had not been consulted about the pros and cons of bringing back Lara. Luckily for Warwickshire, Donald's fearsome pride in performance, love for the club and respect for Reeve as captain led to a memorable season for him, as Warwickshire won two more trophies in 1995.

The sequel in 1996 reflected badly on Warwickshire. Lara, worn down by the relentless demands of the international calendar, dipped out of his 1996 contract, while Donald decided to take a coaching job at Edgbaston and play in the Lancashire League, so he was also unavailable. So the club floundered and failed to win a trophy for the first time since 1992.

No doubt Amiss was acting with the best interests of Warwickshire at heart when that flawed decision was taken. It was the same motive when he got things right as chief executive. One of his strengths was to surround himself with excellent administrative staff and back them loyally through the various vicissitudes. That loyalty was always reciprocated. Keith Cook epitomises that quality. Having joined Warwickshire from school in 1973, Cook moved from the marketing department to be Amiss's number two in 1994, staying with him till his retirement in 2006. Cook, now the club's cricket operations manager, believes Amiss always did what was best for Warwickshire CCC, even when it led to mistakes.

'As a former player, it was difficult for Dennis early on to get his head round a lot of complex administrative issues. In those days he was answerable to a powerful general committee, a lot of them ex-players with strong views. It's only in recent years that it's been replaced by a modern business structure, so that you can make changes without so many things being referred to various sub-committees, then the general committee. Dennis had a fine balancing act trying to get things right. But his heart was in the club. He didn't always get things right, but he tried his damndest.

'Jill, his wife, has always been an absolute rock for Dennis, there with him when he needed support. I've seen him in tears after having to let a member of staff go. He's a big softy, like your favourite uncle – jovial and friendly, but aware when necessary he had to put on the tough outer clothing. But Dennis has always seen Warwickshire like his extended family. He made it clear when he took the floor at his barbie back in '94 when he stood there, a glass of red wine in hand, setting out his vision as the new chief exec. He was as good as his word, despite the inevitable mistakes.'

It was entirely fitting that Jill and Dennis celebrated their golden wedding anniversary at Edgbaston in October 2017, and the gathering of the great and the good that day in the Chairman's Lounge spoke volumes for the respect and affection so many hold for a couple that has always appeared joined at the hip.

Dennis still talks enthusiastically about the game that has brought him so much, extolling the quality of the fielding and the expanding range of batsmanship, an art that still fascinates him. 'I'd love to have played 20/20 cricket. It's a batsman's game, 20/20 ... Roll up on good pitches and you're encouraged to smash the ball over the top? Lovely! And I'd have played the reverse sweep, too. At times in championship run chases in '94, we played 20/20 cricket before its time. We were tremendous chasing a target then.'

He's still a regular at Edgbaston Golf Club, trying out a new theory every week, as he did all through his marvellous batting career. When he pops into the cricket ground, he's delighted to come across any of the young players for a natter, oblivious to the fact they are mostly unaware of his tremendous deeds. Last winter, he bumped into one such tyro and, after an illuminating chat, the youngster asked Keith Cook, 'Who was that, Cookie?' He was told in no uncertain terms to go and look him up, and grasp what he did for Warwickshire from 1958 onwards.

As an epitaph, most runs and centuries and then most trophies as the boss of Warwickshire constitute a handy enough reference point.

Twenty punters

It was not just the players who did well financially out of winning the treble. Some club executives and committee members made a killing, trousering £5,000 each from a fiver bet!

Within a few weeks of Warwickshire's impressive start to the '94 season, the chairman MJK Smith had a letter from a bookie, asking if he had thought about insuring against the club's potential success. There would be some substantial bonuses to be paid to the players if they continued to win games across several fronts. Had the club thought about covering itself?

Smith, not a betting man, pondered and sought advice from the new chief executive, his former team-mate Dennis Amiss. 'I said to Dennis, "I fancy us to win something this season. Let's do a Yankee on us to win the championship and Sunday League and get to the two one-day finals."' Very prescient, indeed. Amiss was all for it and so the chairman went up to the committee room, took a fiver off all those interested and placed a £100 bet with the bookies' firm, Surrey Racing.

Warwickshire did not have to win either of the two Lord's finals, just to get there. In fact, the players surpassed the expectations of the betting syndicate by winning three of the four trophies, when two specific ones would have been enough to scoop the jackpot.

The twenty punters at Edgbaston stood to hoover up £224,000 for just a hundred quid. The longer the season progressed so triumphantly, the more MJK Smith was hailed as the club Nostradamus.

In August, Smith had a letter from Surrey Racing. They were getting twitchy. One Lord's final had already been won, progress in the NatWest Trophy and the two league competitions was now a procession of victories, and Surrey Racing stood to take a substantial hit.

The firm wrote to say that Smith needed to be aware there was a maximum pay-off of £100,000 on the bet. This both outraged and baffled Smith; how could Surrey Racing be allowed to realign the goalposts? What about the other £124,000?

Two committee members with legal backgrounds were enlisted by the club to take on Surrey Racing. Chris Tickle was a barrister and Jamie McDowall a solicitor. McDowall, a Cambridge graduate who had played a dozen county games for Warwickshire as a wicket-keeper/batsman, felt they had a good case.

Jamie McDowall

'We went down to London to argue our case to the tribunal, which was in fact the *Sporting Life* paper. Surrey Racing's defence was that it was a speciality bet, but they had solicited the bet by contacting MJK and then accepted it without informing us of their rules and limitations. We argued that they were under an obligation to pay out the full amount. Also they had never defined to us what in fact constituted a speciality bet. That just appeared in August, when it looked as if we might win the bet as specified.'

Although the tribunal severely criticised the bookies, they won the case, which was an interesting volte-face. Soon afterwards, Surrey Racing went out of business ('I didn't shed a tear,' McDowall says sardonically), but not before paying out £100,000 to the Warwickshire syndicate.

It still rankles with MJK Smith that the full amount was not paid out. 'It's bent, isn't it? Those bookies were urging us to place that bet, and they forked out far less than what we legitimately won. When they looked like losing the bet, they looked for an excuse to pull the ladder up on us.'

McDowall, as befits a man steeped in the complexities of the law, sees both sides of the argument. 'I felt we had grounds for complaint, but we were on thin ice. If you are having a bet with bookmakers, you are deemed to be operating according to their rules. For example, if you go into a bookies' shop, their rules are on the wall. I believe Surrey Racing should have enclosed a copy of their rules to us when we placed that bet.

'I must admit we were all very happy at getting £5,000 each for a fiver's outlay, but it could easily have been double the amount. And we had a long wait before we could celebrate.'

Till the last day of the season, in fact. Just because Warwickshire had enjoyed such a tremendous summer did not mean that the bet was secured. The championship may have been landed on 2 September, but the Sunday League still had to be won, at Bristol, on 18 September before the corks could pop. And when the Bears were 3/3 early on, the twenty punters were twitching. For them, the recovery orchestrated by Brian Lara, Trevor Penney and Dermot Reeve, then the crucial bowling spells from Gladstone Small, Neil Smith and Dickie Davis to nail the win constituted the most nerve-shredding afternoon of that season.

And no, the players did not get a sniff of any of the winnings. The relationship between players and committee may have been harmonious in '94, but it wasn't that close!

Alex Davis – the scorer

Alex Davis, a retired surveyor, was the Warwickshire scorer through the 1990s. He also scored for England on two overseas tours – and is thought to be the only person to have seen every ball of Brian Lara's 375 in Antigua in April and his 501 at Edgbaston in June. He died in 2015, but the 1995 *Wisden* recorded his memories of the two innings:

> For me, the two innings were very different, because the first I was doing manually in a scorebook, whereas the second I was doing on the computer and a manual scoresheet, so I was working twice as hard. And the second was scored at such a rate, we kept having to answer the phone to the press to give the details of each of the 50s.
>
> The advantage of the computer is that it does do the adding-up for you, so you don't have to do so much cross-checking. When there's 800 runs on the board, that makes a difference. There wasn't a problem of space, because I was doing it on a linear system down the page. But then I copied it onto the standard scoresheet. Fortunately, with the 375, Simmons and Williams were out for 8 and 3, so there was loads of space to spread Lara. With the 501 it wasn't so easy because of the runs the other players made, so I had to dodge round the spaces.

Tim Munton

It is rare that a sports reporter gets the chance to impart some good news to a performer. When it transpires, you savour the moment.

When the editor of *Wisden Cricketers' Almanack* rang me in September 1994 to discuss Warwickshire's remarkable season, Matthew Engel asked me who was their single most influential player.

Unhesitatingly I replied, 'Tim Munton.' Matthew said, 'Good, I agree. That's why he's going to be one of *Wisden*'s Five Cricketers of the Year.' He asked me if I would write the feature on Munton and would I care to break the news to him. A nano second elapsed before I accepted.

Munton's reaction when I broke the news to him was typical. First incredulity, then blushing pride. I told him he had to keep quiet about it till the following April, on publication of *Wisden*. There was a look of mild panic, then a plea: 'Can I tell my Dad? He won't say anything, but I want to see his face.'

That summer Munton had taken 81 championship wickets, leading the attack nobly in the absence of Allan Donald, and Warwickshire had won eight of the nine matches in which he captained the side. Dermot Reeve, the club captain, won just three.

It was Munton who held the group together from June onwards as the antipathy between Reeve and Lara threatened to blow the momentum off-kilter. He was soon nicknamed Captain Sensible, a reflection on his desire for compromise and consensus in a dressing room with its fair proportion of forceful personalities. Unlike Reeve, whose form had tailed off in the wake of accumulating injuries, Munton could lead by example in 1994.

Some of the old sweats had been through some fallow periods at Edgbaston with Munton, and they knew he wasn't a dilettante, someone only visible and vocal when the sunny uplands were in sight. Men like Andy Moles, Paul Smith and Gladstone Small were firm friends and admirers. The younger ones only needed a glimpse of Munton's personal example and calm, altruistic leadership to appreciate he was just the man to steer the Bears to treble triumph.

Paul Smith, hardly an Establishment man or attuned to compromises, says Munton did not put a foot wrong as stand-in captain. 'If Munts wasn't

the person he was, we wouldn't have won eight out of nine under him. He was unselfish, brought us all together and led by example on the pitch. A top man. You wanted to be part of his side. Brian Lara respected him greatly; he would never have talked to Munts the way he did to Dermot.'

Lara showed just what he thought of Munton in the Bristol dressing room on the evening when Warwickshire completed the treble by winning the Sunday League. He signed a Bears shirt and handed it to Munton, with the inscription, 'My Player of the Season, thanks for everything'. One can think of another contender for that title, but Lara knew what the big fellow had done for the club.

So did Neil Smith. An easy-going man, but with solid principles, Smith's opinion carried weight. He was firmly behind Munton as the baton of captaincy was passed over. 'Tim had been the ideal vice-captain. He had everyone's respect, and the way he bridged that gap between management and players was crucial. It's easy for management to lose the dressing room and vice-versa, but it never got to that point. Issues were ironed out and quickly.'

Stuart Nottingham, the team's physiotherapist, viewed the dynamics at close quarters and, from the perspective of someone who knew nothing about cricket, offers a telling insight into Munton's leadership. 'Tim was the most influential person in that dressing room, without making any noise. Some of the players would be brash and get on others' nerves, Bob Woolmer would sometimes come in and charge into somebody, and there was Tim, the unsung hero, the glue holding all the egos in check with a shrewd sentence or two. You don't have to be the chief executive officer or managing director to wield the most power. Tim didn't have a title, but he wielded the most control, effortlessly. Everyone shut up when Tim had something important to say.'

It was typical of the self-effacing Munton that, when I sat him down for that *Wisden* article, he insisted on reeling off the names of cricket figures who had done so much for him earlier in his career.

It had not been smooth progress. Born in Melton Mowbray, he had always wanted to play for his home county, but Leicestershire did not offer him a contract

after playing for the seconds. Off to Warwickshire and valuable tutelage from the former England fast bowler David Brown: 'He toughened me up, a great old-school influence with terrific values.' Then Bob Cottam taught him to swing the ball. 'How lucky was I to have two former England bowlers helping me at a crucial age?'

Cottam returns the compliment. 'Tim was a great man to coach. Fantastic work ethic, willingness to learn. When I'm asked about perfect pros I have worked with, I begin with Tim Munton.'

Cottam's technically excellent coaching set Munton on his way, and within a couple of years he was in the England side. It was to be a fleeting experience, and that is why he is phlegmatic about not making an England tour after his 'annus mirabilis' of 1994. 'If I wasn't going to be picked for an England tour in 1992, after being in every Test squad that summer, then I wasn't going to allow myself to be optimistic two years later, even though I had become a better bowler.'

Hard work underpinned Munton's splendid career and, in the winter of 1993/94, he put in the hard yards that set up his outstanding season. The cricket management, aware that they would be missing the cutting edge of Allan Donald, discussed Munton's responsibilities for '94, and it was agreed that he needed to take wickets quicker than in his usual stock role. He also needed to fire out the top order in the manner of Donald.

'I worked hard on the weights during the winter, building up my stamina and strength, because I was preparing for a strike bowler's role, rather than being the usual support as a miserly stock bowler. I was prepared to concede more runs, attack the stumps more and bowl more bouncers. I also went round the wicket on occasions – something I've always been loath to do – and it got me a few wickets at vital times. I was definitely a yard quicker and could still bowl as many overs.'

Munton led from the front impressively, taking five wickets in an innings six times, two more than any other bowler. He also dismissed many of the opposition's best batsmen cheaply. A great bowler and team-man like Donald would always be missed by Warwickshire, but Munton filled the gap superbly. John Emburey, no stranger to winning titles with Middlesex, believes Munton was the key to winning the championship. 'He was like Martin Bicknell at Surrey when they were so good. Just wind him up and he'd still be there at the end of the season, running in hard. And Tim had learned to swing the ball. That's what got the best players out.'

When he took over from Reeve, Munton had a clear idea of how the responsibilities were to be divided with Bob Woolmer. He was a huge fan of Woolmer, and there was no chance of the coach being downgraded in what was expected to be just an interim measure. 'I did the team chats in between sessions during a day's play – what we were looking for in the session ahead. Short and sweet, you don't want to bore players. Bob would outline things in the morning and have plenty of one-on-ones at various stages. His preparation for the games ahead was fantastic. There were a lot of leaders in our dressing room, and Bob and Dermot would have some strong disagreements, but we got there in the end. On the field I never lacked support. Andy Moles could easily have captained the side. Neil Smith, Roger Twose also. Glad was a fantastic support, and I could always rely on Keith Piper to be in my ear!'

But Munton also knew his own mind, and he dug his heels in over an important issue once he was told he was captain. His first game, at the end of June, was against a strong Lancashire team that had genuine designs on the championship, with John Crawley, Neil Fairbrother, Mike Watkinson, Peter Martin, Glenn Chapple and the great Wasim Akram all down to play. The day before, Munton met with Bob Woolmer, Dermot Reeve and Dennis Amiss to select the eleven, and it was made clear to him that the championship was not a serious target. Reeve was already out injured, and Lara would be missing,

resting his sore knee. It was put to Munton that other players should be rested for the Lancashire game, to preserve them for important one-dayers ahead.

Munton was not impressed. 'They made it clear the championship wasn't a priority, that our best chance that season was in one-day cricket. I disagreed. I felt we now had a really good chance of winning the championship and stood my ground. We ended up picking as strong a side as we could and beat Lancashire. We won the next three championship matches in a row and got on a roll, with the collective self-belief getting stronger every game. At the end of that little run, after beating Derbyshire, we went top of the table and stayed there for the rest of the season.

'So that Lancashire match was a fork in the road for me, and I got what I wanted. It gave me the confidence to prove I really could lead the team, with the players I wanted.'

It was fitting that Dermot Reeve should insist that the championship pennant and trophy was presented to Munton after Hampshire were beaten by an innings on 2 September. 'Why not?' says Reeve. 'Tim deserved it. He hadn't missed a match, took 81 championship wickets and led from the front all season. He also captained us to so many championship victories.'

Munton is equally keen that Reeve does not miss out on the plaudits. 'He and Bob were brilliant together, and I really liked Dermot's insistence that no one should take the mickey out of any team-mate on cricketing issues. We should challenge ourselves to try new things, and Dermot was great at encouraging that. And when he came back fit the following year, he proved what a valuable all-rounder he was and led us brilliantly to two more trophies.

'Team spirit often gets referenced when our '94 success is analysed, but for me all the hard work and performances created that team spirit. We were successful – winning engenders team spirit – and then opponents started to be intimidated by us.'

Munton was too equable to bother about ruffling opposition players, leaving that to other, more combustible characters like Reeve, Piper and Twose. 'We had a team of different characters and temperaments. Some enjoyed getting into players' faces, but I couldn't be bothered with all that. Not my style – but also I needed to save my breath if I

Dermot Reeve shares the glory with Tim Munton when the Treble is won at Bristol

was bowling! We weren't a popular side with all the opposition because of the edge we had, but that was the same with sides like Essex and Surrey during their successful seasons around that period. I guess some were just envious of success.'

That may be so, but no player on the county circuit begrudged Munton his success. He had long been acknowledged as a fine exponent of his trade. A conscientious representative of his county for the Professional Cricketers' Association, his dextrous negotiating skills had been tested enough before he took over from Reeve, and his tenacity was admired as much as his good manners on the other side of the table. David Graveney, an executive with the PCA, who played against Munton many times, summed up his qualities pithily: 'A real nugget, an outstanding person and team man.'

By the time the media spotlight had started to shine on Munton and his confrères towards the end of the '94 season, he was perfectly at ease with his public relations responsibilities. At close of play he was a model of patience and cheery good nature with supporters, no matter how the day had panned out on the field. The modern obsession with selfies would be easily indulged by Munton if he was playing these days. He would just be endearingly baffled.

His winter trade at that time, as a sales representative for a local brewery, also equipped him with the necessary perspective on life, honing the people-skills that were already pleasingly apparent. I can also confirm that occasional summons to this quarter for tasting sessions were always favourably received.

Sadly, that sunny September afternoon celebration in front of ecstatic Warwickshire supporters in 1994 proved to be one of the last major highlights of Tim Munton's career. As the season ended, the club entered into some enthusiastic celebrations, with Munton deservedly to the fore, brandishing the three trophies at various functions. But for him it would never be glad, confident morning again.

Injuries meant Munton only played 10 championship games in 1995, but he still took 46 wickets at 19 and he was selected for Nasser Hussain's England 'A' tour to Pakistan. He was firmly in the frame for an England recall the following summer until breaking a wrist in a Benson & Hedges Cup tie against Derbyshire. Then in 1997 a slipped disc ruled him out for the whole season.

Brian Lara returned to take the captaincy in 1998, and Munton insists he was not upset. 'I was part of the decision-making process and was comfortable with the club's position that it was difficult to appoint me as captain, unsure if I would play again after my back op. It was me that suggested Brian for the role. As it transpired, I only got back into the side in the second half of that season, and I was more than happy to play under Brian.'

At the end of the following season Munton asked to be released early from his contract and subsequently joined Derbyshire. Although injury dogged his final season, his contract had been extended earlier and he was appointed vice-captain, playing every game until August 2001. He retired just short of his 37th birthday.

He was proud of his 18 seasons as a professional, but it is his years at Warwickshire that have a particular poignancy for him. 'A big part of me regrets not staying at Edgbaston. In the winter of 1999 I flew out to Cape Town to speak to Bob Woolmer, who was returning as the coach for the 2000 season. We spent three days discussing what was behind my decision to leave, with Bob encouraging me not to leave but to work closely with him, preparing me to become his successor. I often reflect on what would have been, had I listened to him. But factions develop when you're not winning, and the chemistry just wasn't there, compared to our great days. I chose to play my final two seasons elsewhere, protecting those great memories of the mid-1990s.'

Munton handled his departure from Edgbaston with grace and diplomacy, and he will not be drawn on the specifics of his decision. The same applies to the strange hiatus after he had become Warwickshire's chairman of cricket in 2005. It seemed the perfect appointment, but Munton was gone after just eight months. His great friend Andy Moles was in for the Director of Cricket job but lost out to Mark Greatbatch. Munton resigned over the process that led to Greatbatch's appointment. He cares too much about Warwickshire to rake over old coals, but it proved to be an unhappy two years under the New Zealander before the job finally ended up with a worthy Bear, Ashley Giles.

By then Munton was embarking on various business ventures. For four years a director of the PCA, he also ran the cricket operations at Sir Paul Getty's stunning ground in Buckinghamshire for several years and now he is Director of Sport at a marketing-and-events agency in his native East Midlands.

He is glad he kept his own counsel about some disappointing times at Edgbaston because he is so fond of the club, his former team-mates and the supporters. As a result, he is delighted to pop in and out, reflecting on the massive change to the ground since he joined in 1985.

No one who followed the Bears will ever forget Tim Munton's wholehearted contribution over the 15 years. If all the autograph books he signed readily were laid end to end, they would stretch all the way down the Pershore Road. Significantly, when the players' names were read out after the championship was clinched on 2 September 1994, the biggest cheer from the delirious supporters was for Munton. Genuine sports fans recognise the intrinsic worth of certain players.

Munton believes the '94 achievement has only really sunk in over the past few years as its historic nature is spelt out to him. 'I've never been a great one for cricket history, but it makes me proud to be in the annals with team-mates who are now lifelong friends. The year 1994 was huge for me in so many ways.

'I can't believe how lucky I was in my career when all I ever aimed for was playing county cricket. But I got to play for England, made *Wisden*'s Five, managed to get a stocked trophy cabinet and made so many friends.'

He is too unassuming to say so, but he also gained respect from all sections of the cricket industry. You cannot put that in a trophy cabinet, but it is obvious whenever you are with Tim Munton in a crowded room. Folk don't give him the swerve, they make a beeline for him. Still, after all these years.

Roger Twose

Only Roger Twose could rival Dermot Reeve in getting up the pipes of the opposition in that '94 season. Not only was Twose the faithful Sancho Panza to Reeve's Don Quixote in charging full-pelt at opposing players on the field – he had to be restrained at times by his captain, of all people. Twose was not one to turn the other cheek.

Even placid characters like David Graveney and Tim Curtis would get annoyed by Twose on the field. Curtis recalls, 'He had a lot of swagger, with no fear. He'd come down the pitch to reverse sweep the first ball he faced and revel in your reaction.' Graveney admits Twose could get under his skin 'even down to him reading the *Financial Times* at the breakfast table. I thought that was just posing. He's the only player I thought of bowling a beamer at. He loved riling you.'

Reeve admits he had to rein in Twose at times. 'Team meetings could be fun with Roger. At times he'd go totally over the top, eyes bulging, veins in his neck throbbing, roaring out, "Yeh! Let's go for them, come on!" I had to tell Roger that the bell hadn't sounded yet, and we still had five minutes to go. Then he'd call me "Big Ears" to take the attention away from himself and that would raise a laugh.

'He was very vocal on the field and could get the red mists very easily. When he came on to bowl, he would often ask for a defensive field and, if I ever over-ruled him, he'd say, "You always get the field you want when you're bowling." I'd have to point out that I was the captain, and he'd spit back, "You're a crap captain," and then I'd say something like "And you're a fat buffalo, Roger." I loved the cut and thrust of sophisticated debate with Roger!'

More importantly, Reeve loved having Twose out on the field with him. They were so similar in many ways. They made the best of their talents, gloried in mind games, ignored the sceptics and loved proving people wrong after coming through various tests of their aptitude to play professional cricket.

Paul Smith, hardly a soul-mate of Reeve, still recognises how much the captain and his first lieutenant gave to the side. 'Roger was a mini-Reeve, even down to carrying Dermot's guitar for him. But Roger gave a lot to the team. Pick out the best bits of Reeve's game, add Roger's batting ability and leadership in the field – then you have a very good cricketer.'

Dougie Brown, another great enthusiast in the Reeve mould, tapped into Twose's defiant character as soon as he broke into the first team in '94. 'Roger was so positive, he was the life and soul of the side. He'd happily do something stupid on the field to make us laugh, then switch straight back to aggressive mode. He could always break the tension, a major focus when the game was going away from us.'

Off the field, Twose was a fine communicator. He would talk in depth about tactics, assess a match situation intelligently and talk articulately about the challenges ahead in the next session. Reeve admits he came to rely on Twose to help get his various messages across. Conscious that the players would probably get fed up with only hearing Reeve's voice, he would happily delegate to his confident consigliere.

There were times when Reeve sensed he might be losing his team-mates, as his form fluctuated and the niggling injuries reduced his effectiveness. That's when the loyalty and vocal support of Twose was particularly appreciated. Once at Southampton, Reeve came in with the side needing quick runs before a declaration. Reeve, spurning the option of quick singles, opted to use the sweep shot to get some boundaries. It worked, and Reeve ended up with 77 not out. As he came into the dressing room Twose said, 'Well played, Skip, nice innings. Great to see you not playing for the not out, but for the team.' Reeve was touched by that. 'Roger spotted that going for the runs was an incidental, and I was even more pleased that he had spoken out about that in front of the rest of the side. This was exactly the sort of team spirit Bob Woolmer and I had been looking for since we came together in 1993.'

Twose was at his most supportive when advocating the use of the reverse sweep. He had a harsh introduction when, in his early days at Edgbaston, one of the coaches ordered him not to play the shot in the nets. Neal Abberley banned him from the rest of the net session when Twose persisted, and he left in tears. Bob Woolmer smoothed it over, encouraged Twose to work on the shot and Abberley came on-side. But it became a mission to Twose to get the reverse sweep in his team-mates' locker during the '93 and

'94 seasons. In team meetings he would say, 'Listen, fellas, it's easy, you've just got to practise it. We should all be playing it, you'll get one run at the very least.' Other counties started to take notice. Matt Maynard of Glamorgan, an England batsman of great elan and destructiveness, congratulated Twose once on having the bravado to play it first ball, and Hampshire's captain Mark Nicholas was equally impressed. 'Roger was brilliant at using it as a touch shot, angling the ball at ninety degrees with soft hands. That made it so difficult to set a field. It was innovative stuff, coming from clear thinking and hard practice. Roger used to say that you could play it at any time in a match as long as you'd mastered it in practice.'

Twose took it upon himself to proselytise the shot. Trevor Penney became a prime target. He was not keen on playing it, deeming it too risky and, if he got out that way, it would look a poor option. He was batting with Twose in a second-eleven game in Taunton and the off-spinner had a 6/3 field, with six fielders on the legside. Although Penney had practised reverse sweeping in the nets, playing it well, he was not keen on trying it out in the middle, even though the shot was on with such a field. Twose impatiently marched down the pitch and barked at Penney, 'Look at that field, Trevor – do it, just do it!' Penney got four with the shot next ball and soon picked up a couple more. He could not believe how easy it had been.

Twose had a split personality on the pitch. He was invariably bumptious, arrogant and over-aggressive when fielding – so much so that Alec Stewart, on England duty once with Reeve, remarked, 'That Twose is a pain in the neck, isn't he?' Reeve was amused at the source of that comment, given that Stewart had played nine seasons of grade cricket in Western Australia, where the aggro can be of high intensity and that Stewart himself was no shrinking violet. Reeve happily put him right. 'He's a hell of a guy to have in your eleven because of his aggression. I'm glad he's in my team.'

And yet ... Twose always appeared remarkably cool in a crisis, when batting. There was no better man to face the final, decisive ball in the 1993 NatWest Trophy Final, with Twose needing to get bat on ball, and the wicket-keeper up at the stumps, negating his instinct to get down the pitch to Franklyn Stephenson. Twose's vocal encouragement had kept Reeve going

during the climactic final deliveries of that pulsating finish, ensuring the adrenalin still flowed. He was again the ideal partner for Reeve at Lord's in 1995, when Warwickshire squeezed home in the NatWest Final against Northants. Reeve gave Twose the reassuring message when they joined forces at 122/5, needing 201: 'If one of us gets out now, we'll lose.' Twose ignored that, stuck his chest out, made 68, adding a vital 54 with Reeve and that won the cup.

Reeve loved batting with Twose. 'Roger was always so confident and smart at the big times. He'd say, "Skip, I'm going positive now, you just knock it around. I'm ready for them." He would look at all the options, like where the wind was blowing, how many overs a dangerous bowler had left, which was the short boundary, who was carrying an injury in the field. A very savvy cricketer, a great team man.'

Bob Cottam was the first important figure to spot that, underneath all the bluster and braggadocio, lurked a cricketer of potential. Before arriving at Edgbaston, Cottam worked for the National Cricket Association in the West Country, coming across the burly lad from Devon in a match he was scouting at Taunton. 'He had something about him, a bit of a strut. He wasn't overawed by other players who perhaps had greater natural talent. He had fight and character, he wouldn't back down. When I joined Warwickshire, I went for Roger on his potential and maturity.'

Twose had to graduate from the School of Hard Knocks when he joined Warwickshire. He soon learned that an aggressive attitude had to be backed up by performances to avoid being dubbed an insubstantial loudmouth. Twose was smart enough to use the winter months playing in New Zealand – a decision that proved to be hugely significant – but, for three seasons in county cricket, he only made intermittent, unsatisfactory appearances.

He was 24 before scoring his first championship hundred. Impressively it was a double – 233 against Leicestershire. Paul Nixon kept wicket that day for Leicestershire and was impressed. 'He knew his game at that stage, set out his stall and batted all day. I thought he would kick on with that strong mental approach, and he did. Roger was one player who encapsulated Warwickshire's success in '94/95. From being a decent young player he looked like a world-beater for two seasons.'

Roger Twose, hitting a crucial 68 in the NatWest final of 1995

Twose had a shocker in the 1993 championship season, scoring just 184 runs at an average of 11.50. He had shown susceptibility to the short ball, and word soon got around the county grapevine. Twose was lucky that his batting mentor Bob Woolmer was so understanding, showing him what was wrong on his laptop, suggesting the remedial work needed. Twose took himself off to New Zealand again, working hard at his technique. His capacity for hard work always struck a chord with Woolmer and Reeve.

When he returned to Edgbaston in April '94 Twose was sufficiently confident in his prospects to pull the leg of Brian Lara. Amid all the hoopla of Lara's first press conference, the great man paid a visit to the dressing room, just to check out his new surroundings. He found a note pinned to his locker door. 'Welcome to the second-best left-hand batsman in the world!' – written by Roger Twose. Lara took it in good part, enjoying the irreverence which epitomised that dressing room. 'I had to give him a challenge, keep him on his toes! I learned such a lot from Brian in '94 ... whether it was on the golf course, batting with him or how to sleep. Observing a batting genius at close quarters helped my batting so much, especially off the back foot. And after my bad season in '93, I needed a major improvement.'

And so it came to pass: 1,395 championship runs at 55.80 in '94 and 1,036 at 45.04 the following year. Twose played in all the championship matches both seasons and became one of the rocks of the team, a lightning conductor for morale that was invariably high. There was one slight wobble in the '94 season, when Nottinghamshire hammered them by an innings at Edgbaston. That left them just nine points ahead of Leicestershire, who had a game in hand. Were the leaders suddenly vulnerable? Twose, who had made a doughty 80 in the follow-on, was wheeled out to fulfil the inevitable media duties, and he spoke brilliantly, deflecting the necessary enquiries about Dermot Reeve's absence from the team, Lara's trough of low scores, the desirability of chasing four trophies. It was a cosmetic exercise, designed to tart up the shop window, with the hard yards needed by the players still to come – but, as an exercise in public relations, it was a masterful effort. Twose: calm down, everyone, nothing to see here, move along now. That day Twose had the air of a future captain. And his breezy optimism proved justified. Warwickshire won their next three championship matches by eight wickets, ten wickets and an innings, and sashayed to the title. Twose made 86* and 137 in two of those games.

So Twose's '94 season ended as triumphantly as it had begun, when he scored 277* against Glamorgan over two chilly April days at Edgbaston. The crowds had poured into the ground for their first glimpse of Lara, and he did not disappoint with a fluent 147. But statistically he was overshadowed by a nuggety left-hander, stylistically Lara's opposite but sharing his appetite for large scores. Twose did not try competing with Lara in their stand of 215, willingly yielding the strike but, when Lara was out on the second evening, Twose took fresh guard and churned out a mammoth double hundred, spread over ten hours. Before April was out, Twose had banished the 1993 demons.

Was Twose the right man to open in the first championship match of the season? Andy Moles, an orthodox opener, was injured, and Jason Ratcliffe would have been a natural replacement, more so than Dominic Ostler and Twose. Ratcliffe recalls the days before the first match: 'A few batters were sent up to Old Trafford for a second-eleven game. I got a 90-odd and a 40-odd and thought I had a chance of a shot in the first team. But, despite that, they left me out which was quite a sea-change and an indication that they wanted to play differently. The argument from Bob and Dermot was that there were three competitions that were one-dayers and that Dominic and Twosey needed to play early on, so that they could get some form for the one-day games. So Warwickshire started off the '94 season with the championship not very high on the wish list. The focus was on the one-day competitions, and Twosey and Dominic were the types who would play differently. You can't argue with the end product, but that was the beginning of the end for me. Next season I was playing for Surrey.'

Reeve was delighted at the resurgence of Twose. 'For the next two seasons he was an absolute rock for me. He was a fantastic competitor, chockful of confidence and yet so cool in the heat of battle. That 277* was overshadowed by the genius of Brian but in its own way was more significant. We now had a serious opening batsman in our ranks; you couldn't ignore the impressive way he had knuckled down to Bob's constructive criticism.'

Paul Taylor, the Northants' swing bowler who was at the time part of a few England squads and tours, believes Twose could have played for England in his two seasons of plenty. 'He was very under-rated, tenacious, gritty, gave you nothing. He performed regularly and was the cement between the bricks. But England selectors weren't great judges in the mid-'90s, were they?'

It would have been interesting to see how Twose's life would have panned out, had England called. Warwickshire's head honchos expressed disappointment that he never got a chance at England level, but they may have been supportive because they knew that Twose fancied a new life in New Zealand. He made it clear at the end of the '94 season that he would only be back for one more season. His parents had emigrated there, he enjoyed the outdoor life offered by such a beautiful country and had played productively for the past six seasons at Central Districts, then Northern Districts. His qualification period fulfilled, he was eligible to play for New Zealand from April 1995. An intelligent, well-read man, with interests beyond the confines of professional cricket, Twose had studied for a Business Management diploma while playing for Warwickshire, and he openly admitted he hankered after a career in business on the other side of the world. At the age of 27 there was no reason why he could not have an international career before the suit and laptop claimed most of his attention.

After making his Test debut for New Zealand in India towards the end of '95, Roger Twose was no longer eligible for county cricket as English-qualified. A realist, he knew that Warwickshire would be aiming higher for a star overseas player from then on, so he left with no hard feelings. He was missed in subsequent seasons, for his gritty batting, committed approach, loyalty and cheerfulness. He would have made a fine county captain if the game had held his attention. Dougie Brown missed him after the 1995 season. 'He was such a great enthusiast and a terrific thinker about the game. Roger worked out his game perfectly, and he was more talented than many thought. You're not too short of ability when your first two centuries in the county championship are 233 and 277*.'

Twose achieved his cricketing ambition, playing 16 Tests for New Zealand and 87 one-day internatiionals before retiring in 2001. The game could not hold a man of such restless energy and ambition for too long. There were other fields to explore. 'I didn't want professional sport to define who I was. I didn't want to be 'that cricketer' forever after. I wanted more to my life and to prove to myself that I could be successful in the business world.'

He started with the National Bank while still playing full-time and, as he began to phase out cricket, moved to Wills Bond in Auckland, project-managing waterside developments. It is fair to say business has been good for Twose. He agrees, though, that cricket has given him transferable skills. 'To survive as a batsman you have to be resilient and philosophical, finding a way to accept that a bad trot is in some ways out of your control. You've got to have a thick skin to absorb those moments, especially in big games when the moment does not go well. Perhaps I was able to transfer that skill to the business world, where you don't always get the results you want and not every day is a good day.

'In cricket you have to break challenges down. In considering how to score a hundred, you've got to break it down to each decision on each ball. In business the hundred is trying to secure a $50 million dollar development and you have to plan methodically a way to get there, break it down, bit by bit, mentally. Am I making the right phone calls? Am I thinking about this strategically?

'I guess I have never missed playing that much because I stayed in contact with those people whose company I enjoyed. But I'd be lying if I said I didn't miss the camaraderie. Business is a different life to playing with your mates in professional sport, experiencing euphoric highs and harsh lows together.'

Roger Twose always seemed able to compartmentalise his life, while playing for Warwickshire. Edgbaston, county cricket, New Zealand, provincial cricket, all the while pursuing a burgeoning interest in business. His briefcase and the *Financial Times* were as familiar a sight at Edgbaston as his ready smile, and he made no secret of his ambitions, while remaining a committed team man. He was always a fascinating cricketer to interview. Agreeably different. Challenging, yet genial.

There was a lot more to Roger Twose than mere bravado and verbals.

Paul Smith

Sometimes bald statistics don't do justice to a player's career and worth to his side. This is certainly the case with Paul Smith.

First-class career figures of 8,173 runs at 26.44 and 283 wickets at 35.72 don't give a true reflection of his worth. Smith proved that a couple of key wickets or a 20-minute cameo with the bat can be more valuable than a painstaking century or cheap wickets, mopping up the tail.

Tim Curtis, captain of Worcestershire and a fine, obdurate opening batsman, was always wary of Smith the fast bowler: 'He had that X-factor. On a flat wicket, with the game meandering along, he'd stir himself and bowl a rapid spell with lift and a sharp bouncer. He loved to discomfit you, just when you thought you were in control.'

Smith was a big occasion player. A Lord's Final was a pleasure for him. He played in five of them, winning four, including the Man of the Match award in the Benson & Hedges Cup Final of '94. Feeding off the atmosphere generated by a capacity crowd, Smith would be galvanised. There were times when a fustian championship match held little appeal for him, and he'd dawdle around in the outfield, scanning the crowd for any chums to have a natter with on the boundary rope. But give him a big occasion with a point and a purpose, and the Muse of inspiration was summoned easily enough.

In this he resembled his hero, Ian Botham. And the similarities didn't end there. Smith revered Botham's ability to squeeze the grape of social opportunity while remaining the most influential cricketer of his age. The pair got on famously, and Smith always defended Botham zealously when the moral majority got on his case, fulminating about his perceived self-indulgences. It's fair to say that, in his time as a professional cricketer, Paul Smith could echo Oscar Wilde: 'I could resist everything but temptation.' But he remained a fascinating character and loyal team man.

He was popular in the dressing room, with a contrary take on life. He was nicknamed Moonman and Wurzel – reflecting that, when the stars aligned on any given day, he could be an inspirational cricketer while his unruly, luxuriant hair, replete with colour changes, called to mind the TV character Wurzel Gummidge. When he captained Smith, Andy Lloyd dubbed him Stingray – 'because anything can happen in the next thirty minutes.'

Smith was perfectly happy to be pigeon-holed. 'I just played the village idiot in the dressing room, getting the laughs, acting the fool. We had some strong characters, all with things to say. But the lads knew I was serious in my own way about my cricket.'

He had become used to being written off when still at school in Newcastle. He was friends with Simon Donald, who later co-founded and co-edited the British comic *Viz*. He too was dismissed as a timewaster. 'We spent all our time together, looking out of the classroom window, just having a laugh. Simon would be drawing his cartoons, and I'd be thinking about cricket. We were both told we'd get nowhere in life, but we were spirited. We just needed a purpose.'

Bob Cottam, a major influence on Smith in his early years at Edgbaston, was always fascinated by his young charge's attitude to life, buttressed by a seriousness of intent that he kept hidden for the most part. 'There was a lot more to Smithy than just being a fine cricketer. He knew more about life than the rest of the blokes. Always worth listening to, once he stopped playing the fool.'

Tim Munton remembers the many unconventional ways of Paul Smith with great affection. 'When I first started in 1985 at Edgbaston, I was a fairly staid 19-year-old, so my eyes were opened by this young lad with blonde peroxide hair, a pink shirt, leather trousers and an MGB soft top. Every morning he'd bring in two cans of Coca-Cola, forty Rothman's cigarettes, and that would be his diet for the day in the dressing room. He'd always have a story from his night out or a quick quip at the expense of one of us. He had some hilarious one-liners and put downs and he was very, very popular.

'Paul loved American cars and music – especially Jim Morrison of the Doors. He had an encyclopaedic knowledge of him. I reckon Paul would have been happier being a roadie in the States or a rock star. That's why he loved Beefy Botham – larger than life, cricket's not everything, live for today.'

Yet Smith was serious about his cricket when he wanted to be. He was steeped in the game, one of

Paul Smith, after hitting the winning run in the Benson & Hedges Cup Final

three brothers to play for Warwickshire, and his father played for Leicestershire. He respected the disciplinarian in Bob Cottam, admired Bob Willis's straight talking when he was captain ('Put the cat among the pigeons when you bowl, Moonman, and don't just go for line and length'), and relished long sessions with Bob Woolmer, usually over the breakfast table when Smith hadn't long been back at the team hotel. 'Bob tried to keep me on the straight and narrow, but he understood I was a free spirit.

He stretched me with our cricket conversations; I really liked his enquiring mind. He kept telling me to prepare myself properly, and I would answer back, saying I'd be ready. He just told us to express ourselves, and he knew I loved the big occasions.'

I can confirm Smith's knowledge of cricket. Out of all those Warwickshire players in that halcyon period, he knew more about the game's history than anyone else. And he asked thoughtful questions about players and teams that he wanted to know more about. One of his more interesting opinions was that the umpires should decide on Man of the Match awards, because they had the best view of the quality on show. He was full of left-field, sharp theories like that.

Too often Paul Smith was judged on what he looked like, rather than his body of work. Of course, he could have been more consistent. If so, one-day international honours would surely have come his way; he certainly had the natural talent. Tim Munton believes only Brian Lara surpasses Smith as a clean striker of the ball during his time at Edgbaston. 'He timed it so sweetly, hitting it straight unbelievably hard, and he bowled very quickly when he was really up for it.'

He didn't have the purest of actions, having a long drag at the popping crease, a tendency towards no-balls and his awkward action put a strain on his left knee. A knee brace was necessary in his last few seasons. Yet when he stirred himself and the fires of inspiration were stoked, he could turn a game. In the '94 NatWest semi-final against Kent at Edgbaston, Warwickshire were slipping to defeat when Smith came on for one last spell. The crowd roared him on, he fired out Trevor Ward and Graham Cowdrey with some genuinely fast deliveries, and in just a few minutes the game was decided. Figures of 2/66 off 10.5 overs don't do justice to Smith's hostile, inspired bowling that day.

Sometimes, he didn't know how he managed a fine innings or bowling spell. At Worcester in 1989, he scored 100 out of 140 while batting with Dermot Reeve, ending up with a six and 24 fours in his innings of 140. He just stood tall and smashed the ball imperiously. Ask him afterwards how he had managed to play with such authority, he'd just shrug and say "my day, mate." He took a hat-trick against Sussex at Eastbourne in 1990, wearing Tim Munton's size 12 boots, which were rather too large for him. When he leapt up and down in celebration of the second of the three wickets, the boots fell apart. He borrowed Munton's spare pair. Then, when he fired out Tony Pigott with an excellent bouncer to claim the hat-trick, he said amid the back-slapping, 'Dunno how that happened – that was supposed to be my yorker!'

That stern taskmaster Steve Rouse used to get on Smith's case when he became head groundsman at Edgbaston. Rouse had played alongside some serious batsmen in his time as a Warwickshire swing bowler

– including the great Rohan Kanhai – and he wasn't easily impressed by the young players coming through in the '80s and '90s. But he saw the quality in Paul Smith. 'I used to tell him he was a lazy b– because he could have played for England as an all-rounder. He was superb when he got it right, like in that '94 NatWest semi against Kent. But Paul didn't seem to care about England prospects, he went his own way.'

Warwickshire did him no favours down the years, shunting him up and down the order. In 1986, opening the innings, he made over 1,500 first-class runs, setting a new world record for opening stands of 50+ in eight consecutive innings (four of them over 100). His partner Andy Moles loved batting with Smith. They had a contrasting approach to the new ball, as Moles recalls. 'I was the plodder, cantering around the racecourse, while Paul did the Hollywood stuff, taking centre stage. He'd say to me, "Just keep batting, Moler, and I'll keep hitting them." And he did ... he relieved the tension brilliantly. Every Christmas he sends me a card saying, "Moler – we're still world record holders!" It was great fun being in the same side as him. He reserved his key achievements for when we really needed them. He wasn't just a party animal, he was a deep thinker. He understood his role in the side, and Dermot and Woolly handled him sensibly.'

More often than not, Reeve got the best out of Smith when he really needed some inspiration from him. 'If you put your arm around him all the time, and were nice to him, you wouldn't get what you wanted. Paul was the one cricketer on our staff that I'd sometimes denigrate for cricketing reasons, telling him to get his left arm up, that the batters were playing him easily off the front foot. He could lose his energy quickly because he'd lose his adrenalin, and that would result in reduced pace and effectiveness. But some days he could be almost as quick as Allan Donald. Paul was a very dangerous, attacking cricketer.'

Smith happily packed down in Brian Lara's camp as the relationship unravelled between the captain and his star batsman. Smith had admired Reeve's imaginative and dynamic leadership but sensed that Reeve's ego was a problem in dealing with the biggest star in world cricket. Smith also liked Lara, having met him on a pre-season tour to Trinidad three years earlier in the company of Dwight Yorke, the Aston Villa footballer who was often in the Warwickshire dressing room. Lara and Smith were soon boon companions in the 1994 summer. Visits to night clubs were at times on their agenda.

'Brian was a good team man. He didn't like conflict and couldn't help that he attracted the attention of males and females. I know that he has raised millions for charities all over the world, without making a fuss about it. With him and Dermot, it was just a case of staying out of it and concentrating on our own cricket. But I treasure playing in the same team as Brian Lara in 1994.

'Throw Brian into the mix in '94, and you can see how special it was for us. We capitalised on the standards we had set ourselves, managed to keep it all together and enjoyed ourselves hugely. That team spirit got us over the line so often. We had spent a lot of time, building up this fantastic feeling of togetherness. We were also serious professionals. I remember Malcolm Marshall once asking me what it was like to play in a team that had achieved so much. I was struck by that. One of the all-time great fast bowlers who had played many years for Hampshire – yet he was still unfulfilled. Shows how lucky we were.'

Yet it ended in anti-climax for Paul Smith. After being so influential in 1994, he only played three championship matches in the next two seasons, and his winners medal from the 1995 NatWest Trophy Final was scant consolation. He became frustrated at his lack of first-team cricket and a degenerating knee. Only 32, he retired in 1996. It was sad that the mercurial career of such a talented, explosive all-rounder should end with a whimper, not a bang. But he sees it in the round, rather than with recriminations.

'I look back at my career as a great education. When I first went into county cricket in the early '80s, I thought the system was set in its ways. I didn't think that a one-division championship worked. Did winning and losing matter enough? There was a feeling that, as a batsman, as long as you scored 1,000 runs you were going to get another contract. It didn't matter whether those runs won the team any matches. It was all a bit comfortable.

'When Woolly joined us in 1991, his philosophy was music to my ears. I felt I'd been playing a different style of cricket from everyone else and been criticised for being inconsistent. I had always wanted to play aggressive, positive cricket – and that's what Woolly wanted. As a group we all embraced that mentality. Everything fell into place.'

It didn't curb Smith's energetic social life, though. He is highly entertaining on his excesses and how they impacted on his ability at times to play cricket a few hours later. He remembers going out to bat 'three sheets to the wind' against his great friend Malcolm Marshall. 'He shouted down the pitch to me, "Don't worry, Smitty boy – this won't take long." And it didn't. Soon I was on my way back, although in the wrong direction, away from the pavilion'.

Smith's autobiography *Wasted?* was published a year after his retirement, and it was a salutary corrective to the usual bland offerings from a former player. To some it was too lurid, while others delighted in the searing honesty shown in cataloguing such a colourful career. The book did not affect Smith's popularity among his old team-mates, but the subsequent admissions of drug-taking ruffled the ECB dovecotes and a ban from working in English domestic cricket followed.

Now, two decades on, Paul Smith has served his porridge and is working hard with underprivileged and unfortunate young cricketers. He has worked for the Prince's Trust, Cricket Without Boundaries, Coachright and the Active Black Country – using cricket to crash through social and class barriers for those who might appear to be without hope or encouragement.

He agrees that the 24/7 social media phenomenon would have caused him a few problems when he was in his pomp as a cricketer who also embraced his fair share of hedonism.

'We were young men with stacks of energy. Looking back, I think "Where did I get that energy from?" If dear old Woolly were alive today, he'd be delighted that I'm now in bed at the same time as he used to be when he coached us. I sometimes look at my watch around 10pm and think, "I used to be out at ten and probably stayed out for another five or six hours." I did prefer going out once I was prepared in my own mind for the next day. But you do wise up when you get older. I have a very different take on alcohol now.'

But at least he stored away enough memories before wising up. That soigné French actress Simone Signoret once wrote, 'Youth is wasted on the young.' I doubt whether Paul Smith would agree.

Andy Moles

In a Warwickshire dressing room full of individualists, few were as distinctive as Andy Moles. A late starter to county cricket, he counted his blessings every day in a splendid 12-year career while resolutely refusing to conform to the stereotype of a lean machine, a sylph-like athlete.

Inferior batsmen to Moles have played for England. They may have had stomachs like ironing boards and gone to bed early, but could they play fast bowling, relishing the battle, with the slips and wicket-keeper dishing out the verbals?

Moles certainly could. He loved the physical challenge. Some openers block out the psychological contests in the middle, getting 'in the zone', as they say. Not Moles. He liked to get his retaliation in first, telling the perspiring fast bowler 'Is that all you've got?' when they bowled a bouncer. He loved rattling them, forcing them to drop it short, then his impeccable back-foot technique would prosper.

He was a very fine opening batsman, Andy Moles. The stats do him justice – averaging over 40 in his first-class career, when county cricket was chockful of world-class fast bowlers – but it was his unruffled technique that stood out. He was well organised, calm, rarely out of position and he seemed to have time to spare.

An ideal technique for a Test match opener, it would seem. It never happened. The other options were certainly impressive, including Graham Gooch, Michael Atherton and Alec Stewart, exceptional players whose approach to training and fitness eclipsed that of the genial, relaxed Moles. Yet Stewart rated Moles highly. 'I would say that around his best period, Andy Moles was unlucky not to have played for England. He certainly had the technique. Obviously, it was his decision how he prepared himself to play cricket, and England would have been demanding for him. But he was good enough.'

Moles emphatically did not fit the preferred physical mould for a modern England cricketer, although an exception seemed to have been made for Mike Gatting. Moles was built for comfort; he did not place conditioning high on his priority list. He took the view that how he fared at the crease, with the ball whizzing past his nose at speed, was more important than doing hundreds of press-ups before start of play.

Yet he was athletic enough. He played decent semi-professional football when younger and for a couple of pre-seasons worked hard with Coventry City FC, the team he supported devotedly. 'I could do all the 10K runs with the Warwickshire boys in late winter and spring, but when the season started in April, I reverted to enjoying my life as a county cricketer. And that included my two weaknesses – curries and real ale. Proper beer, none of that fizzy rubbish!'

He would like to have been selected for an England 'A' tour when in his pomp, but it was not to be. He was categorised as a fine player, but a singular spirit who would not buckle down to the expected levels of commitment. He nearly made the England team, though, when he was in particularly fine form, in 1995 when the West Indies were touring. The England selectors plumped initially for that outstanding middle-order batsman Robin Smith to open, rather than a natural fit like Moles.

It did not work, and Moles was slated in for the Old Trafford Test. Just before the squad was announced, Moles ruptured an achilees tendon and missed the rest of the summer. He found out a couple of years later how close he had been to an England cap. 'I was doing my level 3 coaching course, and Micky Stewart took one of the modules. Micky was still close to the England set-up at the time, and he told me I had been in for Old Trafford. A fast, true, bouncy pitch against the West Indies quicks would have been perfect for me, but it was not to be. I was in great nick, too. But Nick Knight, my opening partner at Warwickshire, got his first cap instead. It is what it is, as they say. No point in moping about it.'

Moles had needed that philosophical streak as he clawed his way towards county cricket from an unpromising background. An apprentice toolmaker from Coventry, he had played for Dunlop in the Coventry Works League, then Kenilworth Wardens. Onwards and upwards to Moseley in the Birmingham League, where he reeled off big scores, including a few against various Warwickshire XIs. He kept thinking, 'I'm as good as this lot', but no one seemed to agree. At the age of 22, he wrote to every first-class county, asking for a trial. He did not get one reply.

He was now unemployed in the summers, waiting for calls that would get him significant games for anyone, hoping that a county might spot him. He would go anywhere for a game of cricket. One morning he got a call from Warwickshire; Dennis Amiss was a player short for a benefit match up in Blackpool against Nottinghamshire. Could he get there today?

Moles sped up the M6, scored 60 not out and after the game, he was approached by Amiss and the county's manager, David Brown. Had he ever thought of being a county pro? 'Only for the past three years!' was Moles' trenchant reply.

After a six-week trial, Moles was given a contract for the 1986 season. He was 25, mature for an inexperienced pro in those days. It did not matter; he had thought about his game long and hard. He made an immediate impression, averaging 49 in county cricket, forging an unlikely opening partnership with the dashing strokemaker Paul Smith. It was a contrasting but highly effective blend, and Moles soon worked out his value to the side.

'I was quite happy being the plodder, blunting the new ball to allow the shotmakers to capitalise when it was their turn. I got a great deal of satisfaction, blocking it, frustrating the quicks. I had waited long enough for my chance and I wasn't going to change my style now.'

He drank in so much knowledge in those early days, just listening to the senior pros in the Warwickshire dressing room. 'There'd be Dennis Amiss, Browny, Norman Gifford and Alvin Kallicharran, talking about the game. I couldn't get enough of that. I was hungry to make up for lost time.'

Moles knew what his role was and barely deviated from it throughout his time at Edgbaston. 'The rest of the boys batted around me as I tried to establish a platform by tiring out the fast bowlers and blunting the new ball. In '94 it worked a treat as me or Roger Twose would ease the way for Brian Lara or Dominic Ostler to cause havoc.

'That was the beauty of '94. Everyone had a role, we were all part of the jigsaw. Dermot and Woolly had explained it to all of us, leaving us to concentrate on our individual roles, without sacrificing the team ethic.'

There were two notable occasions in the '94 season when Moles played his part to perfection. The Edgbaston wicket for the NatWest semi-final against Kent was slow, a grafter's pitch. Moles assessed the situation swiftly and, as Lara, Ostler and Paul Smith all failed, forcing the pace, Moles dropped anchor to give his team something at least to bowl at. Warwickshire

265/8 in their fifty overs, Moles 105*, and a thrilling victory by eight runs. Warwickshire's brilliant fielding and Dermot Reeve's inspirational captaincy were vital elements in that pulsating win but, without the nous of Moles, Kent would have won in a canter.

Three weeks earlier, he had made an invaluable double hundred to set up a significant championship win at Guildford against a strong Surrey side. Moles knew that the wicket would deteriorate so, with a lead of 103 on first innings, he reasoned that occupation of the crease would be decisive. His 203*, spread over almost ten hours, was the slowest double century in county cricket history, but it kept Surrey in the field as the pitch grew tricky. Victory by 256 runs confirmed that there is more than one way for an intelligent, mature batsman to influence a four-day match.

By 1994 Moles had become an adept batsman in one-day cricket. He had been converted to the reverse sweep by Woolmer and Reeve and bought in totally to the bold approach to spinners. It gratified captain and coach that such a senior batsman should be so open-minded.

'We practised long and hard on the sweep variations in pre-season, and we really took the opposition bowlers apart. After a time they'd say, "Oh, all Warwickshire's batsmen do is play the reverse sweep." Not true, but it rattled many of them. All we needed was guidance, then support in playing those shots, and Dermot and Bob were brilliant at that. If you failed at it but gave sound cricketing reasons for playing the shot, there would be no recriminations. It was a very open, democratic dressing room.

'It was a rare environment in which every player, from the most senior down, derived great pleasure from seeing all the others doing well. Everybody totally respected the others' abilities. Look at Trevor Penney – in one-day games he didn't get the big scores that others did because he went lower down. And then he scored brilliant 20s and 30s that won us the games. He was a great finisher at the death.'

Moles can now smile ruefully at the bad luck that dogged him in that '94 season. Before pre-season in Zimbabwe, he was diagnosed with Type 1 diabetes, which brought its own challenges and a need for lifestyle reorganisation. Then, in a match in Harare, his arm was broken by Paul Smith, inadvertently. 'Paul hit one straight back with enormous power, and I saw it too late. A blistering drive hit me smack on my arm guard, and it was so hard that it broke my left arm. So I was out for a month after that. I was just getting over that when I suffered appendicitis and missed the next six weeks. On my comeback I was chuffed to make a big hundred against Northants 2nds. Dermot and Woolly had told me my first-team place was there for me, as soon as I got fit. I walked off with 164 to my name and shouted to our coach Neal Abberley, "Tell them I'm ready now," only to receive the crushing reply, "Forget that, mate, they're not bothered about you – Lara's just smashed 501." Sums up my career, really. It was an eventful summer, that one.'

Moles is too modest to mention that he averaged 50 in that '94 championship season. He relished his role among all the dashers. 'I wanted to make a statement that I understood my role and that I could play an important part in our season. My job was to create the best situation in the match where the freescoring batsmen could prosper.'

His best friend at the club, Tim Munton, believes that Moles was very under-rated, not least of all by himself. They had been very close since the 1980s, when David Brown put the two young players into the same bedroom on away trips, because they both snored so loudly and the other players were complaining about the noise. Munton was always Moles' biggest supporter. 'Moler was more naturally talented with the bat than I was with the ball, but we prided ourselves on being reliable cricketers. I loved it when he chirped the fast bowlers, then blocked it for session after session. Opening bowlers love putting their feet up while your top order batters just blunt the opposition.

'Moler had a fine, structured cricket brain. He used to say "I'm keeping those shots in my locker today" after sussing out the pitch but, when the occasion merited it, he'd play some classical cover drives or expansive flicks through mid-wicket. Moler was a very fine batsman and a great team man.'

Munton has a stack of stories about Moles' Gattingesque appetite for food. Once, up at Chester-le-Street for a championship match, they had been out for a few pints and Moles decided that the best way to prepare for the next day's play was a curry. The hotter the better. 'We were in Darlington, and Moler challenged the chef to make him the hottest he could cook. It took him half an hour to wade through it, but he wouldn't be defeated.'

Moles' eyes light up when reminded of that Darlington curry. 'It was a chicken Madras, and it came out with a large, ripe chilli on top. The waiter was smiling when he brought it out. He kept asking if I wanted some milk with it, but I said I wasn't a child, that I was happy with him topping up my beers. The staff kept walking past, checking I was ok but I wouldn't shirk the challenge. I polished it off, even the chilli. I did have a bead or two on my brow at the end, though! I wonder if modern county cricketers ever prepare the same way for a match. I doubt it. They miss a lot of fun.'

And Moles has enjoyed himself throughout his professional career as player and now as coach. He was enormously popular with the Warwickshire members, because he was basically one of them, a fan who never forgot how lucky he had been. He mingled happily with the supporters, took the leg-pulling about his weight with good grace and then ordered another pint. No other Warwickshire player entered with such gusto into the sojourns to the Extra Cover Bar. He was equally appreciative and welcoming to the supporters whenever he spotted them on away trips, coming over to thank them for being there. 'I was the local lad from club cricket, just down the road, who did well as a pro. But I was still the same bloke.'

With his sharp, forensic brain and fine personal values, Moles was to prove a natural coach. But he did not stroll straight into a coaching post when he retired at 36 in 1997. He was making a living by selling fire extinguishers when one day Bob Woolmer said to him, 'Have you ever thought about going into coaching? With your character and strengths, you should do.'

That got Moles thinking. 'When someone like Bob says that to you, then you sit up. I learned so much from so many great people at Edgbaston that I felt I could now go for it. They gave me the tools to be a coach myself. I have been so lucky.'

Moles has made his own luck, by his skills and willingness to work across the globe. He is now Development Coach for Afghanistan, charged with identifying emerging young talent to assist that troubled country's ascent to Test status. It is his second stint with Afghanistan, having coached them in the last World Cup. Tim Munton was very worried for his great friend when he first went to Kabul, as the febrile situation became more intense. 'I'd be ringing Moler every day, checking on him. He'd be holed up in his hotel, only venturing out to do his coaching, then back, under lock and key. But he never complained, just got on with it. That's Moler, all over.'

He has built up an impressive CV in coaching – in South Africa, New Zealand, Kenya, England under-19s and Scotland. He was in for the Director of Cricket post at Warwickshire in 2005, but missed out to Mark Greatbatch, with disastrous effect for the next two seasons. 'I thought I'd got it, and I would have been thrilled. But there were political manoeuvrings. Instead I ended up coaching the New Zealand national side after doing well at Northern Districts, so it all turned out well enough. Things happen for a reason.'

Tim Munton hopes his mate will end up with a county job in this country. 'He is so good at identifying, then encouraging young talent. That stems from what he had to learn when struggling to make the grade. Moler has a passion for organising things meticulously. And, of course, he's got such a likeable way about him.'

Of course he has. He was always one of those player singled out by the Warwickshire supporters as they chanted 'You Bears!' on big days in one-day matches as the beer took effect. He was always easy to spot on the field, after all.

Moles is unashamedly sentimental about his time at Edgbaston, especially in the '94 summer. 'We were a band of brothers who looked out for each other with trust and affection. That management group of Woolmer, Reeve and Munts operated seamlessly. No excuses were ever given, we held ourselves accountable if anything went wrong with the cricket.

'When I'm asked for my favourite memory, I never name one innings or one match. It's being part of that family in our dressing room who enjoyed all that success in '94 and '95, after working so hard for it. I doubt if it will ever be repeated.'

If it is repeated, I hope those successful players can look back with as much affection on their time in the sun as the gregarious Andy Moles.

Trevor Penney

August 1989. Edgbaston. The semi-final of the NatWest Trophy. Warwickshire v Worcestershire. The first time I ever saw Trevor Penney field.

During the innings interval, I had popped down from the BBC Radio commentary box to the players' dining room. In those far-off, friendly days, a reporter could wander into such areas. I espied the Warwickshire captain, Andy Lloyd. I asked him what he thought about his side's total of 220 on a slow wicket, given that Graeme Hick and Tim Curtis were dangerous players for the visitors. 'We'll be fine, make us favourites. Watch us in the field. Kalli can't field, and a young lad called Trevor Penney's coming on as sub fielder. I think you'll like him, Patrick.'

Alvin Kallicharran had been hit in the face by a throw from the outfield before he had scored. He battled his way through his innings, but the 40-year-old Kalli decided that he was too groggy to field. It suited him, as well as Warwickshire, to get the young shaver Penney on for the whole of those 50 overs. It was to prove a memorable introduction for the blond, reed-slim 21-year-old in front of a raucous, packed Edgbaston. It was the first of countless times that Penney demonstrated why he was to prove such a popular player for the next decade.

A strong Worcestershire side were simply swept away. Local derbies between these two in that period were always tense, tough affairs, with friendships laid aside. The noise was deafening, especially when Allan Donald nailed Curtis lbw for nought in the first over. I cannot remember such a din at Edgbaston involving Warwickshire in my time as a reporter. Only the closing, climactic stages of the NatWest Trophy semi-final against Kent in 1994 come close.

Penney dominated in the field. From the off, Kallicharran wasn't missed. I had hurriedly done some research on Penney in the rest of the interval. Born in Zimbabwe, attended the same school as Graeme Hick (two years younger), played for Blossomfield and Camp Hill Old Edwardians in 1988, turning out for the county's second XI in 1989, qualifying for England over the next four years.

I later found out he had shared a house on the Colts Ground with Allan Donald. Two close friends from Southern Africa, both with impeccable manners, charmingly approachable towards the Bears supporters and with a remarkable ability to down pints of beer without any effect on their impressive, wiry physiques. Hollow legs, the pair of them. I could never grasp how much Penney and Donald could put away, yet still be so outstanding at the county's fitness programme. Neither could Stuart Nottingham, the team's physiotherapist. 'Trevor was a wonder all those years. He was off the scale in the bleep tests, an amazing athlete.'

Within a few overs of Worcestershire's innings in that 1989 semi, it was clear that Penney was an extraordinary fielder. Stationed at backward point, the ball seemed to be magnetically attracted to him, but we didn't grasp at that stage his gift of anticipation and remarkably agile footwork that got him so unerringly into position. He galvanised a Warwickshire team that at that time was hiding a few camels in the field. The Worcestershire batsmen panicked whenever the ball was in Penney's area, and their innings declined shambolically. A star was born that day.

Looking on with delight was the Warwickshire head coach, Bob Cottam, eminently pleased that his scouting had pulled out another plum.

Cottam was coaching England Under-19s in Australia for the 1988 Junior World Cup while Penney was captaining an ICC Associates side, made up of countries not yet of Test status. Against an England team captained by Mike Atherton, containing Chris Lewis, Nasser Hussain and Mark Ramprakash, Penney made a mature 55 in an honourable defeat. Cottam was impressed. 'He looked the best player on view. And then there was his fielding. I thought we needed someone like that young lad at Edgbaston.'

Cottam offered him a four-year contract and, for a teenager with no real career path ahead, it was too good to turn down. He was working for a tobacco firm at the time, and a career in professional sport was mightily attractive. His father George was all in favour and told him to go to Warwickshire.

George was a huge influence on Trevor. He had played rugby for Rhodesia and, although good enough to play first grade cricket, it was not his paramount sport. But George Penney's fielding was legendary in Harare cricket. Penney Senior used to rave to his son about Colin Bland, the remarkable fielder who illuminated the South African side in the mid-'60s. George knew and admired Bland hugely and bought his son Bland's book on fielding techniques. Trevor devoured every page and put it into practice devotedly.

'I used to go to my club, Edwardians, at least a month before our season started and practise my fielding, using that book as my template. My elder brother Stephen, Eddo Brandes and Graeme Hick would help me out, hitting balls into the distance. If you dropped one of them, then you had to do the hitting till your arm ached. Then I'd take just six balls and aim at the stumps at narrow angles and work out how to throw fast off-balance.

'I would happily field all day. While waiting for my Dad to pick me up for practice or matches, I'd throw stones at the signposts, aiming for a particular spot. I got beaten at school quite a few times because I had a ball in my hand so often!'

Every old cricketer who has seen both Penney and Colin Bland field says the same thing – only the star of the '60s can rival Warwickshire's dazzling fielder of the '90s. Steve Rouse, former Warwickshire swing bowler and head groundsman at Edgbaston during Penney's time, cannot separate the two. 'Trevor read the batsmen so well, watching his feet, anticipating where he'd play the shot. He was so fast and deadly accurate with his throw.' MJK Smith played for England against Bland, then watched Penney dominate batsmen season after season. 'I can't split the two of them. Colin made such an impression when he came in to the Test arena and Trevor never got that exposure, but he was equally good.'

This lack of international exposure may have counted against Penney when comparisons were made with his contemporary Jonty Rhodes, that marvellous South African fielder. A personal view is that, although Rhodes was a wonderful stopper of the ball while off-balance, Penney shaded him because he hit the stumps more often. Allan Donald played with both Penney and Rhodes and concedes that point. 'Trevor ran batsmen out when there was easily a run there, but they got spooked by his reputation. But Jonty was superb as well. How lucky was I to bowl with those two in my team?'

Gladstone Small gives the accolade to Penney. 'He won us games by throwing out top-order batters. They refused to run to him once his reputation had spread. Trevor saved at least 20 runs per innings in the field. He was so fast, so accurate with his throwing. Jonty was fantastic, but Trevor got more direct hits. And he loved to practise.'

Paul Taylor played many times for Northants against Warwickshire. 'Trevor's influence on us was there to see, we were so wary of him. He turned certain twos into ones because of his reputation. These days, every county eleven has a fielder in Trevor Penney's class, but back in the mid-'90s he was exceptional. Out on his own.' Worcestershire's Tim Curtis agrees. 'He was a vital part of their armoury in the field. If you have someone that special, you're never out of the game.'

It seems amazing that Penney's predatory work in the field still caught some batsmen unawares. Tom Moody was run out by him for 47 in the '94 Benson & Hedges Cup Final, which helped win the game. A year later, Glamorgan's players had a long, involved meeting before their home NatWest Trophy semi-final against Warwickshire. The mantra was 'Don't run to Penney, don't run to Penney.' David Hemp and Matt Maynard still took Penney on and perished to direct hits. Glamorgan all out 86, defeat by eight wickets. 'It's days like those when all the practice pays off,' is Penney's modest reaction.

Penney is too genial and grounded to be bothered about all the concentration on his fielding, rather than his under-rated, intelligent batting, but he can surely be categorised as an all-rounder. He feels he could have been an even better batsman with greater awareness, opportunity and preparation. 'Cricket wasn't the sport that I was best at during my teens. I played hockey for Zimbabwe when I was 17 and made the all-Africa team. I was much better at hockey than cricket and was a good squash player, too. That's where I developed my wristiness when batting and my hand-eye coordination. That helped me later when I started to play the reverse sweep.

'I reckon that I'd have been twenty per cent better as a batsman if I'd put more work into it. With my batting, I just relied on my talent. My form would come and go, and I just accepted that. I should have worked how I could get back into form. That's something I tap into, now that I'm a coach. It's all about working with your talent, developing it, then

Trevor Penney in the 1994 Benson & Hedges Cup Final when he ran out Tom Moody with a direct hit from square

building on it. I just loved fielding so much, it was never a hardship to work all day on it. I expected to hit when aiming at just one stump.'

Penney may have undervalued himself as a batsman, but the opposition did not. Worcestershire's Tim Curtis was a big fan of his tactical intelligence. 'He really maxed out on his batting – fast hands, adaptable, flicking the ball into empty spaces with his strong wrists. He'd play doggedly early on, then go through the gears, manipulating the ball. Jos Buttler reminds me of Trevor, although Jos does hit the ball harder. But Trevor was a smart batsman.'

Stuart Nottingham, the Warwickshire physio, was fascinated by Penney's wiry athleticism. 'Genetics had something to do with it, plus growing up in an outdoor culture in Zimbabwe where you could play sport all day long. His movement patterns were so

smooth, he'd turn little rings while running between the wickets to save time. His hockey expertise obviously helped. A wiry, silky mover, he could change direction very quickly and never jolted his body when he ran. He was fantastic at the bleep test, gaining a metre on his turn. No one bothered trying to compete with Trevor on the bleep test.'

Penney was the archetypal team man, never complaining when shunted down the order to allow the expansive hitters more scope to prosper. In one-day cricket, he was a tremendous 'finisher' – expert at coming in with just a few overs left, the game in the balance, nudging and nurdling, running the fielders ragged with his speed between the wickets. He seemed to judge the match exigencies coolly, expertly shepherding the team to a victory when it had seemed in the balance twenty minutes earlier.

He does feel unfulfilled, though, with his batting. 'In one-day cricket I made the number-six role my own, which was a bit frustrating because, if you go in there, you can't really get more than 40 or 50. I am proud of my contribution to those great years at Edgbaston but, looking back, I think I had a lot more to give.'

He certainly did that with a crucial contribution to Warwickshire's '94 championship success in the home match against Lancashire. With Brian Lara and Dermot Reeve out injured, up against a Lancashire side justifiably eyeing up the title, Penney came in at number four to play what he considered his finest innings for Warwickshire: 111 off 130 balls, combating a fiery Wasim Akram with his tail up. Wasim again bent his back in the second innings as Warwickshire chased a target, with rain imminent. Penney orchestrated the victory charge with a cool 31*, and he is still proud of his role in that excellent victory. 'I was extremely happy to have performed like that. With Brian absent, someone had to stand up against a very good attack.'

Penney's partnerships with Lara in that '94 season epitomised what he brought to the side. Penney realised he could never compete with the dashing genius so he contented himself with chugging along in his slipstream, forging valuable partnerships of contrasting styles. The highlight was the stand against Durham of 314, in which Penney made 44. 'I reckoned being able to count to six was the key to that partnership. Brian was a team man, but he was playing so securely by the time he passed his hundred that I only had to run near the end of each over to give him the strike again. We've remained very good friends, and I often remind him he would never have got his 501* without me blocking it at the other end! I had the best seat in the house.'

Once he qualified for Warwickshire in 1992, Penney had five splendid years in the first team, averaging over 40 in championship cricket. After that he was increasingly pigeon-holed as a one-day specialist, despite ending up with a first-class average of 39. The plus side was that it freed him up to develop his coaching skills.

In 2005, on the morning of the C&G Final at Lord's – Penney's final big game for Warwickshire – he took a call from Tom Moody, his old team-mate at Edgbaston. Moody offered him a two-year contract

as assistant coach with Sri Lanka. His new career was up and running.

Since then Penney has coached with England, the USA, Netherlands and India as well as teams in the Premier League, Big Bash in Australia and the Caribbean Premier League. Now based in Montreal, he is much in demand among the world's elite coaching fraternity.

'Cricket is a unique game. It is so much about practice and processes and the mental requirements. It's all about giving yourself the best possible chance to succeed.'

He attributes his burgeoning reputation as a coach to what he learned at Edgbaston. 'For a few years, we had the most fantastic time, and I'm so proud of what we achieved. I coach all over the world, and someone brings up that '94 season somewhere, regularly. I tell them my stories, and they are amazed. "Gee whizz," they say, "that was a hell of a year for you." It was and I doubt if anyone will ever emulate it.

'We all knew in that dressing room what we had to do. Bob Woolmer was so innovative and Dermot Reeve an inspiring captain who made you feel good about yourself and your contribution to the team. At Christmas in 1994, Dermot sent me a card with the message: "You average 50 with the bat and save us 25 runs an innings in the field. Can't wait to work with you again next year." As a young player, I was thrilled to bits and couldn't wait for the new season to come.'

No day ever seemed too long to Trevor Penney. He would bound into the Extra Cover Bar at close of play with a genial word for everyone. He was beloved by the supporters, who relished his ability to sink a few pints, stay on for prolonged banter and still look like an advert for health foods the next morning, as he practised slavishly on the outfield.

'I loved going into the Members' Bar to hear all their stories and have a laugh. I hope I get there in 2019. It's been a few years now.'

If he does, the members will welcome him warmly, reminding him of countless spectacular run-outs and tremendous run chases, overseen by the smiling charmer, still with a flat stomach, still with that enviable thirst. No one ever had to approach Trevor Penney with trepidation for an autograph or a cheery word. He always gave the impression that the pleasure was all his.

Keith Piper

The shimmering brilliance of Brian Lara's batting illuminated the '94 season, but one Warwickshire player eclipsed even Lara for sustained excellence.

Keith Piper had hinted at consistently high quality of wicket-keeping for a few years, but the 1994 summer was his apogee. It is hard to imagine anyone keeping better in a long season.

Piper's elasticity of movement, his peerless work standing up to the spinners, the certainty of his glovework and athleticism standing back were breathtaking. The ball seemed to disappear into his gloves without a sound – the hallmark of a master craftsman.

Bob Cottam signed him for Warwickshire as a teenager on the strength of just a few overs. 'I thought, "Who's this lad?" I'd never seen glovework like his. He was the best I have ever seen.'

He was an absolute natural behind the stumps, the best of his generation. His contemporaries from other counties agree. Fellow members of the Wicket-Keepers' Union queue up to pay homage to Piper.

Jack Russell: 'One of the most gifted wicket-keepers of all time, absolutely brilliant. He made it look so easy. He showed his real class standing up. He was on a different planet.'

Paul Nixon: 'The most naturally talented keeper in the world at that time. Some of the catches he took standing back were outstanding. And when he stood up at times on slow pitches to Gladstone Small and Tim Munton, he was fantastic.'

Alec Stewart: 'An excellent gloveman, lovely hands, he made it look so easy. The ball just melted into his gloves. It must have been tough at times keeping to Gladstone or Allan Donald with the ball wobbling after it passed the bat. He was an artist.'

Glamorgan's Robert Croft enjoyed a fruitful relationship with Colin Metson, who was superb at reading his off-breaks, but he is unequivocal about Piper. 'The best keeper around' is his simple summary.

You would expect Piper's team-mates to be biased, but Allan Donald's testimony is relevant, because he worked with other keepers while on duty for South Africa, then coaching all round the world. 'Pipes had the best pair of hands of any wicket-keeper I have seen. Some of his work off my bowling was unbelievable.'

'Allied to his exceptional glove work,' Gladstone Small says, 'Pipes was also able to unravel batsmen's technical flaws. He was my sounding board whenever I wanted a critical eye on my bowling action.'

Tim Munton, in awe of Piper's natural talent, pinpoints his value to the side as a lightning conductor to the sustained aggression which characterised Warwickshire around that period. 'He was our cheerleader, the guy who got in the face of the opposition. He would throw in an acerbic comment, walking past the batsmen at the end of the over, designed to get under their skin. Pipes was one of the main reasons why we weren't over-popular during that period. But he got us going when the game was drifting.'

Ashley Giles, while acknowledging that Piper was the best keeper he has seen standing up to the stumps, admits Piper was an annoying opponent. 'Pipes could be a real ratbag, he irritated batsmen. We were respected but not generally liked in '94, and Pipes had a bit to do with that. But what a talent.'

The game in '94 that epitomised Piper's all-round value to the team was the NatWest semi-final against Kent when, with defeat looming, he galvanised the players. It appeared a routine victory for Kent as they advanced with untroubled tread on a target of 265 in 50 overs on a slow pitch. With 14 overs left, they needed just 83 with eight wickets in hand.

But Piper wouldn't give up. He bullied his team-mates back into the game, making a string of sensational stops to save byes. After Neil Taylor fell to a remarkable catch in the deep by Dominic Ostler, Piper produced a stunner to dismiss Graham Cowdrey – leaping astonishingly high to snare a snick two-handed off a sharp lifter from Paul Smith. It was a jaw-dropping take which inspired Piper's team-mates and electrified a noisy, partisan Edgbaston crowd.

As Kent's batsmen shrivelled in the crucible, Piper caught the dangerous Matthew Fleming, smartly stumped Steve Marsh and Warwickshire won a match by eight runs in a manner that defied the natural order. Piper's leadership and example behind the stumps were inspirational. 'We knew if we pressed them hard, they'd fold,' he recalls. 'We had so much confidence in each other that we never knew when we were beaten.' It also helped to have a keeper in that indefatigable unit that appeared infallible that season.

Piper was also smart enough to help create cricket history in 1994. When Lara made his astonishing 501* against Durham, he wasn't the only Warwickshire batsman to compile his career-best score in that innings. Piper's 116* in an unbroken stand of 322 for the fifth wicket has stayed under the radar for the past quarter of a century, with such monumental batting coming at the other end. He was only batting up the order at number six because Dermot Reeve was nursing a groin tweak and wanted to ensure his fitness for a Benson & Hedges Cup semi-final two days later.

By early June, Piper and Lara had forged a close friendship and the junior partner proved an excellent foil to the dazzling pyrotechnics, happily yielding up the strike. 'He didn't say much, just told me to keep concentrating. He was so relaxed about everything that I felt none of the pressure I expected, batting with someone who scored 390 that day.'

As Lara glided serenely on to 497*, just two runs short of the highest individual score in first-class cricket, Piper showed an awareness that surprised some, brilliant wicket-keeper though he was. Piper had checked with both umpires that, with a draw certain, the extra half-hour could not be claimed. As the clock neared 5.30 pm, the over being bowled by John Morris would therefore be the last of the match. There were two deliveries left in the over, and Lara needed at least three runs.

'So I went down the wicket to tell Brian that he was almost out of time. He just nodded and smashed the next ball through the covers for four. History was made, and I was proud to be out there to see it from just a few yards away.'

It was no surprise that Piper should cash in for a century on a very flat pitch. He was a good batsman, even if his career statistics suggest otherwise. Just two first-class centuries and an average of 19.99 over more than a decade suggest a mediocre batsman, but he always hinted at a talent superior to his ultimate figures.

Getting under the skin of Northamptonshire's David Capel

One innings by Piper lingers in the memory of this writer. At Southampton in '95 he came in as nightwatchman and promptly unfurled some glorious textbook shots. He continued in the same vein next day till Shaun Udal bowled him for 99. It was a bold, stylish innings, suggesting that, at the age of 25, he was destined to do himself justice as a batsman. That never transpired. Concentration, not a faulty technique, often proved Piper's undoing with the bat.

At the start of the 1994 season, three wicket-keeper/ batsmen were vying for the England role. Alec Stewart's first-class average was 38.66, Steve Rhodes' 31.71 and Jack Russell's 27.48. Piper's lagged behind on 18.88. That England team wasn't strong enough to dispense with the runs that Stewart et al could offer, in addition to their sterling qualities as competitors, in favour of the superior keeper. Bob Taylor suffered with similar comparisons two decades earlier. Piper would bat no higher than number nine if he ever played for England.

Tim Munton reluctantly concedes the point. 'Pipes' average was short by ten runs an innings, compared to the other three, who were not as good as keepers pure and simple. It was frustrating, though, because Pipes played good-looking strokes. He handled the short ball very well and it was always a disappointment when he was out cheaply.'

Dennis Amiss considers Piper the equal of Alan Knott among all the keepers he has seen. 'I was amazed he never played for England. I was mesmerised by his talent.'

The closest Piper got to England recognition was a couple of England 'A' tours: to India in 1994/95, then Pakistan the following winter. He acquitted himself well enough, but there was too little cricket played on the tours for him to make a major impact.

Piper was the only Warwickshire player to be picked for one of two England winter tours after the 'annus mirabilis' of '94, and he always played down talk of an international career. On several occasions I mooted it to him, only to be met with a wrinkled nose and sceptical words. 'It's not going to happen, someone from my background just won't fit in.'

There lies the conundrum of Keith Piper. Such a confident character on the cricket field, but insecure off it. He was the product of his tough North London upbringing. With little formal education, he would bunk off school and wait for someone to organise a game of cricket or football. Joining the Haringey Cricket College gave him some shape and structure to his teenage life. A local councillor had recognised how many youngsters didn't realise their potential as cricketers, as they played unsupervised in parks. It became a registered company with charitable status and a production line of talent – Mark Alleyne, Steve Bastien, the Rollins brothers and Piper – was rolled out.

Piper once admitted to me that Haringey College helped keep him away from the fringes of criminality, giving him some respite from what could be described as a challenging upbringing. I wonder just how much he has managed to banish memories of those tough early days as he encountered subsequent vicissitudes. Certainly his grandfather – known to everyone as 'Pop' – was a steadying, loving influence, bringing up the boy almost single-handed. 'Pop' Piper was a regular presence at Warwickshire games, justifiably proud, but the subject of his grandson's early days always remained off-limits.

Ashley Giles looks back with sympathy on Piper's younger travails. 'They undoubtedly held him back, there was definitely baggage there. Pipes was very insecure, despite the confident front as a cricketer. He needed support at times from the dressing room, and Dermot and Tim looked after him as best they could.'

Dermot Reeve's pastoral care for his brilliant yet troubled charge was admirable. He counted Piper as a close friend and cared for his welfare. Yet even he could get aggravated by Piper's occasionally fiery outbursts on the field or when he had too much to say. 'I sometimes had to come out of the slips because he was saying too much, like the need for a third slip or dogmatic comments about a bowler being crap in that spell. At times I felt like throttling Keith, even though he was such a good mate. He had to be pulled aside at times for a strong word. He could be a little combustible at times, so had to be treated in a certain way.'

Such sensitive man-management by Reeve worked, and Piper remains hugely grateful. 'In any other side in the world, I wouldn't have had the career I had, despite my ability. That group of Warwickshire players trusted each other, helped each other out. Dermot, Tim and Bob Woolmer were fantastic at man-management. They understood me, accepted I was different, that I really didn't have a great deal of self-belief.'

That lack of self-belief dogged Piper once his palmy days at Edgbaston passed. He became more unreliable after being banned for one match in 1997, for testing positive in a random drugs test, while an achilles tendon injury affected his lightning footwork behind the stumps.

His benefit year in 2001 was a trial for him and his committee. Piper found it hard to commit himself to the many functions organised on his behalf. Keith Cook, then in charge of the players' welfare while working with Dennis Amiss, tried his best to keep Piper on track but found it hard. 'Pipes worried about attending those functions, standing up and saying a few words. It was a bonus whenever he turned up. He just hid from the world when he wasn't playing.'

Keith Cook remains enormously fond of Piper and does his best to keep in touch with him. 'He's a lovely lad. Caring and genuine. To look at him as a player you wouldn't believe he lacked self-confidence but, deep down, I think he didn't really believe in his skills. Obviously his upbringing is relevant, but that's a closed book and I respect that.'

Piper retired in 2005 after testing positive for cannabis in the opening round of championship games and banned for the next four months. Warwickshire CCC did its best to keep him in the fold, taking him on the coaching staff until 2008, when he took voluntary redundancy. After a stint coaching at Leicestershire CCC, he left the game in 2018.

It may be that Keith Piper was one of the many ex-pros who struggle with life after they finish playing cricket, needing to adjust and adapt. All who knew him wish him well. At his best he was a cheerful, bubbly character with a good heart. As a wicket-keeper, he was in the highest class, an integral part of a great team. Piper set the fielding standards that defined that side.

Jack Russell played a similar role for Gloucestershire just a few years later when they scooped so many one-day trophies, adopting the Warwickshire prototype. He has no doubts of Piper's enduring value. 'When we batted against them, we used to think "Where are we going to get a run here?" Dermot's field placings were brilliant, but Piper was a fantastic orchestrator behind the stumps. He created and sustained the pressure. Never gave us a moment's peace.'

Hopefully Keith Piper will eventually find peace, away from cricket – and will realise how many of his team-mates and friends from that golden period still care for him.

Neil Smith

It's entirely fitting that the final, decisive delivery of Warwickshire's historic '94 season should be bowled by one of the side's most self-effacing players, one who epitomised their boundless team spirit.

Bristol, Sunday 18 September. Mike Smith c Munton b N.Smith 7. Gloucestershire all out 137, defeat by 46 runs. Warwickshire win the AXA Equity & Law League, their third trophy in 1994.

It had been a triumphant Sunday League for Neil Smith. Midway through the campaign he had been promoted to open the innings, with licence to biff the ball in his customary uncomplicated fashion. Smith, making it clear he was happy to bat anywhere in the eleven, was assured it didn't matter if he went in the first over, as long as he provided impetus, clearing the way for the heavy artillery in the middle order.

With a penchant for clean, straight hitting, Smith was a success. Not for him the deft, nimble reverse sweeps – 'with my suspect knees I wouldn't have been able to get up from the shot to run down the other end' – but his front-foot power was more than enough to get the innings off to an explosive start.

But it was his intelligent off-spin that was so crucial. In the Sunday League he took 26 wickets, the joint highest in the country, a reward for his ability to turn the ball. While other off-spinners settled for containment, Smith gave the ball a genuine rip and he was paid the compliment of front-line batsmen deciding just to see him off, get through his allotted eight overs and try to plunder the runs elsewhere. In three successive Sunday League games, his combined analysis was 24-3-80-10, absolute gold dust for any captain.

Dermot Reeve had no doubts about Smith's value to the side in all competitions. 'We called him "the Iceman" because of his cool temperament; ask him to do anything with bat or ball and he'll try it without any fuss.'

And yet, five years earlier, Smith looked to be heading out of Edgbaston at the age of 22. An innings of just 15* reprieved him. The fact that it came in the pressure cooker atmosphere of a Lord's one-day final, with rain and gloomy light swirling around Lord's, meant it was a precious cameo. Indeed, it could be said that one mighty blow of Smith's straight back

past the bowler's head for six in the final over saved his career.

We have to go back 48 hours from that dramatic Saturday Lord's finish to establish the sequence of events that brought Smith to centre stage. There's a case for saying that, if Tim Munton hadn't failed as night-watchman up at Headingley on the Thursday night, then Neil Smith would not have had the opportunity to make his name.

Warwickshire, 198 behind Yorkshire on first innings, faced a long final day in the field trying to stave off defeat, hardly the ideal preparation for the trek down to Lord's on the Friday night. Tim Munton was sent in on the penultimate evening to protect the accredited batsmen. Usually a brave, tenacious tail-ender – an ideal nightwatchman – Munton failed on this occasion, fired out in the first over by the rapid Paul Jarvis. Enter Neil Smith to see out the day. At that stage, Smith was deemed a promising off-spinner who had batting potential. He was only in the side because the first choice spinner, Adrian Pierson, was injured. In that Yorkshire match, their opening batsman Ashley Metcalfe had batted more than six hours for a hundred and Smith's captain Andy Lloyd had remarked tersely to him, 'You should try that sometime.' Smith was well aware that after just two championship games in the previous couple of seasons, the key decision-makers in cricket terms were none the wiser about how far he could progress. Was he a bowler or did he have genuine batting potential? Could he become a valuable all-rounder?

Time was running short for the 21-year-old Smith to lay out his credentials. His father, Mike, the former England and Warwickshire captain, had been chairman of the cricket committee when Neil was taken on the staff in 1987 and, while no one talked publicly about nepotism, there were a few whispers about his prospects. He had been good enough to represent the county's Under-11s and Under-12s, but that buttered no parsnips when Paul Jarvis was steaming in at you in a championship match. Could Neil Smith survive among les grandes fromages?

He certainly did on that final day at Headingley, making the first century of his first-class career and with added interest, playing some handsome shots in

his 161. It remained his highest score in a 17-year career. So Munton unwittingly did Smith a huge favour by getting out the night before. 'I was bowled middle stump, never saw it. I often joke with Neil that I helped kickstart his career that day!' Having played in both the quarter- and semi-finals, Smith would probably have played next day in the Lord's final, but this knock gave him massive self-confidence that he could tap into when the pressure was really on him 24 hours later.

'It was a nice net for me. I had licence to bat all day, the top batters didn't want to be out there really but I did. I needed to get my feet moving, work on my timing. At the end of that Yorkshire game, I felt I could back myself at Lord's.'

When Smith walked out to bat next day in stygian gloom, Middlesex were favourites to lift the NatWest Trophy. On a slow pitch, in dreadful light, Warwickshire needed 20 from 18 balls. Ten were needed off the last over, to be bowled by Simon Hughes, who was renowned for his slower ball in tight situations. Asif Din took a single off the first ball ,and Smith knew it was now his responsibility.

'Gunga was the more experienced by far, but he couldn't help me now. We were on a hiding to nothing, and there was no other way to play it at this stage. It would have been better to have him back on strike but we were running out of balls, with just five left. I knew Simon would try the slower ball but when? I saw Desmond Haynes gesture to try it from mid-on, and I took a deep breath. The light was shocking, but somehow I connected and got it over long-off. It was a horrible shot but I didn't care.

'The problem now was that Gunga and I had to keep calm. We were now favourites but we still had to win the thing and keep the adrenalin at bay.'

He need not have worried. Hughes conceded a legside wide, then Smith smashed the fourth ball of the final over for the winning runs. It may have been just 15*, but Smith had hit the only six of the match when it was desperately needed. The legend of Smith the Iceman began that day in September 1989. Time and again he would add to it.

But first Smith had to secure his future. He was offered only a one-year contract, but he stood his ground and finally won a two-year deal. 'I was gutted initially, but with all the euphoria surrounding that Lord's victory I wasn't looking at the bigger picture. I needed to prove myself after three years in and around the first team.

'It was a psychological thing. I hadn't been able to control my mental processes. In those early days I was still in awe of the older players like Norman Gifford, Geoff Humpage and Alvin Kallicharran. It was daunting. When the old guard left and team-mates from the seconds came into the first eleven, I relaxed a little and the mental barrier was removed. It helped hugely that I now knew so many of the guys from the past few years.

'There is no doubt, though, that Lord's '89 saved my career – just like Gunga Din in '93. I reckon without that I would've been released at the end of the '89 season.'

Andy Lloyd says that Smith would have played at Lord's, no matter how he fared on that final day in Headingley. 'We needed the variety his spin bowling offered. And he brought increased confidence from that innings into all aspects of his game at Lord's. He bowled well and got us the key wicket of Desmond Haynes. At that stage, you never really knew what you were going to get from Neil, he was very inconsistent. When he was on his game Neil was a very good cricketer, but he wasn't always as he appeared. With our excellent seam attack at that time, there often wasn't scope to use Neil's off-breaks, so he needed more self-confidence. Headingley and Lord's came at the right time for him.'

So the Iceman wasn't always the calm, self-contained cricketer of those glory years in the mid-nineties. It's not as if he wasn't steeped in cricket. Neil remembers talking cricket at home with his dad but never in depth. 'He was always there with his thoughts if I wanted them, but he never pushed them on me. I often went to Edgbaston when he was playing – I remember sitting on dad's cricket coffin in his white Ford Capri, as he drove me to the Indoor School for coaching.' Steve Rouse, MJK's team-mate and later head groundsman, was a willing mentor to young Neil and one summer the great West Indian batsman – and Warwickshire legend – Rohan Kanhai lived with the Smith family. So the youngster inevitably absorbed a great deal of cricketing commonsense. That proved one of Neil Smith's key characteristics as a player.

His father never pushed his name forward at Edgbaston. 'I knew Neil was a good cricketer with lots of promise – and the fact that he played 17 years of county cricket and represented England in the 1996 World Cup bears that out. Once he established himself in the side after '89, it was clear he was worth his place. With his rate of scoring and his off-spin, he had a particular value in one-day cricket.'

And that is as close as we will get to praise of his son from his laconic, understated father. It is of no account. The two remain close, with Neil joshing 'The Old Man', as he calls him, as he cruises through his 80s with the minimum of fuss, as sharp as ever mentally. They remain the only father and son to have captained Warwickshire and, if you press them on that, they will admit to a smidgeon of pride.

Once established in the first team, Smith became a dependable all-rounder, admired for his undemonstrative, supportive nature, embodying the values he felt constituted being a true Bear. 'A lot of our success was built around solid, good blokes like Moles, Munton and Small – fantastic, dependable guys who loved the club. They were great with the supporters in the bar at close of play. I thought it was a great idea to introduce the club rule of going to the Extra Cover Bar. It meant a lot to me, having been at Edgbaston since I was a kid.'

Smith's value to Warwickshire in 1994 was incalculable. He was helped by the decision to sign the slow left-arm bowler Dickie Davis from Kent. For too long Warwickshire had lacked a cutting edge in spin bowling, with oppositions batting out for a draw in four-day games or picking off the sole spinner. Now they were covered in both bases. 'Dickie and I complemented each other very well. He was a flight bowler, whereas I could get the ball up and turn it. So we had variety from two spinners to add to our excellent pace attack. And Dermot could always slip in his cheeky stuff if the game was drifting.'

Before the '94 season the cricket management calculated that the absence on international duty of Allan Donald all summer meant that 80 championship wickets had to be found from somewhere. The signing of Davis and the continued development of Smith garnered exactly that number. Six times the pair took five wickets in an innings. Only Munton – also six times – got near that tally.

Smith also added his unselfish batting to the mix. 'I happily embraced the cricket management's positive philosophy. They appreciated that I would bat anywhere and do what they wanted. It didn't matter to them if I got out for nought in the first over of a one-day match, as long as I was trying to play the appropriate shot, having practised hard at it. We were mostly young, enthusiastic guys, enjoying ourselves – and the pressure never seemed to bear down on us.'

One of those young players, Graeme Welch, warmed to Smith's positive outlook when he came into the side, wide-eyed and just 22. 'The game never stood still when Neil was involved. I thought he was a top-class spin bowler, who never got the credit he deserved. He always tried to spin batsmen out, never took a step back, looking to contain them. Always attacking, he never hid when there was tap flying around. Neil wanted to bowl all the time.

'I got so much encouragement from Neil when I came into the first team, not knowing much about my game. He had a very good tactical head on his shoulders; he really understood the game.

'He was also very brave to bat the way he did in the one-dayers, sacrificing his wicket for the team by playing boldly. He was ahead of his time then. His type at the top of the order became known as pinch-hitters, but Neil set the standard from 1994 onwards.'

Ashley Giles, just 21 in 1994, could not get into the first team because the Smith/Davis axis was too strong, but he watched and learned and appreciated Smith's unselfishness. 'He was brilliant at giving me little titbits and general advice about how to kick on. Hugely supportive. I admired the way he cashed in as a game went into the final innings. That's when the footholds started to wear and loosen, and he'd drop the ball so accurately in the danger areas. Neil attacked with the ball, had a nice loop and turned it sharply. He was an integral part of that team.'

Yet Smith appeared unfashionable at England level. Just seven one-day internationals was his meagre reward. Raymond Illingworth, who knew a thing or two about off-spin, clearly did not rate him as much as Shaun Udal or Mike Watkinson, and Smith is not about to cavil at that. 'What I do feel is that we didn't talk enough about cricket when I was part of the England set-up. Coming from Warwickshire, where

Dermot and Bob created such unity, it was strange to experience team meetings that didn't last very long or the opposition were barely mentioned. Everyone was encouraged to pitch in during team meetings at Edgbaston. I suggest that might have contributed to our great success. Being allowed to express yourself in such a positive environment was fantastic. I never had that with England.'

No matter. He was highly regarded in the Warwickshire dressing room, especially by his captain Dermot Reeve. 'We looked for unselfishness within the framework of efficiency, and Neil Smith was the best example of a team man. In championship games, he sometimes batted as low as number ten and then, in one-day matches, he'd be our wild card, opening his shoulders from the first over. Another player might have muttered about having to throw his wicket away, but not Neil.'

It was inevitable that Smith would captain Warwickshire, given his upbringing, tactical nous and the respect in which he was held. Sadly those two seasons (1999-2000) were not a success, and he was unceremoniously sacked within 24 hours of the latter season ending. The fact that he was the county's fourth captain in five seasons illustrates the lack of direction dogging the club, compared to the 1993-96 period, but there would be no bleating about it from Neil Smith – not even when he ended up with only a one-day contract as his career wound down, retiring in 2003.

Smith never took himself too seriously, but his team-mates valued him enormously. His one-day performances were excellent, but he also made crucial contributions to Warwickshire's two triumphant championship seasons in '94 and '95, scoring 848 runs and taking 85 wickets. 'I would never consider myself to be one of the better players, but I felt I was always competitive, wanting to be involved.

'That was the best period of my career and all those years later, wherever I go, those are the years Warwickshire supporters want to talk about. We just worked together. We had a great atmosphere and whenever we went on the pitch everybody in the side had a collective goal to win. We didn't all get on, and there were issues off the field on a few occasions. The Reeve/Lara issue was there of course, and it could have derailed us, but the cricket management kept us on track, so hats off to them.

'That collective will-to-win underpinned everything. I don't think you can have 15 to 18 guys, travelling around the country for five months and spending ten hours a day together, without having a few issues. They were dealt with.'

Neil Smith has been associated with Warwickshire cricket for more than 40 years. Typically, despite that messy end to his playing career, he bears no malice – or, at least, keeps his own counsel. He has coached at schools and clubs in the county, is a regular at Edgbaston matches and never succumbs to the trap of comparing present with past. A big supporter of Warwickshire Old Cricketers' Association events, he will willingly yarn over old times, indulging the veterans with a twinkly eye and a kindly word, teasing the Old Man that his memory is getting worse.

He is at ease with himself and his fine career, happy to have chugged along in the slipstream of the sleek, glamorous liners. Neil Smith knew his worth to Warwickshire but has no intention of trumpeting it.

Besides, he knows how close he came to having a short career, had it not been for two innings on successive days in September 1989. 'I was heading for the chop. Those two innings helped me have a decent career.'

Typical of Smith, that word 'decent'. It describes him perfectly as a man, but his team-mates will say it undersells his cricket career.

Dominic Ostler

It may appear bizarre to dub an all-rounder someone who took one first-class wicket at a cost of 295 in a 15-year career, but Dominic Ostler should be viewed as just that. I base that assessment on the remarkable standard of Ostler's fielding in all areas of the field. Think Ben Stokes, if you want a modern equivalent. Ostler was brilliant in the slips, specialising in snaring edges off Allan Donald's searing pace, while in the outfield he was intimidating. He could throw at speed over a long distance, running out many a dozy batsman who had not done his homework. There was never 'one for the throw' with Dominic Ostler. His speed around the boundary rope and brilliant anticipation were breathtaking. His team-mates struggled to remember him dropping a catch in the deep over more than a decade.

MJK Smith, a superbly brave short-leg fielder himself, and Dennis Amiss have both been associated with Warwickshire CCC for more than 60 years, and both are unequivocal that Ostler is the best all-round fielder they have seen in the Bears' colours. Amiss says: 'He caught everything in the slips, and they came at him from AD at the speed of light. In the deep, he was so fast to the ball, athletic, great with the dive on the boundary rope, saving hundreds of runs a season. And he'd get on his feet rapidly after a tumbling stop and hurl it in fast and straight. He had a magnificent arm.'

Tim Munton is just one of many bowlers grateful to have Ostler in the field. 'What an all-rounder! He took so many wickets for me in the slips, with fantastic reactions. And in the one-day games, when the scouts are sent out to patrol the boundary, he remained a threat. He'd arrow in a fast, flat throw if anyone was daft enough to take him on. Dom gave us so much in the field, alongside Trevor Penney. Trevor was a specialist, brilliant at backward point, but Dom was sensational anywhere.'

Ostler was always endearingly modest as a player and even now he plays down his fielding prowess. 'I didn't bowl, so I thought I needed another string to my bow when I first got into the side. Being a bit lazy, I liked being able to switch on and off in the slips, have a bit of banter with Keith Piper, then get ready for the next ball. I loved taking those one-handers to

AD, standing thirty yards back. I preferred second slip, keeping third open, so that I could get the dive in to my right when necessary. In the deep I knew I had a strong arm and I liked tumbling around, going for the spectacular. I had minimal practice; it all just seemed natural to me.'

In 1994 Warwickshire fielded brilliantly. They were a constant threat, nagging away at opposition batsmen. In Piper, they had the best wicket-keeper in the country, the slips and gully cordon populated at different times by Ostler, Dermot Reeve, Roger Twose and Dickie Davis missed very little, they had the outstanding backward point in Penney, and in Ostler the supreme outfielder. Topped off by the best captain in Reeve.

'Dermot was one of those instinctive captains who would make things happen. He knew that we would normally pull something out of the bag in the field when it was really needed. We gelled as a group, and we felt unbeatable at times.'

Ostler was predominately a front-foot batsman, specialising in booming straight drives. At his best he would bully the ball, dominating the bowling. Yet he needed encouragement often. A shy young man when he first came into the side, inclined to blush when called upon to speak at team meetings, he relied a lot on his captain's support in those early days. 'Andy Lloyd was brilliant for me, giving me so much self-confidence. All I ever wanted to do was play for the Bears. Born in Solihull, played league cricket for Moseley, my Dad a Warwickshire member, me a Birmingham City supporter – what a thrill even to think about playing for the county. And when Andy promoted me to number four in my second season in the first team, I felt he really believed in me.'

So did Dennis Amiss. He admired Ostler's destructiveness but felt he should score more runs. 'Dennis walked past me one day and just said, "You're a bloody good player but you don't get enough hundreds." It was hard to argue with that and I was flattered, but in my defence Andy, then Dermot encouraged the batters to go for their shots and play for the team. I liked that collective unselfish attitude, whereby you had to go in and whack it – where quick fifties were more important than a slow century. We

Dominic Ostler in the slips

weren't going to play dull cricket, letting games peter out.'

Dermot Reeve was also a big fan. 'If I ever had a bad patch, Dermot would come up to me and say, "Look, mate, what are you worried about? You're going to play every game this season, so relax." That was great, it made me believe I could go out and play with freedom, with no recriminations if I got myself out.'

Reeve was as good as his word. Ostler played in every match in seasons '93 and '94 and missed just a handful in '95, through a knee injury. In return Ostler signed up to Reeve's campaigning zeal over using the reverse sweep. It was, initially, antithetical to Ostler's robust style of play, but Reeve eventually got through to him. 'I saw the point of playing the spinners with more finesse, messing their fields around. I was getting just as many runs playing cleverly rather than launching into booming drives that got me just a single, because they hit the fielder on the rope too quickly for a second run. We played it with so much confidence as a batting unit that we'd sit in the viewing area, calling the shot before it was played because we would notice how the field was set. Dermot and Roger Twose led the way brilliantly, and almost all of us followed suit.'

Ostler remembers particularly an innings of 78 against Northants in the Sunday League in 1994, when he played with a new deftness. 'I tried it every ball in one over, rotating the strike, disrupting the spinner's field. Dermot was amazed and clearly chuffed that I'd bought into the reverse sweep.'

There was another reason why Ostler became a convert to the reverse sweep. Bob Woolmer. Ostler revered Woolmer's tactical nous and imagination, reasoning that, if the coach was a devotee, he had better sign up. 'Bob knew how to manage people as well as offer theories. He knew just a word in my ear was enough, whereas others wanted more technical advice from him. All I needed from Bob was support and reassurance. He was a massive part of any success I enjoyed. If you look at my career, I was at my best when Bob was the coach.'

The Woolmer/Ostler combo was not quite in the Samuel Beckett/Billie Whitelaw bracket, but the coach was certainly the perfect mentor for the buccaneering Ostler. And the facts back up Ostler's assertion that he was at his best when Woolmer was on hand at Edgbaston. In seven full seasons over two spells, Woolmer guided Ostler to championship averages varying between 34 and 48. When Woolmer was elsewhere, Ostler's average fluctuated between 4.75 and a highest of 27. He became confused, lost confidence, was dropped several times and looked forlorn without his guru. A knee injury also reduced his effectiveness.

At the end of the 1994 season, Ostler was among several Warwickshire players with reasonable aspirations of an England call. Only Keith Piper got the call – for an England 'A' tour to India. Ostler had to wait till the following year, putting in another impressive body of work as Warwickshire garnered two more trophies. He was picked for the 'A' tour to Pakistan before Christmas. He missed the first two internationals due to illness, scored 68 in the third, acquitted himself well in the one-dayers – but that was it. Eleven of that touring party, under the captaincy of Nasser Hussain, went on to play Test cricket. Not Dominic Ostler.

He needed a good start to the 1996 season to press his international case, especially for the one-dayers, but a knee operation hampered his season and 712 championship runs at 27.38 didn't exactly hammer home his credentials. 'No complaints. I had to hit the ground running that May, but I started poorly. That was probably my chance, but it had gone.'

That suspect knee hampered Ostler for the rest of his career, although the return of Woolmer in 2000 kick-started him into some consistency, as he banged out some big hundreds – as Dennis Amiss asked him to do a few years earlier. But by 2003, just 33 years of age, the dodgy knee was playing him up. 'I couldn't play four-day cricket anymore. I didn't want to be the sort of player who sloped away and played second-team cricket for years. I wanted to say "Thank you, I loved playing for Warwickshire, it's my time to go."

'I will always treasure my time with the Bears, especially winning all those trophies in the space of two years. We were idolised like footballers for a time. Walking down the street or in the pubs we'd get so much attention. It was proper big-time. We never thought we'd lose a game; winning became a habit. If we were bowled out for 150, we still felt we'd bowl them out for less. Chase 300-plus? We can do that. We had this amazing rapport within the side. Living in each other's pockets for six months was bound to lead to some tensions, but we stayed close-knit, even when Dermot and Brian Lara were at odds. We just stayed out of it and concentrated on our game. It came down to eleven guys going out on the park, united – whatever else was going on.'

Ostler, in common with his team-mates, was awestruck at Lara's talent. When he made his 501* against Durham, Ostler's early dismissal for 8 ushered in the batsman who made history. 'I was caught behind after thumping a couple of boundaries. I'm claiming an assist for Brian's innings! Just to watch him build an innings, then take an attack apart was an education. We all fed off Brian, he gave us so much confidence. There was nothing we wouldn't chase with him in our team. Brian was unbelievable – he picked the ball up so much quicker than anyone else. That massive high backlift! He hit the ball so hard.'

One of the reasons Ostler was so popular in the dressing room was because he was so happy to play for his home county and he radiated modesty. The supporters picked up on that also; he was one of their own. He would pitch up at the Extra Cover Bar at close of play and chat to the members, taking the banter about being a Bluenose from the Aston Villa supporters. He is at ease with his 15 years at Edgbaston.

'OK, I averaged only 35 and should have scored more hundreds. But in the early '90s the home pitches were quite sporting and we all played unselfishly, giving the ball a whack, not thinking about our averages. Runs per balls were more important than heavy scoring. I picked up eight winners' medals and feel privileged about that. It was an amazing time to be a Warwickshire player.'

And he's still a true Bear. After learning the coaching ropes while captaining Berkswell CC (two Birmingham and District Premier League titles in three seasons), with the club acting as a feeder for promising players on the Warwickshire pathway, he is back at the ground he knows so well.

Ostler is now coach to Warwickshire Women, having previously coached their Under-17 squad. 'I have really enjoyed it. I love coaching, though I never thought I would. I want to improve young cricketers, for the benefit of Warwickshire – male and female.'

I suspect the fielding standards of Warwickshire Women will improve markedly. They could not have a better mentor.

Dickie Davis

The night at the Botanical Gardens in leafy Edgbaston was a classy affair. The mood was celebratory, and no wonder. The great and the good of Warwickshire CCC had gathered there to celebrate the tenth anniversary of that remarkable 1994 season.

Brian Lara had flown in from Trinidad, Roger Twose from New Zealand, Dermot Reeve from Australia. Andy Moles, Allan Donald and Trevor Penney had all travelled thousands of miles, primed for an evening of nostalgia and merciless leg-pulling.

Only one relevant figure from 1994 was missing. Dickie Davis. A life cruelly snuffed out a year earlier due to a brain tumour. Just after Christmas. He was only 37.

Sam, Dickie's widow, had been very touched by the invite to the dinner. The club had been at great pains to make her realise her late husband was not forgotten, nor his contribution to the Treble Season. Neil Smith, who had been very close to Dickie in his time at Edgbaston, had assured Sam that she would be looked after sensitively if she agreed to attend.

'I wrestled with the decision, knowing it would be hard for me. Neil and his wife Rachel put me up, and everyone was so kind to me. Rich was mentioned in the speeches, and it was clear he hadn't been forgotten, even though it was nine years since Rich had left the club after just two seasons. I felt closer to him that night for being there.

'The way I was treated so kindly that night summed up our time in Birmingham. Right from the start we were made to feel part of an extended family. The year 1994 was one of the happiest of my life, and I know that for Rich it was also memorable. He played for a lot of clubs and he always said that Warwickshire was the first time he felt a family atmosphere.'

Dickie Davis made an immediate, favourable impression when he joined from Kent, not just because of his skilful slow-left-arm bowling. He was popular because he was a dependable, low-maintenance team man. Certainly he was hungry for success. Two years earlier he had been the country's leading spinner, taking 74 championship wickets, but the emergence of Min Patel sidelined Davis and he turned down a one-year contract to join Warwickshire. It would not be the first time he decided to up sticks to further his career.

Davis brought flight and guile to his spin bowling, with the ball seemingly on a string when he was bowling at his best. His signing solved a problem that had hampered Warwickshire's progress for some time. They needed an experienced left-arm spinner to complement the off-breaks of Neil Smith. Now they had a balanced attack at last, with the head groundsman Steve Rouse well aware that wickets which would turn late in the game would suit the cricket management very nicely.

Davis also brought doughty, brave batting and excellent slip catching to the package. 'Just as well he had hands like buckets,' Dougie Brown recalls, 'because he had the slowest twitch fibres I've ever seen. Dickie was a big lad and couldn't run all that quickly, but he was a brilliant slip fielder. A great solid pro and just the nicest man you could ever meet. He was a great signing for '94.'

Davis had been approached on the day of Warwickshire's momentous NatWest Trophy victory at Lord's the previous September. Bob Woolmer kept an eye on the playing talent at his old county and noticed Patel was keeping Davis out of the team. Woolmer rang Davis from Lord's as the champagne corks popped and opened negotiations. Sir Alex Ferguson, a committed opponent of resting on laurels in the immediate aftermath of victory, would surely have approved of Woolmer's forward thinking.

Sam Davis remembers how well Woolmer and Dermot Reeve sold the club to them. 'We were both Kentish people, but Rich felt he needed a new environment. He loved Bob's positive philosophy and, when we met Dermot for the first time, we thought Warwickshire could conquer the world! They were both so infectious.'

Initially Neil Smith was anxious, sensing a rival for the main spinner's berth. 'I saw Dickie and Sam at Edgbaston before the end of that season, and I wondered what it would mean for me. But we quickly became great mates, roomed together on away trips and supported each other. When you become friends in a team environment, you're not resentful of the other's success. We were different sorts of bowlers – Dickie a slow, flight bowler and left arm while I gave the offies a bit of a rip. Whenever both of us were

Receiving congratulations for a caught-and-bowled in the match against Hampshire that secured the championship title

picked, we gave the side options. Our slip fielding was pretty smart before Dickie arrived but, when he got in there and started to catch pigeons, we were tremendous. He also got useful runs, too.'

Ashley Giles also struck up a happy relationship with Davis, despite the fact that his signing had thwarted Giles' hopes of a breakthrough into the first team. 'It was never personal between me and Dickie; he was too nice a bloke to allow things to fester. He was just a solid, good all-round cricketer who fitted in straight away. He was a confident lad from the south who could handle himself if necessary, but I remember above all a bloke who liked a beer or two and made us stronger as a unit.

'I just had to grin and bear it and try to battle my way into the side later on. I wasn't then superior to him with the bat and certainly not as a catcher. Dickie was more experienced and deserved to be playing ahead of me.'

Sam Davis recalls with affection the friendship that Dickie and Giles enjoyed. 'I remember one time driving them both to play at Knowle and Dorridge for a second team game, and I took a wrong turning. They didn't have time to go into the dressing rooms to change at the ground so they ended up clambering into their whites in my car like a pair of naughty schoolboys!

'One day, after Rich had left Warwickshire, we were watching Ashley playing for England on the TV. I said to Rich, "That could've been you" and he said, "Not at all – Ashley got his chance, took it well and I had just had to move on to another county. No problems at all." There was never a hint of personal rivalry between the two.'

The Davises settled happily into life in Birmingham, Dickie playing in more than half the championship games that summer, with his personal highlight his 6/94 that helped secure an important victory at Scarborough. Sam was there for that and for the final game at Bristol, where his 2/28 alongside Neil Smith secured the Sunday League, trophy number three that season.

He did not make either of the Lord's finals, but Sam says he took the disappointments with equanimity. 'Rich would have been gutted at missing out on Lord's finals if he'd still been at Kent, but personal rivalries were set aside at Warwickshire because the

team spirit was so good. The younger players and the newcomers all felt part of it, and I and the other wives were made to feel so welcome. Everyone wanted the team to do well, even those not in the final eleven.'

That remained the case with Giles and Davis, but the following season Giles' bowling started to click and he went up the pecking order at his friend's expense. Davis's value as a flight bowler was primarily in one-day and three-day cricket, where the batsmen would usually come at him and at times self-destruct. He was, above all, a slow bowler who didn't turn the ball a great deal. Towards the end of four-day matches Giles, who bowled quicker, was getting crucial turn and bounce.

Neil Smith understood why Giles was pulling ahead of Davis. 'Dickie wouldn't run through a side, especially in four-day games, while Ashley had served his trade and knew that greater speed was needed when the wicket started to help the spinners. And there were times when Dickie and I both felt we should play, but only I got the nod. But that was never an issue between us; we were too close and supportive.'

In that 1995 championship season, Giles and Davis played 11 games between them, but it became clear that the younger man (by seven years) and the bigger spinner would pull clear of Davis. And Davis's relationship with Dermot Reeve started to unravel, culminating in a disagreement on the field during the match at Durham. Davis, still very popular with his team-mates, realised his time was up at Warwickshire when he barely featured in championship games after May that year. He hardly figured in Sunday League games or the Benson & Hedges competition and not at all in the NatWest Trophy. The writing was on the wall for a talented bowler who, at the age of 29, rightly refused to fade away in second-eleven cricket.

His team-mates were sorry to see Davis go, but Gloucestershire offered him a two-year contract. He spent two seasons at Bristol, then had a few one-day matches for Sussex, before becoming cricket development officer for Greater London, then getting into coaching with the England Women's team, St Edmund's School in Canterbury and then player/coach with Berkshire.

There was one last hurrah on a county field for Dickie Davis and, in doing so, he made cricket history. In August 2001 he turned out for Leicestershire against Northants on a raging turner at Northampton, becoming the first to play for five first-class counties. A youthful Graeme Swann and Monty Panesar each took eight wickets in the game, but Davis wasn't eclipsed, taking 6/73 in the second innings.

Not a bad way to end your county career, but a fortnight later Dickie Davis had far weightier matters to encounter. He had an epileptic fit. A month later, he was told he might have another five years left. The tumour was inoperable.

After a year of radiotherapy, Sam and Dickie began to hope with justification, because the tumour had shrunk markedly. In January 2003 the oncologist told Dickie he did not need to see him for another year. When he looked at Sam, aware of her mixed emotions, he said, 'Ok then ... for Sam. July.'

By midsummer a second tumour in Dickie's frontal lobe had developed. Radiotherapy was now impossible. In September they had the bleakest of diagnoses. Dickie had around four months to live.

By now Sam's sister Claudine was engaged to David Fulton, Kent's captain. They brought their wedding forward so that Dickie could be part of it. He said Grace at the wedding on 19 December.

Sam and Dickie managed to spend a peaceful, loving Christmas at her mother's home near Canterbury. But he had a stroke on 28 December and died the following day.

More than 500 attended the funeral, including an impressive turn-out from Warwickshire. For years afterwards Sam would receive letters from the Bears' scorer Alex Davis and his wife Chris as well as Roy French, the players' dressing-room attendant when Dickie was at the club. Affection and respect from the dressing-room attendant is usually a reliable guide to a player's popularity. They see a great deal, often with emotional players under strain.

Sam finds it cathartic to talk of Dickie and his desperately sad death. 'He never talked about dying, wouldn't ever let it get to him. Just once. He said to me, "If I do go, just make sure they play Van Morrison's *Bright Side of the Road*." That was the tune they used to play on the public address whenever Rich walked out to bat in Sunday League games for Kent. He and Graham Cowdrey were huge fans of Van Morrison. Rich was so courageous when dying, never fearful.'

Sam uses Dickie's fatal illness as an example of Brian Lara's caring nature. When Lara made his remarkable 501 in 1994, he made it wearing Dickie's helmet because his was broken. In 2006 David Fulton decided to donate half the proceeds from his benefit year to Brain Tumour Research in honour of his late brother-in-law. Sam got in touch with Brian Lara, asking him if he would kindly donate that historic helmet for an auction to boost the fund. Lara happily agreed.

'I met him in London. He was with his great friend Dwight Yorke, the Aston Villa footballer, who knew Dickie and all the Warwickshire boys from 1994. Brian brought along a letter of authentication, bought me a drink, chatted affectionately about the old days at Edgbaston and gave me his blessing for the auction.

'We raised £6,000 from the auction, and the helmet has been donated to the Lord's museum. It was so thoughtful of Brian. Whenever I see him at functions, he always comes over for a chat. I think it's lovely that such a legend still remembers Dickie, after playing just one season with him a quarter of a century ago.'

It also tells you a lot about Mr and Mrs Davis and the friendships they forged in Birmingham. Sam is now a fundraising executive with the Professional Cricketers' Association – 'trying to help those in the cricket world who really need help' – and she keeps in touch with Warwickshire folk. 'Jason Ratcliffe worked for a long time for the PCA, and we still reminisce fondly. Ratters took Rich's death particularly hard.

'A couple of years ago, I was at Edgbaston on PCA business and bumped into Keith Cook. Big hugs and smiles, and then he took me on a conducted tour of the new museum. He loved talking me through all the history. And he was kind enough to focus on 1994. Wonderful man, Keith. Wonderful club.'

The memories cascade out of Sam Davis when she talks about that short period she and Dickie spent in Birmingham. 'Going down the chippy in Worksop for all the second team because they didn't like the food. Trotting off to Buckingham Palace in the winter to celebrate winning the championship. Those two finals at Lord's that summer, when the wives and girlfriends had rather too many drinks! Sharing a few glasses with Rachel Smith throughout that summer. It was so lovely that our husbands were such great friends.

'The whole Edgbaston experience was a lovely part of Dickie's short life – and mine.'

Gladstone Small

'Gladys!'

Cue for Gladstone Small to turn around. Wherever he is in the world, he knows what that shout means. 'It'll be a Warwickshire supporter. Only they have ever called me that. So I know it's time for some nostalgic talk with a Brummie. It was also my mother's name, so it's guaranteed to get my attention. I'm constantly amazed how often I get recognised around the world. I stopped playing twenty years ago.'

There are two reasons for the immediate recognition of Gladstone Cleophas Small. The first enables me to usher the elephant out of the room and then get down to assessing his career and winning character.

'Gladstone Small ... isn't he the cricketer with no neck?' How many times has that comment been aired? Unkind folk have described him as looking as if he has a coathanger inside his jacket, wondering how he ever managed to play professional cricket for 20 years.

It's called Klippel Feil Syndrome. A cervical spine condition, usually present from birth, resulting from the fusion of two of the seven cervical vertebrae. In layman's terms, a shortness of the neck.

Gladstone was born with this condition but has never made anything of it, other than a couple of articles to help raise funds for more research. He used to say he only thought about it when he put on a new shirt and the collar would come up a bit high. Having known him for forty years I have never seen any evidence of distress from him over the condition. It never hampered his cricket; it's just there.

He could see the funny side of it when the Warwickshire supporters, who loved him, would sing an affectionate tribute as he fielded on the boundary edge. To the tune of the Lambeth Walk, the ditty would end with 'Doing the Gladstone Small', the fans hunching their shoulders up and down in unison. It was only ever a good-humoured acknowledgement of how much they loved him, no one ever meant to be disrespectful. And Gladstone would smile, wave and join in the shoulder finale. That only made the supporters worship him even more.

It's that affection from the public which is the second part of Gladstone Small's recognition factor – his easy manner, natural chuckle and unforced approachability.

I cannot think of a more popular cricketer with Warwickshire supporters in my time at Edgbaston, nor when he was an England player. At airports around the world, with England players hanging around, waiting for luggage, shades on and eye contact minimal, I have heard so many parents reassure their autograph-hunting children that at least one of the stars would oblige. A couple of minutes later, Gladstone had made more fans for life.

Gladstone never forgot where he came from, remaining grateful for the chance to be paid playing the game he loved. Growing up in the Barbadian sugar cane valley of St George, he took advantage of that perfect climate by playing cricket every day – except Christmas Day, when Gladys insisted her boy went to church.

He came over to Birmingham when he was 14. That was a culture shock, and the shy, bespectacled boy took some time to develop his natural talent as a fast bowler. After playing schoolboy cricket as a batsman who bowled off-spin, he was given a trial at Edgbaston for Young Warwickshire Amateurs. Rain forced them into the Indoor School and, with the ball skidding through, a tall blond lad – Robin Dyer – suggested to Small that he could bowl a bit faster. By the end of the trial he was the fastest bowler on view.

When he turned out at the Oxbridge Festival just short of his 17th birthday, one of the umpires was particulary impressed. Derief Taylor had been wise counsel, coach and confidant to many young players at Edgbaston down the years, and it was due to him that Small had a winter trial in 1977/78. He was on his way to a 20-year career with Warwickshire and 70 appearances for England in Tests and one-dayers.

Gladstone's relaxed manner and readiness to learn endeared him to his mentors, two of whom knew a bit about fast bowling. 'Bob Willis was great to me. He understood the mechanics of fast bowling, that I was still growing physically. He advised me when to pace myself, then really go up a gear. He warned me against bowling too many unproductive overs when the game was going nowhere. Bob also did his best to keep me out of second-eleven cricket, trying to stay fresh.

'David Brown, my first cricket manager, was another who gave me so much great advice. Another former England fast bowler, full of good sense, very strong on the mental demands. He would set up contests in the nets, bowling at Dennis Amiss and Alvin Kallicharran, and I'd watch the battles for hours, observing how Browny would try to dismiss these top batters. I watched and listened. And then I had to bowl at Dennis in the nets, after he had just scored 150! Dennis just loved to bat. Priceless experience.'

In 1980, his first season on the staff, the 18-year-old Small was the leading wicket-taker in the side that won the John Player League under the Willis/Brown axis. He also learned how to party. On the night of Warwickshire's triumph at Leicester, the squad and coaching staff decamped to the Prince of Wales in Birmingham. Warwickshire's first trophy for eight years was celebrated raucously, with Kallicharran dancing on the bar (handy being so diminutive) and Brown heading off to his home in the Worcestershire countryside, leaving the trophy behind for the bar staff to take care of.

Gladstone always liked a party as a player, but only when it was justified.

The rest of the '80s was hard going for Warwickshire, even though Small graduated to the England Test side in 1986. Not another trophy till 1989 and, for the bowlers, many games slogging away on unproductive Edgbaston pitches too much in favour of the batsmen. By the time he was 20, Small had played more than 50 championship matches, a steep learning curve when the county's bowling resources were threadbare. His workload throughout the '80s needs to be borne in mind in relation to the injuries he picked up towards the end of his career.

Paul Smith shared a house with Small for three years in their early days on the staff and remembers how much work Small put in: 'We played a lot of drawn games on wickets with little bounce, where the batsmen could just get on the front dog and accumulate. Glad was dying to get the ball whistling around their ears, and it's a measure of his ability that he got into the England side, having to drag something out of those slow Edgbaston pitches that favoured the batters far too much.'

By the time the Woolmer/Reeve influence started to gel, Small was in his 15th season. He had respected the hard work and positive influence of Andy Lloyd and Bob Cottam, relishing the two NatWest Trophy wins at Lord's. But he wanted more from what was left of his career as he approached his 33rd birthday.

'Bob and Dermot took the team to new heights. They created a unique atmosphere. We just knew that, when we went on the field, the other team would have to play a hell of a game to beat us – as long as we played well. For me, as one of the old guard, it was fantastic.

'By 1994 I still loved playing county cricket – aware that my international career was over – but I wanted inspiration to keep going for Warwickshire. Andy Lloyd had taught us it was fine to gamble, and Dermot pushed on even more. We had some success in the 1980s but a lot of failures. We had never got close to winning the championship, and that's the one I wanted. It means you've played consistently as a team for months. To have such a squad getting so much success in my 15th season was fantastic.'

Small was even prepared to put up with the ribbing about his seniority from the cheeky young pups in the dressing room, who were amused at his fondness for a nap and the ministrations of the physiotherapist, who invariably got him on the park in 1994. That joshing was underpinned by immense professional respect for a craftsman of an opening bowler who helped Tim Munton to surmount the loss of Allan Donald all season. Small knew his prime job was to fire out the best batsmen, especially with the new ball, and, starting with the first championship match against Glamorgan (5/46 in the second innings), he did just that.

His work in one-day games remained influential. In the NatWest semi-final against Kent, a desperately tense low-scoring game, his analysis of 12-3-32-0 suffocated the life out of Kent early on. The Benson & Hedges semi-final against Surrey (11-2-38-0) and the final against Worcestershire (11-4-26-1) were testament to his craft and experience. The final day of the season, when Warwickshire defended 183 to win the Sunday League (8-2-25-3) at Bristol, was a perfect example of his enduring skills. The adjective 'evergreen' was bandied about many times in 1994 when assessing Small's contribution.

'Unselfish' is another word. Dermot Reeve greatly admired Small's professionalism and loyalty to the cause when he travelled with the team to key games when unfit to play. Not for him Teletext and feet up at home, keeping half an eye on the Bears' progress. He wanted to be in the dressing room at all times.

'Gladstone had the assorted knee, calf and thigh injuries a fast bowler gets after being in the game a long time, yet he and the other senior players would talk to the younger ones, offering advice and showing joy at their team-mates' successes. Gladstone had to put up with Twose and Ostler calling him Grandad. He was brilliant for team morale.'

Typically he slides any praise towards others, especially the coach. Small admits he needed persuasion from Woolmer and Reeve about the merits of the reverse sweep, but he was a happy convert when he saw the havoc it played with opponents, until they caught up in later seasons. 'I was old school, improving by watching and talking to the older players, rather than have my game dissected and put back together again. But the way that Bob inspired the younger players, giving them options and the tools to improve, was tremendous.

'Dermot and Bob were at that time the best in their fields. We usually found ways and means to win a game.

'One great regret from those days is that more of my Bears colleagues weren't selected to play for England. Paul Smith, Tim Munton, Andy Moles, Dominic Ostler, Keith Piper would all have performed creditably and might even have become stars at international level had their cricket skills been duly recognised.'

After the triumphs of '94, injuries started to dog Small, as they do to almost all opening bowlers in their 30s with so many miles on the clock. But he still showed his plumage when called on, especially in the successful capture of the 1997 Sunday League, when he and Donald bowled so skilfully in the middle of the innings, to telling effect.

A feature of Small's latter years was the affection shown to him as he loped back to the boundary after bowling an over. The applause was warm and genuine and Small's courteous response every time confirmed the touching mutual regard. Those Warwickshire supporters could recall the days when Small had bowled his heart out in a limited attack and still related to the fans through thin and thin, ever cheerful, grateful for what he had achieved.

'I've always had a great affinity with all those in the Extra Cover Bar, respecting how so many members would turn up to away games, dossing down in dingy digs, letting us know they were with us when we took the field. It could be Taunton, Scarborough, Canterbury, Cardiff and you'd hear the chant of "Come on, you Bears!" That meant so much when you were going through a tough time out in the middle. That chant isn't some wheeze by a marketing guy in the office, it comes from the heart. They dragged us through.

'During those great years, I don't recall any player saying "Do we have to?" when we'd finished play and the Members' Bar was suggested. I'm glad we didn't have to go through all this modern stuff of ice baths twenty minutes after coming off the pitch – by then, I'd be eyeing up my first pint in the Members' Bar! I'm so glad I played when I did.'

So are countless Bears fans, now middle-aged or in the sere and yellow, rheumy-eyed as they look back at that '94 season. The public's fondness for Gladstone Small is still obvious when he pops into Edgbaston on match days or when he turns up for the annual golf day, when serious sums are raised for youth cricket in the area. Gladstone has always had delusions of adequacy as a golfer, but the swing remains as smooth as his batting, even if the ball ends up in strange places. And – of course – he has all the right gear. 'You've got to look the part if you can't play the game decently!' Collar up, and a cool dude amble.

After retiring, he worked as a director of the Professional Cricketers' Association, turning out in charity matches and as a popular host of discussions with old players for the punters' delectation at breakfasts and lunches during international matches. And he still manages to escape some of the English winter's rigours by leading supporters' parties on England tours. His enviable knack of being able to remember so many of his punters' names remains a source of wonder, as does his famed affability during

the inevitable travel glitches that would drive others to distraction.

After picking up so many aches and pains, he doesn't miss playing nor does he envy current players for the fortunes they are amassing from the worldwide opportunities. He does miss the camaraderie of the dressing room, the intimate nature of growing up together and, of course, the laughter – which invariably followed Gladstone around.

Press Gladstone for special memories from his long career, and he'll gloss over taking five wickets in an innings in successive Ashes Tests in 1986/7, being an integral part in Jamaica of the England side that inflicted on West Indies their first Test defeat in 16 years, playing in the 1987 World Cup Final or winning seven trophies with Warwickshire.

But he will mention a maiden over he bowled against Viv Richards at Taunton in 1985. That day Richards plundered 322 off 258 balls for Somerset in an astonishing display of thunderous strokeplay. No one could bowl at him, apart from a few minutes after Richards had passed 200. 'Somehow I kept him quiet for a maiden, when the ball had been flying everywhere. I hope he wasn't just having a breather. At the end of the over he said, "Well bowled, Smally!" and I was walking on air. Much as I loved Brian Lara, a fabulous player, Viv remains the greatest I ever saw. He was so intimidating, destructive and proud. Viv would pinpoint the opposition's best bowler and try to take him apart. Usually he succeeded.'

Small was certainly the best Warwickshire bowler that day, as he often was during those fallow seasons in the '80s, long before the trio of Donald/Munton/Small became the best seam attack in county cricket.

For that longevity and durability alone, Gladstone Small deserved the many days of glory during the 1994 season. But even if he had been just a mediocre player, only passing through Edgbaston for a couple of seasons, he would be remembered affectionately for his personality and decency. Instead he is revered for many reasons, and for 'Gladys' the feeling is mutual.

'Is part of me still a Bear? All of me! Just because I don't live in the area anymore doesn't lessen my love for the club. I'm always checking the scores and keeping in touch with old friends at Edgbaston. Playing for Warwickshire gets in your blood. It's given me so much in my life.'

Dougie Brown and Graeme Welch

It's a sign of a highly successful team in sport when young, inexperienced players come in and make an immediate impression without the collective standards dropping one iota.

So it was with Warwickshire in 1994, with Dougie Brown and Graeme Welch. In fact, on results alone, these two tyro all-rounders strengthened the side.

Dermot Reeve, at his best good enough then to be an England all-rounder in one-day cricket, was nevertheless struggling with both form and fitness by the end of June, as the side continued to fight four separate campaigns.

There was a danger that the Edgbaston express could be derailed, with almost three months of the season still to go. Could the cricket management take the risk of sidelining Reeve for the championship games to come? They managed to keep the lid on their concerns about Reeve's baffling decline in form, dressing it up as a succession of wear-and-tear injuries, keeping him fresh for the one-day games, inspirational captaincy still vital ... blah, blah, blah.

Amiss, Woolmer and Munton knew that the dressing-room atmosphere would be less tense with Reeve and Lara both out of each other's hair, but would Welch and Brown step up to the plate?

Neither had yet played a championship match, despite having been on the staff for several years. They had served a tough apprenticeship in the second XI since 1989, under the watchful eye of Neal Abberley, but everyone knew that the leap from the seconds to the first team was a mighty one, especially at a time when so much world-class talent was populating the county championship.

Within three weeks Welch then Brown had made impressive debuts, helping to win vital games at Northampton and Guildford. The side's winning mentality hadn't missed a beat, and their all-round talents had not only strengthened the lower-middle order batting, but their different styles of bowling had broadened the bowling options even more. Brown the tall seam bowler, Welch the swing bowler with the ability to move the ball late.

Welch stayed in the side till the end of the season, while Brown was never overawed in his appearances. Both went on to have long careers at Edgbaston.

Brown is grateful that the squad's positive environment encouraged the newcomers. 'Abbers in the second team, then Bob and Dermot were brilliant in the way they allowed us to express ourselves. It was all so new and exciting, and the seniors seemed to feed off our youthful energy. It was proving a long haul for them, competing on all four fronts, and a couple of young whippersnappers with no fear galvanised them. There was no pressure on us. Just be as professional as you could.'

Welch admits he was in awe of some of his teammates when he made his debut at Northampton. 'They were legends to me, yet they made me feel so relaxed. I could hardly believe what was happening, it all happened so quickly. I was only expected to chip in with a wicket or two, bowling third or fourth change and bat down the order, but Dougie and I had been in good form in the seconds and we got on the rollercoaster.'

Welch made an immediate impression in the Northants match, making a composed 35* at number ten, adding 68 with Tim Munton for the last wicket. He took four wickets in the match and handy ones they were – Allan Lamb, Rob Bailey and Mal Loye (twice). Warwickshire beat a strong Northants side by four wickets in a run chase, and it was all a blur to Welch. 'Just being on the same pitch as Lara, Lamb and Curtly Ambrose was a big enough thrill.'

Brown felt the same three weeks later at Guildford, coming up against Alec Stewart, Graham Thorpe and Adam Hol[lioake. But he didn't appear cowed, rescuing his side from 131/8 in the first innings, adding 110 bold runs with Welch. They unleashed a fusillade of shots, taking the attack to the bowlers in the manner preached by Reeve and Woolmer. Both made fifties, sparking a recovery that saw Warwickshire again see off dangerous rivals, with victory by 256 runs.

'It was great to change the momentum of the match with someone I'd grown up with,' recalls Brown. 'I was champing at the bit, down to bat at number ten. I couldn't wait to get out there. Graeme, a veteran of three matches in the first team, played a couple of fine shots and I thought, "Let's see if I can do the same" and then we were off and running, matching each other shot for shot.'

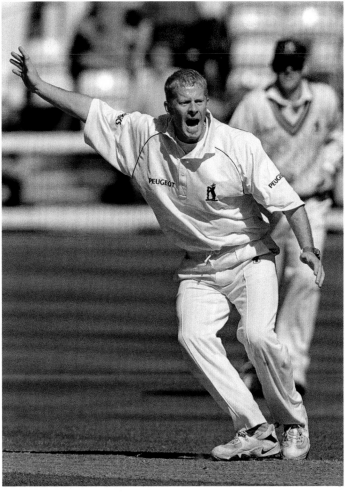

Dougie Brown (above) and Graeme Welch (right)

Welch admits there was a contest within a contest going on at Guildford. 'Me and Dougie were always competitive. He seemed to want to beat me at everything, growing up at Edgbaston, and although I was more laidback I backed myself against him. I suppose we were competing for just one place, with Dermot presumably returning soon. Dougie was desperate to get to the top, while I just backed my ability. But we stuck our hands up in that Surrey game and we certainly didn't weaken the team.'

They were chalk and cheese as characters. Brown, academically bright, a qualified physical education teacher, was frustrated by a series of injuries in his early 20s and, after five years of second-eleven cricket, was still to make his championship debut as he neared his 25th birthday. He was anxious to make up for lost time.

Ashley Giles shared a house with him during that time and recalls his intense drive to succeed. 'He had a bad ankle and several other injuries and he went through a dark phase, wondering if he was ever going to make it. It held him back for more than a year, and he was starting to think about having to fall back on his teaching qualifications. He'd been a chubby young lad but, when he came to Edgbaston, he took fitness very seriously. He'd do a lot of running – too much sometimes. When he finally got himself fit, he was just Mr Cricket – so much energy, for so many years. He loved the contest. Dougie was a great mentor to me when we shared a house because I was wet behind the ears then, a bit spoiled by my parents. He really toughened me up, starting with tidying up after me.'

Bob Cottam remembers the day when he decided to sign up Brown, and it stemmed from an incident that had nothing to do with his cricket ability. 'Every year I'd have a triallists' day at Edgbaston and I saw this tall, ginger-haired lad steaming in off the longest run-up I had ever seen. On the hottest day of the year. He then went about his fielding practice with great enthusiasm. Then he batted. There was a huge jug of orange squash beside the lads and some were slurping away after bowling just one delivery. Not Dougie. I had to force him to have a drink eventually. I said to Neal Abberley, "We'll have that lad – he's so enthusiastic." And Dougie never lost that as a player.'

Cottam was also responsible for bringing Welch to Edgbaston. At 14 Welch was playing second-eleven cricket in the North-East league. His dad Robert was a pro for South Hetton, and he made sure that young Graeme moved to a better club when just a boy. Doug Ferguson, a National Cricket Association scout who knew Cottam, recommended the lad, and he came down to Edgbaston for a trial. 'I first batted in the indoor school and I just couldn't hit the ball, it came at me so fast. Bob must have seen something in me because he made me bat twice. We then had an inter-squad game outdoors against players like Andy Moles and Gladstone Small. Roger Twose and Keith Piper were also having trials, and they got two-year contracts that day. I thought my chance had gone but, a fortnight later, my contract was posted to me.'

That contract brought a pleasing little windfall to Doug Ferguson. Cottam had a scheme whereby any scout who found him a good enough youngster would get £300 from Warwickshire CCC and, if that player was eventually capped by the club, he would receive £3,000. 'Doug had told me that Graeme was an even better player than Peter Willey at the same age, who came from the same area. Warwickshire weren't sure about Graeme but I said, "Wait till he gets strong enough, he's still raw but there's something there." Within a couple of years, he was playing for England Under-19s.'

Welch loved Cottam's tough love. He relished his straight talking. In 1990 he took Welch down to Lord's as twelfth man for the championship match, just to have a close look at him and see his true mettle. Welch came on as sub fielder, snaffled a couple of great catches. 'I'm out there in the field, watching Desmond Haynes and Mike Gatting bat, and I thought, "This is for me." They were looking at how I would handle the situation and my two catches – at short leg and diving full length at cover – were worldies. I was only eighteen.'

By then he'd willingly embraced the social side of professional cricket. On his first day as a pro at Edgbaston, Allan Donald and Trevor Penney took him a mile down the road to Selly Oak and their favourite pub, the Old University Tavern. 'I couldn't believe how much those two natural athletes could put away. With their help I made up for lost time!'

He was soon known as 'Pop', partly through his fondness for a beer and because that was the nickname for both his father and grandfather. It's one nickname that has stuck down the years. 'I smoked as well – and so did many of that '94 side. I know Bob Woolmer didn't really approve of my lifestyle, but I was fit enough. I was on good money, getting into nightclubs for free because I was alongside Brian Lara. I didn't want to go home when the cricket ended. Walking into the Members' Bar at close of play with no segregation, chatting to the supporters, a few beers. Who wouldn't want all that at the age of 22?'

Dougie Brown remembers Lara in '94 equally fondly but for different reasons. 'I really enjoyed Brian that year. You've got to remember he was young and inexperienced in the ways of the world so that he was guarded and stuck to his close friends, but he was great with the younger players. He was a big encourager and very generous to me with his time and energy. I know he and Dermot looked to steal each other's thunder at times, and that must have been a management challenge. But as a batsman he was out on his own. A ridiculous, awesome talent.'

Brown and Welch quickly tapped into the culture of winning. Brown says, 'We had an uncanny knack of winning when the chips were down. Somebody stuck their hand up. Pop and I were just young lads, but we appreciated how good those experienced county pros were. We stayed flexible and competitive. A highly enthused and motivated group of players kept the Woolmer/Reeve ethos intact all summer, even when Dermot wasn't playing.'

Tim Munton, who took over the captaincy from Reeve during the introduction of Welch and Brown to the championship side, believes Welch was one of the most talented young bowlers he has played with. 'And he was better with the bat than many thought. Above all, they fitted in perfectly into a confident, positive dressing room, and contributed a fair amount.' Andy Moles looked on approvingly at the young jousters. 'Their brashness and self-confidence summed up our environment. They just breezed in and didn't need to bed in. And they spurred each other on.'

Welch quickly assimilated himself into the culture of getting up the opposition's noses, even though he was just 22, and a genial, laidback sort. 'When I got into the team, I fielded at silly point to the spinners for the rest of the season and, once I heard all that chirruping from Keith Piper, Roger Twose and the captain, well I just piled in. I remember they used

to give Richard Illingworth and Steve Rhodes some awful verbals whenever we played Worcestershire around that time, and I felt obliged to give it out as well – not that I had any right to do so. Years later, when I got to know those two Worcestershire lads, I felt a little sorry. But nobody ever felt comfortable against us when we gathered round the bat. We'd happily have a beer with the opposition afterwards, but they soon started to take us seriously on the field.'

Looking back on his playing career, Welch admits he under-achieved. 'If I knew then what I now know,' he smiles. 'As a bowler I lacked two to three mph and got exposed when the ball didn't swing. There wasn't much technical coaching around in those days, and I lacked pace. As a batsman I was technically flawed, getting into some weird positions. Dougie was a better technician, more robotic and manufactured, while I just relied on natural talent. He worked so hard, so fair play to him. I didn't have Dougie's drive and passion and probably thought I'd be ok eventually, after that great start in '94. And I wasn't all that confident inside. I was in a dressing room of legends, great mates, but at times I felt I didn't belong in that company.'

Ashley Giles feels both young players brought a lot to the team. 'Pop was a very under-rated batsman. He was excellent off the back foot, pulling the quicks with ease. At one stage, he looked like being a batting all-rounder. He had great skill as a bowler. When he swung it late, he was a handful.

'Dougie was focussed and disciplined, polar opposite to the free spirit that was Pop. Dougie had a high action and hit the seam, making it go either way, and was a fine, correct batsman who hit the ball very cleanly. Their rivalry for that one spot in the team was fierce. Opposite ends of the spectrum but both very talented.'

A tough experience the following summer in the Benson & Hedges Cup did nothing for Welch's fragile self-confidence. Against Lancashire, he returned figures of 11-0-103-0, becoming the first bowler to concede over a hundred in that competition. He was unimpressed by his captain's handling of him that day. 'I remember during the interval thinking surely Dermot wouldn't ask me to bowl my remaining four overs when I was getting so much stick. But he did and I was exposed. By then Dermot was playing for England in the one-dayers and liked to get his overs out of the way, returning reasonable figures while the rest of us got pasted late on. That's what he did against Lancashire.

'Dermot didn't like competition in the team, and there were a few all-rounders pressing him hard, including me and Dougie. I never really got on with Dermot, I thought he was selfish. But he was a brilliant tactician, made the most of what he'd got and was a born winner. He liked Dougie, his enthusiasm appealed to him more than my laidback style.'

Welch was never slow to offer an opinion when the occasion demanded and it's refreshing to hear a different take on Bob Woolmer from one of his former charges. He admired Woolmer's knowledge of the art of batting and his espousal of a positive approach, but didn't really warm to him. 'I felt Bob was a bit political and liked to get his sort of blokes gathered around him for protection. He never really stood up to be counted. Bob Cottam was more my kind of coach. Coming from the north-east I liked straight talking, knowing where I stood. He was as straight as a die. I remember warming up at Northampton once and, after bowling just one delivery, Bob said to me, "That'll do, Welchy, that's good enough for me!" The others may have preferred Woolly's quiet arm around the shoulder but I preferred Cottam's toughness.'

Brown agrees that Woolmer lacked finesse in certain areas. 'He could be a little wishy-washy with the players, then blunt next time. But Dermot's man-management of us was excellent. Between them they had the full package.'

Brown has now accumulated vast experience as player and coach and can assess Warwickshire's achievement better from a distance – specifically from the United Arab Emirates, where he is the Director of Coaching. After 20 years playing for the Bears, then another decade as Academy Director then Director of Cricket, he still believes 1994 was a remarkable achievement.

'If anyone wins three trophies again in a season, they thoroughly deserve all the accolades. Some teams prioritise the championship or a one-day trophy. Warwickshire scooped three and missed out on the fourth, courtesy of the toss of a coin. Gloucestershire were a wonderful side after our great years but they never won the championship – and that's always been the one for me. The greatest test of a county cricket team is how you compete over four days. Our tally of championship wins in two successive years was ridiculous.'

Good enough to play one-day internationals for both England and Scotland, Brown still can't believe the lack of England recognition for some of his 1994 team-mates. 'Moles, Piper, Neil Smith, Ostler, Munton – all at the top of their game. Piper was by far the best keeper in the country and all he got was an 'A' tour. The rest got nothing that winter. What we accomplished in '94 was extraordinary, and yet England didn't think so.'

Welch has his '94 winners' medals from the championship and the Sunday League boxed up at home. 'My proudest possessions. We had a common goal, and that was to win. It was a fantastic time to be coming into the first-class game. And the quality of overseas players that season – Wasim, Ambrose, Haynes, Hooper, Moody, Azharuddin, Mushtaq Ahmed, Walsh – was far higher than today. They really raised the overall standard.'

He's now back at Edgbaston for his third spell there, having captained Derbyshire, then coached at Essex, Derbyshire and Leicestershire. He's recognised as one of the best bowling coaches in England now, enjoying a particularly good rapport with the dressing room. After clocking up 15 years in Warwickshire's service, he believes the presence of former Bears in the backroom cricket management is crucial. 'Growing up as players we all respected the traditions of the club and all the great players who'd gone before us. Neal Abberley made sure of that and it was a terrific grounding. We're trying to get back to that ethos now.'

He's a throwback to a simpler, less scientific period of the English game. If he'd possessed more of Dougie Brown's mindset, getting the very best out of himself over a long period, then perhaps Welch would have kicked on to greater things as a player. But he's content with his playing career, channelling the experience of his frailties and mistakes into coaching. He'll never lose his strong ties with the Durham area, nor that warm, friendly accent, but the feeling is that Graeme Welch is happily ensconced at his cricketing home.

Keith Cook – Cricket Operations Manager

Keith Cook at his desk but not in 1994 – no computer then

When you've joined the club straight from school in 1973, you can be described as part of the nuts and bolts at Warwickshire CCC. But Keith Cook is far more than that. He is the engine room, the man who has done more for generations of players at Edgbaston than anyone.

Ian Bell calls him 'a phenomenon. In twenty years on the staff here, I've never seen him lose his rag. He's the glue that holds it together behind the scenes. Cooky just gets on with it, helps you focus on your cricket. He's fantastic for overseas players, helping them fit in straight away and he connects the traditions of the club with the modern. He's an absolute Bears' legend.'

Keith Cook's official title at the club is Cricket Operations Manager. In effect, he is Mr Warwickshire, a description that would make him blush and move the subject along to his beloved Aston Villa's fortunes. If there is an issue that needs a second opinion or a thorny dilemma at the club, the traditional response is 'Ask Cooky, he'll know.'

In 1994 he was assistant marketing manager before becoming number two to the new chief executive, Dennis Amiss, later that year. It was a shrewd move by Amiss; as a senior player, he had seen at first hand Cook's knack of defusing tense situations, liaising amicably with key club sponsors and charming the players into representing the Bears at important functions. In return Cook would happily sort out administrative hassles that professional sportsmen think bedevil only them – like paying parking fines, getting a new mobile phone or sorting out a car.

He loved 1994. His great friend Asif Din had rescued his career after that epic hundred in the NatWest Trophy Final in September 1993, and the subsequent award of a benefit for the 1994 season meant that Cook would be busy from the start of the year. 'I really enjoyed going around the various functions with Gunga, showing off the trophy, so chuffed he'd played such a vital role in winning it. We seemed to be everywhere that winter, with my job to remember to pick up the trophy at the end of the evening. I forgot it one night – when I went back to the Botanical Gardens in Edgbaston, I found it propping open a door'.

And then came Lara. From April onwards, that year was a frenzy for Keith Cook, and he relished every challenge. 'For the marketing department, it was a fantastic opportunity. On the day that Brian arrived for his press conference just after scoring his 375, we couldn't move for TV crews, and his first press conference was surreal, almost as if a rock star had arrived. And after he got his 501, the phones just went off the hook. Everybody in the local commercial world wanted to be associated with Warwickshire and, being a local lad, it was fantastic, great fun.

'From a commercial aspect, it was almost like printing your own money. Budgets were easily met, membership soared and so many wanted to be part of our success.

'I think Brian was bewildered initially by all the attention, but he soon got used to it, trying to keep his head down. He had a certain detachment towards me, because I was the one who had to try arranging all the media interviews. So when he saw me approaching him, he'd dread it because he knew what I was going to ask him. But after '94 he's always been very pleasant to me.'

Perhaps it had dawned on Lara that Cook was deservedly popular with the rest of the players. In those days the administrative staff used to have lunch in the players' dining room in the old pavilion, and Cook barely got his cutlery wielding before one of them was asking for a favour or advice.

'I loved the banter with the players. I'd socialise with them, having dragged them out to functions and I'd class them all as friends. That '94 squad were full of great characters. I was almost the same age as some of them, having grown up with them at Edgbaston. The captain was terrific fun – Dermot was a naughty boy but always made me laugh. What a blend they were – some mercurial, some sensible, some off the wall. Yet they all came together on the field that summer. There was a special affinity.'

The same applied to his relationship with Amiss. They worked closely together until Amiss's retirement, and the mutual respect and affection were tangible. 'Dennis always did his best for the club and at times he had a tough balancing act, but his heart was in the right place. We gave all we could to each other because of mutual loyalty. I couldn't have asked more from Dennis. He was incredibly supportive when my personal life fell apart at one stage and I was determined to repay him for that.'

Only once did Keith Cook waver in his total commitment to Warwickshire CCC. In 1987, after 14 years at the club, he left for nine months to work for the club's physiotherapist, Bernard Thomas, just a mile from the ground. He soon realised it was a mistake.

'No offence to Bernard, who head-hunted me to run the admin side of his business, but it was like working in a bank from nine to five. I missed the variety of cricket. At five to 11 I'd be looking at the clock, thinking, "The boys will just be running out now to field. I wish I was there." In the end, I was delighted to be asked back. And lucky.'

Not really. Cook has been invaluable for too long. Ashley Giles has known him for a quarter of a century as player and Director of Cricket and cannot comprehend Warwickshire without Keith Cook. 'Down the decades, the players have revered him. He epitomises everything we value at Warwickshire. If you asked Cooky to work 35 days in a row, he'd smile and say "no problem". He always seems the last to leave and lock up.

'Here's an example of how much he loves his job. When I first took over as Director of Coaching in 2007, there were many rumours of upheaval of the staff, with jobs going. One day I called Keith to come over to the indoor school for a chat about several things. I thought no more of it, but he arrived, pale and worried. I twigged that he thought he was going to get the push and I said, "Cooky, don't be daft, we can't survive without you!" Everyone at Edgbaston would say the same.'

Cook diffidently swerves analysis of his vital contribution to the club but will admit 'putting a smile on colleagues' faces and helping others here makes me happy.' He is more precise about what he calls the Warwickshire Way. 'We are friendly and respectful of the players, while we want them to be aware of the traditions and history of this club. Ashley was very big on that. He told the players they were part of a chain that goes back to 1882. When we signed Dominic Sibley from Surrey, he was very impressed by the pride we all felt at being part of the Bears' history and our desire to keep adding to it.

'I know that other counties feel the same way, so I can only talk about mine. We all have an ambassadorial role, doing the right thing for our colleagues when no one is watching. Help each other out with your heart, rather than for cosmetic reasons.

'I can't think of one player at Edgbaston in my time that I didn't like. There have been some interesting challenges but, when you get to know the blokes, it's worth it. I'm no Christian bible-basher, but cracking away at problems and solving them makes me feel better and my job worthwhile.'

Now that the revamped Edgbaston stadium is continuing to attract high-profile international matches, Keith Cook's role has expanded. He is the first contact point for the various international boards on behalf of players, umpires, commercial partners, supporters' groups, broadcasters and all the other interested parties, all determined to get what they want. Cook's sunny disposition has defused many a potential flashpoint. Many in his position might find reasons for thwarting requests, but he relishes resolving problems.

Ashley Giles appreciates Cook's value in this area. 'Cooky is one of the reasons Edgbaston now has such a fine international reputation. Some sides come there with a long list of demands, and invariably he is the first club official they meet. His natural attitude is "No problem, we can work that out." I've never met anyone with a bad word about him.'

His popularity with former players is obvious when the Warwickshire Old County Cricketers Association golf days are staged, usually with his organisational skills to the fore. Many of them are from the class of '94, and they make a bee-line for him in the bar. They may be mature adults now, but some of them have to stop themselves from saying, 'Cooky, can you sort this out for me, please?'

Massive respect underpins that affection. Tim Munton speaks for countless past and present players: 'The most hard-working, level-headed bloke you could ever meet. When you talk about true legends of that mid-1990s era, you can bet 99% concentrate on the players, but he's one who had an equal effect on us and the members, on and off the field. We may well have won a few trophies in our glory years without Keith Cook, but he didn't half make it easier for us.

'And he still looks so young! Ageless. The Peter Pan of Edgbaston.'

Among Edgbaston staff, retirement does not bear thinking about for the modest bulwark who started in the era of Rohan Kanhai, Lance

Keith Cook with his two children in 1993, the summer when the AXA Equity & Law League introduced coloured clothing. Steven and Louise modelled the junior sizes that the club shop was selling.

Gibbs, AC Smith, John Jameson, Bob Willis and David Brown. The Dorian Gray of B5 7QU still has the picture in the attic, the embodiment of the maxim that hard work keeps you young. Among other things ...

'Having a young wife keeps me busy! And your own body and mind tell you when to pack up. No sign of that yet, I'm glad to say.'

Not too late then for the club to honour Keith Cook. He would be horrified at such a suggestion. Other counties have awarded testimonials to a groundsman and a scorer in the past decade; surely sailing devotedly before the mast of the SS Warwickshire for more than four decades deserves a fitting tribute? I can think of many who would volunteer for that testimonial committee.

Steve Rouse – Head Groundsman

Steve Rouse has never been the sort to gush, but he did allow himself the occasional tight smile as he perched on the Edgbaston roller during the summer of '94. A tough Welshman (rugby union, karate, weightlifting), disinclined to show his sensitive side (opera buff, keen gardener), Rouse was in his 30th year with Warwickshire CCC when the club was storming the domestic citadels on four fronts. And he's still quietly pleased with the role he played that season, his first as Head Groundsman.

He joined the groundstaff in 1964, played in the championship-winning team in 1972 and coached various age groups in the indoor school so Rouse developed distinct opinions on how to improve Edgbaston's pitches when he took over that responsibility.

A left-arm swing bowler, part of a dressing room occupied by batsmen of the calibre of Kanhai, Kallicharran, Smith, Jameson and Amiss, Rouse always felt they were unduly favoured by the placid home pitches. He was never slow to bemoan the lot of the bowler, certain that Warwickshire wouldn't prosper in county cricket unless there was a more equitable contest between bat and ball. The redoubtable, trenchant Rouse was nicknamed 'Rebel' with good reason.

Dennis Amiss was his room-mate for years when they played together but, after Amiss graduated to the Chief Executive's role in 1994, Rouse made it clear he wouldn't be doffing his cap at his old chum in their new respective posts.

A regular, short exchange of this nature would ensue: AMISS: 'Rebel, I want you to take some grass off for the next match.' ROUSE: 'Piss off, Dennis – go and do your job and I'll do mine!'

No one told Steve Rouse how to prepare his wickets, not even the captain, Dermot Reeve. 'Rebel was very much his own man, with his own ideas of what constitutes a good cricket wicket.'

Bob Woolmer came closest. Woolmer was savvy enough to go more than halfway with Rouse, seeking his opinions and valuing them. They had played against each other many times in county cricket and then would meet up regularly during an English winter in Cape Town, where Woolmer had his family home and Rouse a holiday bolt-hole. Woolmer realised that, underneath the terse, macho bluster, Rouse was a thoughtful, loyal individual with high professional standards and a burning desire to see the Bears become more than just a dangerous one-day side.

'I learned such a lot from Bob about coaching during our chats in Cape Town over a glass or two. He'd not been involved for a few years in county cricket until he came to Edgbaston in 1991, and he was intelligent enough to ask my opinions about opposition players and sides. Bob would listen, take it all in very calmly, very respectful. He made me feel I was still part of the playing unit. He made it clear when I took over as groundsman that I was more than just that to him.'

Rouse also came to understand Reeve's 'modus operandi', the methods the captain used to gain an extra half a per cent over opponents. 'He used to ask me if the players could practise alongside the pitch for the next game. He knew that wasn't allowed up to two days before day one, but I turned a blind eye. I would tell him I'd be gone from the ground by 5.30pm and what happened after that was nothing to do with me.'

In turn Woolmer appreciated Rouse's efforts, preparing for that historic season: 'It was a revelation to play on some beautiful net wickets and on a middle which encouraged batsmen to play their shots and bowlers to take wickets.'

Neil Smith, who had been coached by Rouse as a boy in the indoor school, was a major beneficiary of Rouse's determination to strike a better balance between bat and ball. 'Rebel relaid the pitches so that they turned and bounced a little bit more. It was nice for me to bowl on. I always felt better operating on turning pitches because I could actually spin the ball. The relaid pitches encouraged me to bowl it slower.

'Rousey bought into our aggressive nature on the field to give us pace and bounce and wickets that turned as the game went on. It was the perfect marriage between those wickets and our attitude.'

Rouse, like many groundsman of his era, knew what to do with Edgbaston pitches to favour the side's major assets. 'Bob would say, "Rebel, we're playing such-and-such in a few weeks. It would be great if it turned on days three and four."' More often than not Bob got just what he'd asked for.

'I was able to prepare the wickets to have the appearance of a traditional Edgbaston pitch but with characteristics requested by Bob. The wicket would be rock hard, flat as a fart, and the opposition would take one look at it, get excited about a typical Edgbaston greentop and put us in. We'd make millions on it early in the game, then spin them out in the fourth innings. Dickie Davis and Neil Smith were very happy!'

That may appear sharp practice, but every successful county is favoured by the black arts of groundsmanship and Rouse is unrepentant. And if Warwickshire were allegedly favoured by his work in their championship seasons of '94 and '95, how to explain the loss of just one match away from home in that time?

Rouse was always splendidly forthright in his opinions. His background was unconventional and shaped his truculent approach to life. His father flew Spitfires in the Battle of Britain, his uncle Hurricanes and his mother was a tracker in the ops room. Dad hoped young Steve would follow him into a career in aviation, but he turned down the chance of pilots' training at RAF Cranwell to start at Edgbaston for the princely sum of just over £4.50 a week, in new money. 'It felt like a small fortune. My family was upset, but I never regretted it.'

He was always happy to march to a different tune in his cricket career. Whenever I was on Test Match duty for the BBC at Edgbaston, I'd resolutely beat a path to Rouse's hut, aware that his refreshingly candid views on the quality of batting he'd watched were gold dust, compared to the clenched-teeth banalities of the players, as orchestrated by their press officer. No one dared to police Steve Rouse when a microphone was pushed his way.

He's the only key figure from Edgbaston's halcyon period to express doubts about Brian Lara's stature. 'You can only judge the amount of time a top batsman has against genuinely fast bowlers. I thought Brian was a touch worried early on by the short-pitched, quick stuff. He'd hook the medium pacers happily enough but not the genuine quicks. I'd love to have seen him up against someone like Mitchell Johnson, who'd make him hop around. Rohan Kanhai was never worried by short, fast bowling when I played with him. He was a truly great player.'

Rouse is no overt sentimentalist but looks back fondly on those early years as Head Groundsman, when the Bears were so dominant. 'It seemed such a long winter after we'd won all those trophies in '94. I couldn't wait to get back to see those guys who'd created history.'

He is big on cricket history, treasuring his 47 years at Edgbaston as young hopeful, first-team player, coach and groundsman. Not that he would admit to that all too readily – got to keep up flinty-hearted appearances. But 'Rebel' Rouse is fooling nobody. He looks forward to reunions of former players as much as anyone.

'I caught up with dear old Gladys at the last Edgbaston Test, up in the chairman's lounge. There we were, suited and booted alongside the various big cheeses, two old players having a yarn. Glad said to me, "Rebel, it's 11.30 – time for a snort", and he brought back four glasses of Pimms. We sat in the sunshine, enjoying the cricket, agreeing we'd had the best of times.'

Odds on, they both concluded it was still a batsman's game. Nothing changes when old bowlers get together.

Stuart Nottingham – Physiotherapist

It's axiomatic that to win two leagues of 17 matches each in one season you need your key players to stay fit. So it was for Warwickshire in 1994, with the exception of Dermot Reeve. Much of the credit for that goes to an unassuming, unselfish man with a ready smile who knew very little about cricket. But Stuart Nottingham's contribution must never be minimised.

He was in his third year as club physio in '94 and 'Fizz', as he was popularly known, was a tremendously positive influence behind the scenes. Fundamentally he got the players on the park. Twelve of the players managed 11 or more championship matches, while only 17 were needed throughout that long campaign. Five played all 17 games, while Brian Lara and Trevor Penney missed only two each.

Various injuries needed to be managed: Reeve's degenerative hip, Lara's knee, Andy Moles' broken arm and tendonitis (plus dealing with his diabetes), Paul Smith's fragile knee and Gladstone Small's wear-and-tear issues stemming from a decade and a half of fast bowling.

Tim Munton, battling nobly against his daunting workload, relied heavily on Fizz from August onwards. 'For those last weeks, it was a case of hot baths then rubdowns from Fizz to get me on the park. No day was too long for him. He was quiet, dependable and caring, with a great passion to keep us going. Fizz was our 13th man.'

Gladstone Small knew enough about physiotherapists in a long, physically stressful career, and Stuart Nottingham has a special place in his affections. 'He'd work on me at the ground, or the team hotel on away trips, at any hour of the day. Such a good bloke. A real team man.'

Nottingham's sporting background was in cycling, and he'd worked with Moseley Rugby Club before coming to Edgbaston. 'That was a great plus for us,' says Munton. 'It was more important that he understood instinctively about fitness training and rehab. He didn't waste his breath asking about cricket, just got on with the job quietly.'

But Fizz was a keen observer, fascinated by the team dynamics. 'There was such a lot of positive energy in that dressing room, masterminded by Dermot Reeve. He was always jumping up and down, making the

Treating Paul Smith during the B&H Final

most noise. I never knew how much of that was attention seeking or just his natural ebullience. But he was innovative and that added to the dynamism in the group. There was social friction between a few of them, away from the cricket, and some flashpoints in the dressing room. Roger Twose could ruffle feathers big time, Bob Woolmer was challenging with everybody, including me, but he only wanted the best. There were strong-minded individuals wherever you looked and not everyone liked each other. But you can do extraordinary things with a group of people who have a common goal and won't be deflected from it.'

Nottingham attributes much of the cohesiveness to senior players who had seen tough times at Edgbaston. 'Andy Moles showed great character in that '94 season, getting himself really fit the previous winter, then breaking his arm unluckily pre-season. Then he was diagnosed with diabetes. But he battled back into the side mid-season, setting a great uncomplaining example, averaging over fifty in the championship. Gladstone was a consummate pro, a delight to work with. Very appreciative, laidback yet focused in what he needed to do to stay fit. But the key figure, the one who did more to hold things together, was Tim Munton. He kept all the egos in check, telling everyone to keep their eyes on the big picture. The unsung hero, he had influence and control without the power.'

The captain was a challenge for Fizz. 'I never knew how fit Dermot was from one day to the next. Clearly he had pain and niggles, and that left hip took a lot of strain from his bowling action and led to his premature retirement two years later. But what is pain and what is functionality? It varies from player to player. Dermot was always stretching when he talked to you, and he seemed to need warm-ups a lot. Was some of it showmanship? I'll never know but to be fair to him, he was only 33 when he was forced to pack up.'

Fizz was such a devotee of the team ethic that he would automatically warm to certain players on a personal level while doing his utmost to treat everyone the same professionally. Reeve and Lara were not exactly his cup of Darjeeling – not that they would ever know that. Their spectacular spat on the field of play at Northampton was witnessed by a few of the players at close quarters, but only Nottingham was present when it continued in the dressing room. 'I had to smile when I read their different accounts of the incident in the books they later brought out. Fundamentally it was two prima donnas having a handbags row. Voices were raised, and two egos were bashed around the room. Brian was tired by then, the season was proving physically hard for him. He hadn't been prepared in April for what was going to hit him, with all the travelling and the marketing hoopla. Dermot felt he was disrespecting him, and so it went on. They never really kissed and made up after that, but Dermot was out of it for much of the final half of the season, so it didn't greatly affect the dressing room.'

Nottingham has a pragmatic theory for that. 'Cricket can be a lazy game when you're winning; you just keep it all ticking over. That's where Tim

was so valuable. The guys were desperate to get on the pitch, partly through pride at doing something special and also there were some handsome bonuses on offer if you played and won. So for me it was a case of patching them up.'

The collective eye on the prizes was another reason why Fizz kept his own counsel about the number of smokers among the regular players. 'I can think of eight of them, plus the occasional social smoker. A few of them liked a drink as well. But I wasn't their keeper, they were adults, even if I disapproved. I just ran with it, did my job – and loved being part of it.'

He had an inkling on the pre-season tour to Zimbabwe that the '94 season might be special. 'Looking back on it now, there were tipping points that proved crucial in the long run. Gunga Din's century to win the NatWest the year before, signing Lara that April. When that happened, I thought to myself, "Hang on, we're at the threshold of something here." A massive advantage was the absence of England call-ups. That certainly helped me in my job.'

He did a great job for Warwickshire and continued to do so for a decade before embarking on a successful career in private practice. Nothing was too much trouble for Stuart Nottingham when a Warwickshire player needed him, as Tim Munton recalls. 'Just before the start of the 1997 season, I couldn't move one morning. My leg felt it didn't belong to me. I rang Fizz in a panic, and he dropped everything to work on me, trying to jog it free. It was a slipped disc, and I missed the whole of that season. But I'll never forget his care and attention to me. He was always on the end of the phone.'

Some cricket physios allow themselves to be distracted once they've acquired a smattering of knowledge about the game, then get embroiled in dressing-room politics. Stuart Nottingham was far too modest, dedicated and intelligent to succumb to that. He was a discreet confidant to any player who wished to unload in private, a valued sounding-board with no agenda to the cricket management. The Fizz never missed a trick around the dressing room, knew where all the bodies were buried – but never betrayed confidences. That's why he was greatly respected.

And, just for the record, he's no killjoy. He likes a pint. Even though, enviably, he still has a stomach like an ironing board.

Roy French – Dressing-Room Attendant

There's been a French Connection in the Warwickshire dressing room since 1993, the year it all started to fall into place.

Roy French and his son Robin have been the dressing-room attendants for three decades now and, as far as Roy's concerned, it was his destiny.

He went to the same school as Dennis Amiss, a year later, and his dad used to take him to Edgbaston as a boy. 'All day long, throughout the school holidays, with my thermos flask and sandwiches. I was never bored. I believe God put me on this earth to do that dressing-room job, I loved it so much.'

The best dressing-room attendants are cheerful, helpful, sensitive enough to stay out of the way when necessary, tactful when there are harsh words exchanged and they can't get out of the door, and ultra-loyal. Roy French ticked all those boxes handsomely.

The players loved him. They joshed him because of his devotion to Birmingham City and teased him whenever the great former Blues player Trevor Francis popped into the dressing room. Roy would be too starry-eyed to say much. And when players with Aston Villa connections – Gary Shaw, Dwight Yorke, Colin Gibson, Mark Bosnich – also stuck their heads around the door, supporters like Gladstone Small and Keith Cook made sure they were introduced to the rabid Bluenose. Just to check how tactful he could be.

Neil Smith summed up the contribution of Roy French to those days of plenty. 'Roy was as valuable as Keith Cook in the office. Totally switched onto us, nothing was too much trouble. He'd put bets on for Glad at Ladbroke's on the ground or go and buy fags for Pipes. We thought so much of Roy that at the end of one of those great seasons, there was a benefit tour to Barbados. We all went on it and clubbed together to fund the trip for Roy. I can safely say he enjoyed it! And he deserved it.'

Allan Donald and Andy Moles put Roy up when he wintered in South Africa once, and Dermot Reeve always included him in end-of-season parties. 'Dermot was great to me. He gave me a lovely photo, signed by him, when he left the club. We both loved the TV programme *M*A*S*H*, and he and I would spend hours watching it in the gym, when he was supposed to be training and me cleaning up.

'Gladstone could sleep for England. I only woke him up when it was time for him to eat. What a man, nothing ever seemed to bother him. When it was his benefit year, I wrote in his brochure, "I've only got one complaint about you, Glad – how come we backed so many losers when you spent so long reading *The Sporting Life*?" He'd leave it till the last minute before punting. And he usually got it wrong.

'Roger Twose doing the haka in the dressing room ... I thought the roof was going to fall in on us. Tim Munton being sensible. You could rely on Tim for a statesmanlike comment. Trevor Penney and his pranks. He once locked me in a big cupboard where all the drinks were stored. I had left the key in the lock and TP turned the key. I was in there for an hour.

'He was like a whippet, Trevor – running two when his batting partner could only manage one. He liked a beer; Allan Donald managed to get a massive consignment of the South African Castle Lager delivered, and I had to find room to stash all the cases of it. Even in the shower area. TP kept wandering off at close of play with a case in his arms. I called him the Phantom Beer Nicker!'

Roy was in charge of the beer consignment whenever Warwickshire made one of their familiar appearances in a final at Lord's. He loaded up the cases onto the team coach, and the players left him at the Grace Gates, oblivious to the logistical hassles of getting all the beers into the dressing room, with the Lord's jobsworths out in force. Roy managed to square it with them, with his usual genial nature and ready wit, but the local constabulary were a tougher proposition.

'What do you think you're doing?' a bobby asked Roy. 'Are you going to sell them outside?' Roy did his best to persuade the constable of his bona fides and was warned, 'You've got thirty minutes to get them off this pavement and make them disappear. If not, you're in the local nick.' Mission accomplished, with the aid of some stewards and other dressing-room attendants, with Roy shrewdly divvying up some of the booty with his helpers. He was a resourceful man.

His duties involved cleaning the dressing room and showers, operating a vacuum, sorting out tickets and any specific requests for food, doing errands to the

Roy French in the old pavilion dressing room, just before it was knocked down in 2009

shops for the players and, in the case of Brian Lara, cleaning his golf clubs.

In 1994 Lara had been bitten by the golf bug and took great care of his clubs. He trusted Roy to look after them at Edgbaston when he was on away trips that season. Once, on his return, he didn't realise Roy had put them away for safe keeping. Lara was consternated, convinced he had lost them somewhere during his busy schedule. Roy knew where to find them but Andy Moles whispered, 'Don't tell Brian – hide them.' He duly did so until it was time for Warwickshire to go out to field. Moles said, 'Put them on his seat, Roy,' and, when Lara came back at the interval, his golf clubs were

there, pristine from a special cleaning. 'He stood there, open-mouthed, as if they'd materialised from nowhere. I saw him a couple of years ago at a charity match, and we had a laugh about it.'

Roy will not hear a breath of criticism about Lara from that '94 season. 'He was young, under a lot of pressure, and it was all so unfamiliar to him. Sometimes he'd just sit in his dressing-room space, looking for some peace, because everybody was after him. I did my best to keep people away from him when they tried to get into the dressing room. Sometimes I'd say to him, "Brian, there are a few things that need signing by you, please," and he'd give me a look. But

I knew he'd do it in his own time, perhaps a day later. He'd come in and say, "OK, Roy, what do you want me to do?" He was as good as gold.'

Roy also handled dressing-room duties during Edgbaston Test matches, and his popularity was acknowledged by many. He recalls doing cigarette duties for Shane Warne, having his ribs crushed by Andrew Flintoff in a victory hug after that dramatic win over Australia in 2005, and Tim Lamb, the ECB Chief Executive, making a beeline for him to thank him for all his cheerful support of the England team. Alastair Cook bumped into Roy after his retirement and invited him into the England dressing room for a farewell beer. Jack Russell gave him an affectionate mention in one of his books. Mark Butcher spotted him in the Oval dining area and insisted Roy joined him for a bite to eat and some reminiscences. Roy also speaks fondly of outstanding overseas players such as Graeme Smith, Kumar Sangakkara, Justin Langer, Anil Kumble and Mohammad Azharuddin. 'Very genuine and caring men. It was a privilege for me to be working alongside so many great cricketers and respectful men.'

But at heart he's a true Bear. His greatest memories surround his Warwickshire tribe, and 1994 still burnishes his memory. 'They were great lads. They reminded me of those superb Aussie teams around that period. Not over-confident, but with an aura about them. They expected to win. Things could get heated at times in the dressing room, but I loved the frivolity and the daftness when we won. There was a great mix of youth and experience in there. They were so good to me. My friends, really.'

Roy retired in 2010 and Robin is now in charge of the home dressing room, a massive area housing state-of-the-art facilities, with a greatly enhanced emphasis on security. Roy wouldn't recognise the serious atmosphere now, understandable though it may be. He had the best of times, although he says wistfully, 'I wish I could turn the clock back to those days.'

His health hasn't been all that sound lately and he's confined to a wheelchair, so trips to his beloved Edgbaston that started over sixty years ago are rare. Some of the Class of '94 still ring him for a natter, pulling his leg about being a loyal Bluenose. Above all, Roy French is a loyal Bear. As much a part of the scene as anyone from that memorable period.

His name may mean very little to Bears' supporters, but he was vital to countless Bears' players. Mention his name to any of them, and they'll smile immediately.

Not the worst of testimonies.

Robin and Roy French

Key Matches in the Season

v Glamorgan, Edgbaston, 28 April – 1 May

Great players adapt and prosper in different conditions. Brian Lara demonstrated that in April 1994.

Just 11 days after breaking the world Test record with his 375 against England in Antigua, Lara purred to 147 with nonchalant ease on his county championship debut. From the Caribbean heat to the dank chill of Birmingham, it made no difference. Lara just sauntered through the gears against Glamorgan, leaving the despairing bowlers cowed in admiration.

The off-spinner Robert Croft was then developing into a fine bowler who would later play for England, and he relished his duel with Lara. One shot, played inside out over extra cover for six, lingers long in my memory and indeed that of Croft. 'An incredible shot, so swift and so certain. There was a bit of rough outside his off-stump and I was aiming for that. He knew it. You had to be patient because he was so quick on his feet. His first stride was like lightning, and it got him into position instantly. That high backlift ... he never gave you an early read on whether he was going to play an attacking or a defensive shot.

'I could have placed every fielder on one side of the wicket, and he still would have found a gap. He could create angles on a straight ball, angling the face of the bat in or out, depending on where the fielders were.' Croft had the eventual satisfaction of having Lara caught at slip, with the ball turning out of the rough, but not before he'd reached his hundred off 99 balls, then accelerated even more ravishingly before he fell.

The Glamorgan captain Hugh Morris had the task of trying to stem the flow from Lara's bat. 'Setting a field to him was a challenge. He just threaded the ball through the eye of a needle. We had a fine fielding side in those days, and I don't remember one of us making a diving stop to one of Lara's shots. He was almost taking the mickey out of us; his control of the ball was astonishing. Very few batters took to Crofty the way he did that day; it was as if he was batting on roller skates against him.

'I'd played with Viv Richards at Glamorgan just a few years earlier, and he was my hero. Brian had the same sort of aura of a great player, a real presence about him.'

The supporters had had to wait a day before seeing Lara do more than just field at slip, after Glamorgan

Brian Lara's first innings for Warwickshire

had won the toss and batted. Another left-hander born in the Caribbean – David Hemp – had compiled a worthy hundred in dismal conditions on a stodgy pitch, but Lara next day simply transformed the match with his peerless strokeplay. He was supported ably by another left-hander, playing an innings that proved more significant than the iridescent genius of Lara's.

Roger Twose gained so much confidence from his 277*, spread over ten hours, that he was to prove one of the side's most durable and valuable players over the next five months. His dreadful 1993 season was soon an irrelevance as his technical improvements against the short ball were clear. Hugh Morris was impressed by this innings. 'He proved to be a very good player in an outstanding county team. A great man to have in your side – tough and tenacious. I can relate to being a workmanlike left-hander, not very easy on the eye – especially when you're batting with Lara – but Roger was nuggety and valuable.'

When Dermot Reeve declared, leaving Twose just 28 runs short of equalling Frank Foster's county record set up 80 years earlier, some of the statistically-minded in the large, shivering crowd felt cheated of missing out on a piece of Warwickshire history. They weren't to know that, just five weeks later, Lara would smash Foster's record, against Durham.

The key to Reeve's declaration was its timing. Glamorgan's players were weary, chasing leather for 176 overs. Four of their bowlers had conceded 100-plus runs and the fifth, Steve Watkin, went for 99. A ticklish 75 minutes of batting before the close on the third day was the last thing Glamorgan wanted and they were soon 9/2 against the craft of Small and Munton – including Morris, for nought.

Small cleaned up on the fourth morning and, with an impressive innings victory in the bag, thoughts of Frank Foster's innings at Dudley in 1914 were firmly on the back burner. It was the perfect start for Warwickshire, with a handsome redemption for Twose and confirmation that Lara meant business with his new employers. His dazzling display meant Warwickshire rattled along at nearly four an over, and that set the pattern for the rest of the season in the county championship. Lara would continue to score at almost a run a ball in the championship, giving the bowlers more time than they expected to bowl the opposition out twice. On more than one occasion, such latitude was to prove decisive.

No one at the start of May could have believed that Lara would progress to such largesse and brilliance over the next few weeks, but he had put down an impressive marker at the first time of asking.

Robert Croft had no doubts about Lara's value to his new team-mates after just one match. 'The superstar rolled into town, and he gave all the TV cameras great entertainment. But he also did what the great Viv did for us – bringing out the best from the players around him. Like Roger Twose in his double hundred. He wanted to earn Brian's respect and he did, with great effect for Warwickshire for the rest of the season.

'Brian was out of this world in that game and it was a privilege to pit my wits against him. And I got him out!'

Warwickshire v Glamorgan, Edgbaston, 28 April – 1 May 1994

Warwickshire won by an innings and 103 runs

Umpires: J.H. Hampshire & J.W. Holder

Glamorgan

S.P. James	c Asif Din b N Smith	19	lbw b Small	61
H. Morris *	lbw b Munton	24	b Munton	0
A. Dale	c Piper b Munton	32	c Reeve b Small	0
M.P. Maynard	lbw b Reeve	5	c P Smith b Small	34
D.L. Hemp	c N Smith b Munton	127	c Twose b Small	2
P.A. Cottey	lbw b P Smith	18	c Reeve b Davis	33
R.D.B. Croft	b Reeve	30	c Davis b Munton	5
O.D. Gibson	b Small	61	c Reeve b Davis	15
R.P. Lefebvre	c Twose b Munton	20	b Davis	32
C.P. Metson +	lbw b P Smith	2	c P Smith b Small	0
S.L. Watkin	*not out*	0	*not out*	0
	b 9, lb 13, w 1, nb 4	27	b 4, lb 3	7
		365		**189**

1/31, 2/53, 3/64, 4/118, 5/158, 6/222, 7/327, 8/354, 9/365, 10/365
1/4, 2/9, 3/89, 4/93, 5/104, 6/126, 7/155, 8/170, 9/189, 10/189

Warwickshire

D.P. Ostler	b Gibson	42
R.G. Twose	*not out*	277
B.C. Lara	c Maynard b Croft	147
Asif Din	st Metson b Croft	42
D.A. Reeve *	lbw b Gibson	18
P.A. Smith	b Watkin	38
N.M.K. Smith	c Gibson b Dale	15
K.J. Piper +	run out	12
R.P. Davis	*not out*	35
G.C. Small		
T.A. Munton		
	b 7, lb 9, w 1, nb 14	31
	(for 7 wkts, dec)	**657**

1/50, 2/265, 3/372, 4/435, 5/531, 6/557, 7/592

Small	27	6	75	1	17.3	3	46	5
Munton	23.4	5	57	4	21	5	73	2
Smith NMK	18	3	46	1	15	4	25	0
Reeve	23	5	61	2				
Davis	21	7	51	0	12	7	24	3
Smith PA	12	2	35	2	2	0	14	0
Lara	1	0	7	0				
Twose	5	1	11	0				

Watkin	32	7	99	1
Gibson	30	4	134	2
Croft	51	13	173	2
Lefebvre	39	11	122	0
Dale	24	3	113	1

v Leicestershire, Edgbaston, 5 – 9 May

Great players score vital runs when their side desperately needs them. It took Brian Lara just two matches to win over his Warwickshire team-mates. In their eyes he was now a special player.

His century in the first innings against Leicestershire was almost routine, if you can take for granted a dazzling 106 off 136 balls when everyone else struggled against a strong attack and the follow-on was only averted with the last pair together.

But his 120* off 163 balls a day later that staved off defeat was of a different dimension. Lara himself thought it was his most satisfying innings of the summer, because of its significance and the challenges set by a very difficult pitch. No one else passed 20 as Leicestershire, credible challengers for the championship, pressed hard for victory.

Dermot Reeve reckons it was the best innings he ever saw in county cricket. Reeve, batting at number four due to Asif Din's leg injury, was one of those swept away in a devastatingly hostile spell of fast bowling from David Millns, at his best a genuine England prospect. He was certainly that on the final day, and he helped reduce Warwickshire to 61/4, well adrift of the victory target of 285 on a hard, fast wicket, with cracks developing. The odd ball took off, and others scuttled through low. It was a pitch light years away from the Antigua one where Lara had made 375 a month earlier, or the blameless one where he scored his debut century against Glamorgan.

Lara radiated serenity and assurance, as the rest of his team-mates were rapped on the knuckles or plagued by shooters. As Reeve recalls, 'Brian made it look a doddle. He adjusted so late that the shooters would be kept out easily and, if the ball took off, he'd either play it over the slips' heads or leave it alone. The bad delivery would just be dismissed to the boundary with no fuss. Brian seemed from another planet as a batsman, and we couldn't believe our luck.'

Lara found a doughty ally in the imperturbable Neil Smith. They added a precious 67, with Smith doing what he was told by Lara. 'I faced one ball an over at the most. That innings showed me just how good Brian was. Leicestershire were a very vocal, competitive side with fine bowlers, and they knew they'd win if they got Brian out. They tried everything. They kept putting the field out to get him off strike, but he judged where to hit the ball so well. He would pick the gaps for four or, if needed, three or one to keep the strike near the end of the over. To be able to control an innings to that degree in that situation was absolutely fantastic.'

There was just one moment of fallibility from Lara, and it annoyed him so much that he gave Smith an earful. Phil Simmons, a fellow Trinidadian, was standing at first slip, trying to work out how to dismiss the masterful Lara. With Millns about to bowl the last ball of an over, Simmons moved stealthily from first slip to third, anticipating a steer from Lara. The wicket-keeper, Paul Nixon, recalls what happened. 'Brian was looking to run it down to third man, and Simmo got it exactly right by moving over. But it went straight in and out, and we couldn't believe it. Simmo never dropped anything. Brian was in the sixties then, and he never looked like getting out after that.'

But Lara was displeased at the Simmons drop. He thought Smith should have alerted him to the switch as Millns was running in. 'Brian told me off, and he was right. Normally I'd have noticed that, but the way he was farming the strike was remarkable so I just switched off mentally. I was facing so little of the bowling that I was just enjoying his amazing innings.'

By the time Smith was out, Leicestershire knew the game was up and, as Lara walked off unbeaten at the end, the respect from the opposition was ungrudging and genuine. Millns said to his captain, Nigel Briers, 'That's as good as Alan Mullally and I could ever have bowled. We'd have won that if Lara hadn't played like that.' Lara said later in the season that this Leicestershire attack was the toughest he faced all season.

Millns, now a first-class umpire and a pro cricketer for 17 years, still exalts Lara's batting in that second innings. 'The best batting I have ever seen in any of my games. He was on 99 for ages, yet he remained calm and just waited for the moment. I remember when he first came in he was wearing side pieces on his helmet and after facing a few balls – and seeing one ball take off to whistle over our keeper's head for four byes – he called for a helmet and grille. He was still on nought but steeled himself for the battle. He wasn't going to go without a fight.

'The way he adapted and went about his business was hugely impressive. I was a 90mph bowler in those days, yet he made me look 70mph. I didn't even manage to ruffle him with the short stuff on that helpful pitch – he just got out of the way. A dot ball to him was an achievement; he gave you such a small target area. You'd try to dry him up by putting him under pressure, set fields to make him go over the top, get him off strike early in the over. It made no difference, he just played the way he wanted.'

David Millns thought so highly of Lara that at home he still has the scorecard of a championship match in 1998 when he dismissed Lara, lbw, for 5. 'A career highlight for me, he was that special. I loved pitting my wits against him.'

Paul Nixon is equally laudatory about Lara's second innings hundred. 'We had a fine attack, but Lara was immense. He reined it in but still hit the same delivery, pitching on middle stump, both sides of the wicket in front of square, then behind square. From middle and leg, he'd hit it down to third man or through extra cover. He had a fantastic eye.

'To me, he's the number one batsman of my time – comfortably. Tendulkar? He defended your best ball; Brian hit it for four. His boundary count was off the chart, especially when he got to 30. He could change a game in a session, and play in all circumstances. If Brian could score 500 in an innings in England, he could have made 1,000 on Indian wickets, where the ball never gets above knee height. And Brian always batted for the team, as he showed against us.'

That hundred by Lara is the one his admirers in the dressing room cited when his commitment to the cause came to be questioned later that summer. Paul Smith was amazed by the innings: 'He played for the team; Brian was determined they weren't going to beat us. What a contrast to Antigua a few weeks earlier – it was freezing cold, very overcast, they were a fine bowling unit, and a red ball was coming at him hard in the gloom. But he took them all on. He massively impressed us all that day.'

Tim Munton makes the point that the course of the Bears' triumphant season might have been altered if Leicestershire had won this game. 'They were a similar group to us – great team spirit, fine bowling attack, the sum of their parts. But, with respect to Simmons, they never had a Lara. It was a pivotal innings, one for the team.'

That hundred set Lara apart from many overseas players. Truly, he was now a man for all seasons.

Warwickshire v Leicestershire, Edgbaston, 5, 6, 7 & 9 May 1994

Match drawn

Umpires: B. Dudleston & D.R. Shepherd

Leicestershire

P.V. Simmons	c Reeve b Bell	9	c Reeve b P Smith	39
N.E. Briers *	c Ostler b Reeve	154	c sub b N Smith	22
T.J. Boon	c Ostler b Small	42		
J.J. Whitaker	c Reeve b Bell	25	(3) b P Smith	4
V.J. Wells	c Piper b P Smith	21	(4) b N Smith	2
B.F. Smith	b Small	78	(5) not out	25
P.A. Nixon +	c Reeve b Small	7	(6) c Piper b N Smith	19
G.J. Parsons	lbw b Bell	6	(7) not out	11
A.R.K. Pierson	not out	26		
D.J. Millns	lbw b P Smith	10		
A.D. Mullally	c Bell b Munton	1		
	b 8, lb 6, nb 10	24	b 3, lb 9, w 1	13
		403	(for 5 wkts, dec)	**135**

1/11, 2/100, 3/162, 4/212, 5/320, 6/341, 7/348, 8/378, 9/402, 10/403
1/73, 2/76, 3/79, 4/79, 5/108

Small	27	3	77	3				
Bell	26	5	89	3	5	0	19	0
Munton	27.2	6	78	1	11	3	25	0
Smith PA	16	2	67	2	9	2	27	2
Smith NMK	13	3	35	0	17	5	52	3
Reeve	14	5	43	1				

Warwickshire

D.P. Ostler	c Nixon b Millns	17	lbw b Millns	14
R.G. Twose	c Nixon b Parsons	51	c Simmons b Millns	12
B.C. Lara	c & b Pierson	106	not out	120
Asif Din	b Pierson	14	(7) run out	9
D.A. Reeve *	c sub b Pierson	0	(4) c Parsons b Millns	3
P.A. Smith	c sub b Pierson	13	(5) c Whitaker b Millns	0
K.J. Piper +	c sub b Pierson	0	(6) b Pierson	8
N.M.K. Smith	c Simmons b Pierson	18	c sub b Simmons	20
G.C. Small	c Millns b Pierson	5	not out	0
M.A.V. Bell	not out	4		
T.A. Munton	c sub b Pierson	5		
	b 14, lb 5, nb 2	21	b 7, lb 3, nb 10	20
		254	(for 7 wkts)	**206**

1/27, 2/129, 3/201, 4/201, 5/206, 6/210, 7/229, 8/238, 9/247, 10/254
1/32, 2/45, 3/61, 4/61, 5/91, 6/120, 7/187

Mullally	20	6	55	0	12	1	57	0
Millns	13	3	52	1	15	4	54	4
Wells	6	1	29	0				
Parsons	15	3	57	1	13	4	41	0
Pierson	17.5	5	42	8	13	2	23	1
Simmons					3.4	1	21	1

v Leicestershire, AXA League, Edgbaston, 8 May

As the players celebrated their Sunday League title victory at Bristol in mid-September, one popular squad member was missing, unable to share in the revelries. Michael Bell had set the Bears on the road to the title in the first game of that Sunday League season, with a devastating spell of 5/6 in just 18 balls, as Leicestershire were routed. But his back gave way over that weekend, and his summer of cricket was over.

A prolonged and painful period of rehab prevented Bell travelling down to Bristol four months later. His stunning spell against Leicestershire must have seemed light years away. 'I just got it right that day. I just glided in and let it go. My action, head and feet were all in the right place. The ball swung for me and they nicked it'.

It was the second successive Sunday League game that Bell had dominated, albeit separated by a winter. In the final game of the 1993 season, he took 5/21 against Nottinghamshire, so he was hardly a wild-card selection the following May, especially after taking 22 wickets in three championship matches that August. A left-arm swing bowler of great natural talent, he could bowl a devastating in-ducker when the stars aligned. With a lovely, smooth run-up and textbook action, Michael Bell oozed class, even though he lacked consistency.

Neil Smith came through the age ranges with Bell at Edgbaston. 'As a bowler, he made it look so easy. Never looked like hard work.'

Dominic Ostler hated facing him in the nets, because of his inconsistency. 'One ball he'd clean you up with an absolute jaffa – next would be a beamer. Not deliberate, he just couldn't control the ball sometimes. But when he got it right ... Lovely bloke, Micky. The coolest dude I ever met in cricket. We nicknamed him Breeze, because he just breezed through life. He was immaculately dressed, either in whites or civvies. Never put coins or keys in his pocket, in case they creased his trousers. Once, on a plane to South Africa, he slept upright all the way and looked as fresh as a daisy when we landed while we all looked like a bag of shit. An effortless bloke.'

And the only professional cricketer to appear in *Only Fools and Horses*, the classic TV comedy. It was as an extra in the 1996 Christmas special. 'My dad worked for the Caribbean section at the BBC's Pebble Mill studios, and he was asked to find some black faces for a market scene. For Peckham, read Bristol City's car park. I thought I might end up on the cutting room floor but I'm in it, after about twenty minutes. Never got to meet David Jason, though! I'm still available for more crowd scenes!'

Someone of Micky Bell's sunny disposition is not one for regrets, but he does wish he could have played a more relevant part in Warwickshire's success. He had the talent but admits he lacked consistency. 'I took wickets in clumps.' There was also fierce

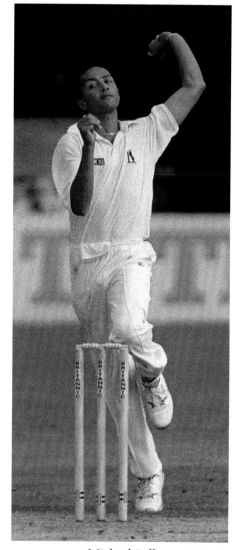

Michael Bell

competition among the seam and swing bowlers at the time at Edgbaston.

He was finished with pro cricket at the age of 32, but his last spell at Surrey ushered him into the property world. He now has a developing property portfolio in the Brighton area, a clothes shop – appropriately enough – in the Lanes and turns out for Sussex Over-50s. No doubt he still has the best action in every game he plays.

Warwickshire 173-4 *(40 overs)* (Asif Din 54*, Reeve 65*) beat Leicestershire 151 *(39.3 overs)* (Bell 5-19) by 22 runs

v Somerset, Taunton, 19 – 23 May

This was the match that alerted the rest of the counties to Warwickshire's ability to chase a target with elan and clear-eyed spirit.

After this thrilling win, no other county declared against Warwickshire for the rest of the season. It was too dangerous. It appeared no feasible target was beyond them after cantering home at Taunton to reach 321 in just 53.4 overs. In 1994, before T20 made anything possible, that was an astonishing rate of scoring.

There were extenuating circumstances in Somerset's failure to rein in the batsmen during their exhilarating run-chase. Rain bedevilled the game, and in the final session, with the run-chase established, the rainy conditions hampered Somerset in the field. The umpires, Ray Julian and Kevin Lyons, were criticised by Somerset's captain, Andy Hayhurst, for allowing the game to continue in what he termed 'unplayable conditions'.

The Lara factor also influenced the result. His sparkling 136 off 94 balls (his century coming off 72 balls) was another masterclass in precise, yet flamboyant strokeplay. After Hayhurst and Tim Munton had cooked up a run-chase of 321 in 95 overs, Roger Twose and Dominic Ostler opened with a sprightly stand of 71 that boded well for Warwickshire if the rain held off. It didn't. No play on the final afternoon, and Lara walked out after tea, just 5*, facing the daunting target of 234 from 31 overs. The positive mindset established since Asif Din's match at Lord's in '93 was going to be tested. So was Lara.

He started badly, running out Ostler for 51 when that powerful striker of the ball was motoring along smoothly. Lara knew he had to win the game now, relying on those flexible hitters Paul Smith and Asif Din for support. Lara's second fifty took just 21 balls and, when he was out, Asif Din twinkled wristily to seal a remarkable win with 20 balls to spare.

Lara played with such luminous certainty in conditions that were so foreign to him that it's easy to overlook the positive contributions of the other four batsmen who all batted splendidly. So it wasn't the wondrous solo performance of the Leicestershire match. The others breathed the spirit of Lord's '93, believing anything was possible. But there was no doubt who was the principal orchestrator.

Dominic Ostler was initially annoyed that Lara ran him out when he was going so well but soon came round. 'I said to him, "Don't ever do that to me again", and he knew he was in the wrong. But you can't say much when he carried on batting like that. It was one of the best hundreds I have seen and the one that stands out for me that summer. I was transfixed as he hit the gaps. They had virtually every fielder on the boundary, and he still hit the fence with such power and placement. It was so good that even Gladdy got off the physio's couch to watch him!

'It was an education to watch Brian build an innings like the Somerset one, then take the attack apart. He was a massive help to the rest of the batters. We all fed off him and we now felt we could chase anything.'

Tim Munton, captain in that game, was still astonished by Lara's innings against Somerset, even though he'd been his team-mate for nearly a month.

A long way from Antigua
Dickie Davis helps Brian Lara to keep warm in the field

Brian Lara flashes a four off Mushtaq Ahmed, as Iain Fletcher jumps out of the way and Rob Turner looks on

'From the defiance of that Leicestershire hundred to that phenomenal innings in a run chase, he was the complete batsman. And he took on responsibility either to earn us a draw or win us the game, against the odds. He just kept on surprising us.'

One wise old sage from Warwickshire's past was equally impressed as he savoured Lara's innings. MJK Smith, the club chairman, watched in awe. 'I think it was Brian's finest innings that summer. When you see something like that, you can do nothing other than sit back, thinking you're a very lucky bloke to be able to watch it.'

So two wins out of three in the championship already and Lara's genius had swiftly entranced his new team-mates. He had clocked up five successive first-class hundreds, beginning with the 375 in Antigua over the past month, batting in princely fashion in radically differing conditions.

Yet in that Taunton game a rift in the lute appeared between Lara and Dermot Reeve that was never really repaired. Within a few weeks there were deepening

fissures between them. It began on the final morning at Taunton, as Warwickshire fed Somerset some cheap runs to set up the declaration which later rebounded on them. Asif Din and Dominic Ostler only delivered 19 balls before the declaration, but not before Lara and Reeve irritated the umpires. Lara had just taken delivery of a new mobile phone and he took it onto the field to see if it would work, as Somerset faced the undemanding bowling.

Reeve, back from England one-day duty the day before so unable to play at Taunton, thought it a good wheeze to call up Lara on his new toy as the batsmen were getting ready to face the first over. Reeve says he checked it out with the rest of the players before they went out, and the jape was willingly embraced. So Reeve rang, Lara answered from his position at first slip and he heard Reeve say, 'Brian, I think you're standing a bit close to Keith Piper.'

Reeve takes up the story: 'Brian looked up at our balcony, saw me and some of the other lads waving and promptly put the phone away. We had a chuckle and thought no more about it, just a harmless piece of fun that you experience in every county dressing room.

'A year after the event, I read in Brian's autobiography that I'd got him into trouble with the umpires for calling him on the mobile in the day's second over. That was nonsense; that call wasn't from me, if he did have another. I only called him before a ball was delivered.

'After the game, the umpires told me to have a word with Brian, that you don't take calls during a first-class match. Brian was very sniffy about it with me, and he said in his book I was having a joke at his expense. He didn't seem to realise it was just a gentle bit of leg-pulling. A sense of humour was always part of the Edgbaston atmosphere in my experience. I realised, though, that Brian would laugh at himself if the joke or quip was from others in the team, rather than me.'

As a camp follower of the Warwickshire players during that period, I can happily confirm that laughter was often heard from their dressing room, that many pranks were played, banter exchanged with vigour and that Reeve was often at the centre of such jolly japes. Some were less fond of the captain than others, but few would doubt his knack of extracting humour from most situations, to defuse tensions. Dermot Reeve was a funny man, a talented mimic with a fecund supply of leg-pulling ideas. At his best, he definitely boosted team spirit.

It may be that if Paul Smith, Keith Piper, Trevor Penney, Neil Smith, Gladstone Small or Tim Munton had made the call to Lara's mobile that morning, it would have been taken in good part by him. Lara may have already decided by then that Reeve was not his favourite captain in his brilliant career thus far and would therefore not appreciate his sense of humour.

What isn't in doubt is that just one month after the mobile call that went wrong, various sub-plots that started to swirl around Reeve and Lara's relationship culminated in the star player telling his captain to go forth and multiply in front of several team-mates in the middle at Northampton. That froideur between Lara and Reeve became an issue that tested the cricket management.

Somerset v Warwickshire, Taunton, 19, 20, 21 & 23 May 1994

Warwickshire won by six wickets

Umpires: R. Julian & K.J. Lyons

Somerset

M.N. Lathwell	c Davis b P Smith	86			
I. Fletcher	c Davis b P Smith	17			
R.J. Harden	c Davis b P Smith	0			
N.A. Folland	c Piper b Davis	21			
A.N. Hayhurst *	not out	111			
R.J. Turner	c Lara b Munton	40			
H.R.J. Trump	c Davis b Small	15			
G.D. Rose	c Lara b Munton	1	(2) not out	13	
Mushtaq Ahmed	c Davis b Munton	2	(1) not out	9	
A. Payne	c Munton b Davis	34			
P.J. Bird	not out	0			
	b 6, lb 19, w 1, nb 2	28			
	(for 9 wkts, dec)	**355**	(for 0 wkts, dec)	**22**	

1/36, 2/36, 3/76, 4/149, 5/249, 6/272, 7/295, 8/299, 9/349

Small	36.2	6	104	1				
Munton	42	17	77	3				
Smith PA	16	7	24	3				
Twose	13	1	42	0				
Davis	25	9	59	2				
Smith NMK	15	6	24	0				
Asif Din					2	0	9	0
Ostler					1.1	0	13	0

Warwickshire

D.P. Ostler	not out	41	run out	51	
R.G. Twose	not out	13	c Turner b Mushtaq	33	
B.C. Lara			b Mushtaq	136	
P.A. Smith			c Lathwell b Hayhurst	39	
Asif Din			not out	42	
T.L. Penney			not out	9	
K.J. Piper +					
N.M.K. Smith					
G.C. Small					
R.P. Davis					
T.A. Munton *					
	lb 3	3	b 1, lb 4, w 1, nb 6	12	
	(for 0 wkts, dec)	**57**	(for 4 wkts)	**322**	

1/71, 2/96, 3/170, 4/296

Bird	7	1	32	0	9	0	53	0
Payne	4	1	13	0	8	1	41	0
Mushtaq	6	3	9	0	14	0	65	2
Rose	2	2	0	0	18.4	1	117	0
Trump	2	2	0	0				
Hayhurst					4	0	41	1

v Kent, B&H Quarter-Final, Edgbaston, 24 – 25 May

Now this was one of those matches where Warwickshire got lucky. The club chose not to use the trusted, usual covering with poor weather forecast and, when it duly rained, the ground wasn't playable. It needed a bowl-out to settle the tie, and Kent failed at the last.

After missing out in the lottery of aiming at the stumps, Kent departed Edgbaston, disgruntled, fired up to write a letter of complaint to Lord's. It was hard to argue with the withering assessment of their coach, Darryl Foster. 'When you come to a Test match ground you are entitled to expect something better.'

The key decision had been taken a few days before the scheduled Tuesday start. With heavy rain forecast leading up to the game, a decision was taken not to use the 'Brumbrella', a huge automated tarpaulin that could cover the entire ground. It had been utilised successfully on many occasions, and Edgbaston had acquired the reputation of a ground that dried quickly. But groundsman Steve Rouse was concerned about fungus fusarium, which prevents grass growth. Some of the pitches needed rain to aid the even growth of grass. Others, including the one for the Kent game, were put under smaller covers. It rained all day on the Saturday before Tuesday's big match, and it got under the covers.

A large crowd turned up for the match and were frustrated that there was no play on a grey but dry day. After all, the quarter-final at Derby, 40 miles away, started at 2pm. But it was too wet to play at Edgbaston, with little prospect for the reserve day.

The phone lines between Edgbaston and Lord's hummed for 24 hours, with the Test and County Cricket Board ruling the match could not be moved. The championship was to resume on Thursday, and there were no gaps before the next round.

According to Tim Munton, Warwickshire suggested going up the A38 to Derby, where the match had been concluded on Tuesday, and playing a 30-over tie there on Wednesday. 'But Kent refused to go to Derby. They preferred the bowl-out option as a last resort. We would have gone to Derby.'

With no play possible on the reserve day, some Kent supporters aimed a few verbal volleys at Steve Rouse as he made his way back from the square to the groundsman's shed. The redoubtable Rouse was not going to shy away from justifying his actions. 'I said, "Come and have a look at the square with me" and told them that Kent were moaning about the follow-through on the wicket next door. We were happy if I covered it, but the two umpires couldn't agree on that and we had a stalemate. Those Kent supporters said, "It's ok to play on that" after I explained it all to them. We definitely could have played on that second day. Chuck a bit of sawdust on some matting, and we'd have been ok. We played in worse conditions, like the Sunday slog, many times. But Kent didn't fancy it; all they wanted was the bowl-out if we couldn't have a full game.'

An impasse. A bowl-out was the only solution. Even then, tempers flared as the paying spectators were denied access to the indoor school, where ten players would be trying to hit three stumps. The media were also barred, although the authorities relented when the sponsors intervened on our behalf. This observer felt a pang of remorse on behalf of the paying punters, who would have loved to be so close to the action, but the club was bothered about the sheer volume of spectators who would be crammed into the indoor school. There simply wasn't enough room. And the sponsors wanted their pound of flesh. Ironically, no play for two days and the consequent brouhaha led to extra media coverage for Benson & Hedges. We media folks do love a row.

It was fascinating to observe close-up the concentration and tension among the players. Even vastly experienced performers such as Gladstone Small, Tim Munton, Dermot Reeve, Carl Hooper, Mark Ealham and Min Patel suffered the gnawing of the lip and the blocking out of extraneous sounds as they prepared to bowl. Allan Donald, on tour with South Africa that summer but a regular at Edgbaston when possible, joined his erstwhile team-mates in support. Standing helplessly alongside Brian, it was poignant to observe two great cricketers experiencing the tension associated with an inability to influence the result.

Warwickshire's bowlers had decided to go round the wicket after practising in the indoor school. Each of their five bowlers hit the stumps on one of their two balls, and the first four Kent bowlers matched them. Then Nigel Llong, a 25-year-old batsman/off-spinner

making his way in the Kent team, was the tenth to try his luck, and both times he missed – narrowly.

Warwickshire's players celebrated with gusto. Donald and Lara embraced as if they had been team-mates for years. Kent's players sloped off, convinced not enough had been done to protect the pitch. It would have taken the hardest heart not to have sympathised with Kent, particularly Nigel Llong. He later became an international umpire, a decade after the Edgbaston heartbreak. His comment after failing in the indoor school encapsulated the cruel nature of what was cricket's version of a penalty shoot-out: 'Now I know what Stuart Pearce and Chris Waddle felt when they missed those penalties in the World Cup.' But Llong didn't have the financial consolation of an earner from a pizza TV commercial.

Kent's protests to the TCCB were in vain, but the rancour lingered on. Matthew Fleming was sufficiently incensed to write to Lord's about the preparations at Edgbaston. 'I was furious that Warwickshire got away with it. They had a waterlogged half of the playing surface, and the other half was playable. Even the indoor school, where we had the bowl-out, was affected by the rain. It was a farce that the host club escaped sanction for such a ridiculous situation.' Fleming's reward for his candour was to be hauled up before a TCCB disciplinary committee to explain himself.

As a result, matches between the two sides took on an extra dimension of competitiveness. There was enough needle in the first place but now Kent thought Warwickshire had sailed close to the wind, while some of the Bears felt Kent were just a bunch of whingers, sore losers who under-achieved.

Ten weeks later, the two sides locked horns again in a titanic NatWest Trophy semi-final at Edgbaston. The bowl-out in May added extra spice.

Allan Donald and Brian Lara look on, powerless

Warwickshire v Kent, Edgbaston, 25 May 1994
Warwickshire won 5-4 in a bowling contest

Warwickshire			Kent		
T.A. Munton	1 out of 2		C.L. Hooper	1 out of 2	
G.C. Small	1 out of 2		M.A. Ealham	1 out of 2	
P.A. Smith	1 out of 2		D.J. Spencer	1 out of 2	
D.A. Reeve	1 out of 2		M.M. Patel	1 out of 2	
R.P. Davis	1 out of 2		N.J. Llong	0 out of 2	

v Middlesex, Lord's, 26 – 30 May

They came in droves on the first day in anticipation of Brian Lara's sixth successive hundred in first-class cricket – but the pyrotechnics from him had to wait until the final day.

Richard Johnson, an England bowler of the future but then only 19, and playing his fourth championship match, had already dismissed Lara a fortnight earlier in a Benson & Hedges Cup match – with his first ball, no less. He then followed that up by having Lara caught down the legside for 26.

Lara had made his customary watchful start and, just as he started to open up, Johnson induced 'a strangle', as the pros call it. A soft dismissal, with a legside tickle landing in the wicket-keeper's gloves, rather than kissing the boundary rope at fine leg.

Lara would make amends handsomely on the final day, with Johnson and the other Middlesex bowlers discovering the slow pitch could be overcome by scintillating batting.

The game had pottered along worthily enough until Warwickshire batted for a second time, 38 runs in arrears. Lara came in early, purring along to reach 55* at close of play on the third day. Next morning a fusillade of brilliant shots brought him to 140 off 147 balls. One stroke in particular lingers in the memory of those who played in that match.

John Emburey was almost 42 in May 1994 – a canny, resourceful off-spinner who had played over 60 Tests. He was difficult to collar, a master of line and length who was rarely smashed around the park, not least because he regarded a looping, slow off-break as an affront to the Offies' Union. Embers believed in keeping it tight. When in doubt, a flat trajectory on a slow pitch was the way to keep batsmen quiet.

Unflappable, wordly-wise, Emburey had seen it all before in his long career, even being launched for a prodigious six into the Lord's pavilion on Cup Final day when he was just 25. Glamorgan's left-hander Mike Llewellyn had smashed him almost into the BBC Radio commentary box in the Gillette Cup Final in 1977. It was an enormous carry, and the consensus among historians was that only Albert Trott's six over the Lord's pavilion in 1899 surpassed it.

Emburey reacted in his usual phlegmatic fashion. A muttered Cockney curse in his best Peckham tones, a cursory glimpse at the footholds and he was ready to bowl again. After all, hadn't Llwelleyn hit Mike Gatting's first three deliveries for 14 in that innings? Mike Brearley, Emburey's captain, rated his young off-spinner highly and, with his encouragement, Emburey completed an impressively mature spell of 0 for 32 in his twelve overs.

Seventeen years and thousands of off-breaks later, Emburey suffered the same fate against a left-hander on the same ground. This time the enormous six was to the left of the pavilion sightscreen, looking back from the middle, landing on the south turret, above the home dressing room.

Mike Gatting, Middlesex's captain in 1994, remembers both sixes vividly and with something approaching awe. 'They were the two biggest sixes I've seen at Lord's. Mike's was over straightish long-on while Brian's had a bit of fade on it, over straightish long-off. If it had gone dead straight, it might have gone over the pavilion. He took two steps down the pitch, and the timing was so sweet, just a gentle click. He smiled at Embers, who didn't smile back! There was nothing Embers could have done about that shot. It was a stroke of genius.'

Emburey, a wry, fatalistic cove, sees the funny side of both punishing sixes now. 'I suppose it's a claim to fame of sorts, isn't it? There was a bit of a fade to it with Lara's shot, as he hit me inside out, slightly to the offside. Otherwise it would have gone out of the ground.

'The funny thing was that I was suffering from double vision at the time after having an operation in the winter for a detached retina. I kept seeing two balls at the same time, so I daren't look at where Lara hit me. I just bowled line and length at him and hoped for the best. He was so gifted.'

Angus Fraser, who had bowled to Lara six weeks earlier in Antigua, recalls the six vividly. 'When we did TV publicity for Middlesex's T20 games, we'd set up the bowling machine, talk about Albert Trott's six over the pavilion and get some of our biggest hitters to try to emulate that. Some of them landed it in the seats of the pavilion, but Lara's hit

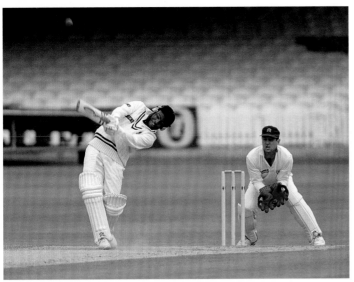

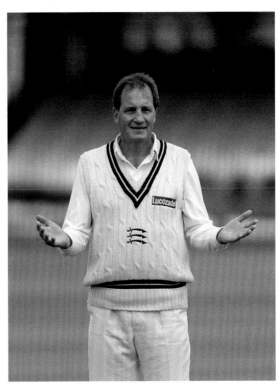

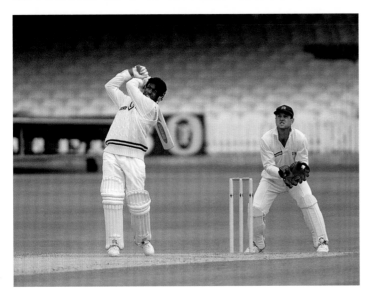

The shot of the season
Brian Lara almost clears the roof of the Lord's pavilion, while John Emburey the bowler looks helpless.

was huge. The ball got wrapped up in the flag above the home dressing room and I reckon, if that hadn't happened, the ball would have bounced over the pavilion. It's the biggest six I've seen at Lord's. I must admit that when it soared away, I had a chuckle because I knew Embers would be spewing. That six was all about timing because, although strong, Brian was quite slight in those days.

'He is the best batsman I have ever seen. He has played half a dozen of the greatest 20 innings in cricket history. When he performed, you remembered it. I was disappointed when he got out, even against England. During his 375 in Antigua, I beat him twice in an over. I stood there, hands on hips and told him, "I don't suppose I can call you a lucky so-and-so when you're on 320!" Brian just chuckled back at me. We got on very well down the years. An amazing batsman.'

And remarkably prolific at that time. This was his sixth first-class century in seven innings – only seven other batsmen in history had matched that. It was only the end of May, yet Lara had already scored ten first-class hundreds in 1994. He was Bradmanesque in his remorselessness but with more dash and daring.

And Emburey had a final, satisfying influence on the match. Aided by Fraser, the last Middlesex pair hung on for a draw, denying the splendid Tim Munton and Gladstone Small. That outcome appealed to the gnarled old pro in John Emburey. Let Lara have his glory and another hundred – but we stopped them from winning at the death.

Not that Warwickshire were unduly perturbed. As May ended with the draw at Lord's, the progress so far in '94 in all competitions was encouraging – played 8, won 6, drawn 2. A solid enough foundation for a historic summer.

Middlesex v Warwickshire, Lord's, 26, 27, 28 & 30 May 1994

Match drawn

Umpires: J.D. Bond & D.J. Constant

Warwickshire

D.P. Ostler	c Brown b Fraser	17	lbw b Johnson	26
R.G. Twose	b Williams	10	lbw b Fraser	1
B.C. Lara	c Brown b Johnson	26	c & b Emburey	140
T.L. Penney	lbw b Williams	43	c Ramprakash b Fraser	11
D.A. Reeve *	c Gatting b Johnson	4		
P.A. Smith	c & b Johnson	24	(5) c Gatting b Weekes	65
K.J. Piper +	c Rampr'sh b Williams	22	(6) not out	32
N.M.K. Smith	c Brown b Fraser	20	(7) not out	22
R.P. Davis	c Carr b Emburey	7		
G.C. Small	b Williams	13		
T.A. Munton	not out	5		
	lb 10, nb 10	20	b 2, lb 3, nb 4	9
		211	(for 5 wkts, dec)	**306**

1/21, 2/47, 3/66, 4/78, 5/125, 6/164, 7/166, 8/193, 9/193, 10/211
1/2, 2/50, 3/129, 4/224, 5/278

Williams	24	4	71	4	10	0	55	0
Fraser	24	10	43	2	17	4	60	2
Johnson	22	9	45	3	17	2	64	1
Emburey	14	5	37	1	20	3	79	1
Gatting	5	1	5	0				
Weekes					11	1	43	1

Middlesex

D.L. Haynes	c & b Small	0	(7) lbw b Munton	24
M.A. Roseberry	lbw b Twose	119	c Piper b Munton	73
M.W. Gatting *	lbw b Munton	52	lbw b Munton	18
M.R. Ramprakash	c Lara b Small	37	b Munton	0
J.D. Carr	lbw b Small	0	(1) lbw b Smith P	32
P.N. Weekes	c Lara b Smith P	3	(5) c Piper b Smith P	29
K.R. Brown +	c Piper b Small	0	(6) b Small	46
R.L. Johnson	lbw b Reeve	4	(9) c Smith N b Munton	0
N.F. Williams	b Reeve	7	(8) lbw b Small	10
J.E. Emburey	not out	9	not out	4
A.R.C. Fraser	c Piper b Munton	3	not out	0
	b 1, lb 10, w 2, nb 2	15	b 3, lb 6	9
		249	(for 9 wkts)	**245**

1/0, 2/77, 3/156, 4/156, 5/163, 6/174, 7/185, 8/201, 9/246, 10/249
1/84, 2/129, 3/129, 4/132, 5/206, 6/221, 7/239, 8/239, 9/245

Small	28	5	70	4	14	2	41	2
Munton	35	12	68	2	17	3	76	5
Smith PA	12	2	35	1	5	0	36	2
Reeve	17	4	31	2				
Smith NMK	3	1	15	0	8	0	33	0
Twose	5	0	19	1				
Davis					4	0	19	0
Lara					2	0	31	0

Results: 28 April to 30 May

County Championship

Apr 28,29,30,May 1   **Edgbaston**   **Glamorgan**   **Won by an innings & 103 runs**
Glamorgan 365 (Hemp 127, Munton 4-57) & 189 (Small 5-46)   Warwickshire 657-7 dec (Twose 277*, Lara 147)

May 5,6,7,9   **Edgbaston**   **Leicestershire**   **Match drawn**
Leicestershire 403 (Briers 154) & 135-5 dec   Warwickshire 254 (Lara 106, Pierson 8-42) & 206-7 (Lara 120*)

May 19,20,21,23   **Taunton**   **Somerset**   **Won by six wickets**
Somerset 355-9 dec (Hayhurst 111*) & 22-0 dec   Warwickshire 57-0 dec & 322-4 (Lara 136)

May 26,27,28,30   **Lord's**   **Middlesex**   **Match drawn**
Warwickshire 211 & 306-5 dec (Lara 140)   Middlesex 249 (Roseberry 119, Small 4-70) & 245-9 (Munton 5-76)

AXA Equity & Law League

May 8   **Edgbaston**   **Leicestershire**   **Won by 22 runs**
Warwickshire 173-4 *(40 overs)* (Asif Din 54*, Reeve 65*)   Leicestershire 151 *(39.3 overs)* (Bell 5-19)

May 22   **Taunton**   **Somerset**   **Won by five wickets**
Somerset 105-7 *(20 overs)* (Smith P 3-18)   Warwickshire 106-5 *(19.2 overs)* (Smith P 41)

May 29   **Lord's**   **Middlesex**   **Won by three wickets**
Middlesex 155-7 *(38 overs)*   Warwickshire 156-7 *(37 overs)* (Smith P 44, Ostler 42)

Benson & Hedges Cup

May 10 *(1st Round)*   **Lord's**   **Middlesex**   **Won by three wickets**
Middlesex 150 *(54.3 overs)* (Munton 3-27, Smith N 3-29)   Warwickshire 151-7 *(53.2 overs)*

May 24,25 *(2nd Round)*   **Edgbaston**   **Kent**   **Won 5-4 in a bowl-out**

Other match

May 14,16,17   **Oxford**   **Oxford University**   **Match drawn**
Warwickshire 303-5 dec (Ostler 149, Smith P 50*)   Oxford University 47-2

County Championship

	P	W	L	D	Bt	Bl	Pts
Surrey	5	4	1	-	14	16	94
Leicestershire	4	3	-	1	13	15	76
Essex	4	3	-	1	9	16	73
Nottinghamshire	4	3	-	1	6	12	66
Durham	4	2	2	-	8	14	54
Warwickshire	4	2	-	2	7	11	50
Gloucestershire	5	1	2	2	9	17	42
Sussex	4	1	-	3	5	11	32
Lancashire	3	1	1	1	4	10	30
Northamptonshire	4	1	1	2	4	10	30
Worcestershire	4	-	1	3	9	14	23
Derbyshire	5	-	3	2	5	15	20
Hampshire	4	-	2	2	8	11	19
Kent	4	-	1	3	4	13	17
Glamorgan	4	-	1	3	8	8	16
Yorkshire	3	-	-	3	8	8	16
Middlesex	3	-	-	3	4	11	15
Somerset	4	-	4	-	7	8	15

AXA Equity & Law League

	P	W	L	T	NR	Pts
Surrey	4	3	-	-	1	14
Warwickshire	3	3	-	-	-	12
Nottinghamshire	4	2	-	-	2	12
Sussex	4	2	1	-	1	10
Worcestershire	3	2	-	-	1	10
Yorkshire	3	2	-	-	1	10
Kent	4	2	2	-	-	8
Lancashire	3	2	1	-	-	8
Hampshire	3	2	1	-	-	8
Durham	3	1	-	-	2	8
Derbyshire	4	1	2	-	1	6
Leicestershire	3	1	2	-	-	4
Glamorgan	3	1	2	-	-	4
Gloucestershire	4	-	3	-	1	2
Northamptonshire	3	-	2	-	1	2
Essex	3	-	2	-	1	2
Somerset	3	-	3	-	-	0
Middlesex	3	-	3	-	-	0

v Durham, Edgbaston, 2 – 6 June

Amid the mountain lava of statistics contained in this match, an observation from one of the Durham players stands out. Wayne Larkins was being driven home to the north-east by his team-mate John Morris, still trying to take in the momentous feat by Brian Lara they had witnessed at close quarters. Both hardened pros, former England batsmen, they were fairly unshockable at this stage of their careers.

Morris switched on the radio to listen to how BBC Radio 5 Live would be covering Lara's innings and, once they had digested the facts, Larkins said in wonder: 'Do you realise, he's just hit half a thousand in one innings?'

A thousand runs in a first-class season was the normal benchmark for a self-respecting batsman in 1994, and Lara had just scored half of that tally in one innings, off only 427 balls! It was the highest individual score in first-class cricket, eclipsing a record that had stood for 35 years, sending statisticians into overdrive. As the Durham spinner David Graveney put it pithily: 'Smoke was coming out of the Edgbaston scoreboard on that final day!'

Graveney's unwilling part in that historic day must be highlighted. He spent the day in the dressing room, unable to bowl, after suffering a thigh strain the day before in the Sunday League fixture, in which, ironically, he dismissed Lara; 'He just had a hack at me, caught deep square leg.' On the final morning Mark Saxelby, a useful swing bowler, slipped in the footholds while practising and damaged his back. So Durham were down to four front-line bowlers, one of whom – the left-arm spinner David Cox – was making his championship debut. So the unremarkable medium-pace trundlers Larkins and Morris had to be pressed into service.

With so few bowlers available, Durham were unwilling to agree to a deal whereby, after a couple of declarations, Warwickshire would face a run chase on the final day. After the third day had been washed out, they were still 346 adrift as negotiations started on the final morning, with Lara 111*.

Geoff Cook, Durham's Director of Cricket, was not disposed to make it easy for Warwickshire when Dermot Reeve and Bob Woolmer, hoping for a deal, knocked on the visitors' dressing-room door.

Cook said he would be happy to set up a worthwhile game, but he had lost his star bowler – which led to Graveney looking around, wondering who Cook was talking about.

Cook remembers Woolmer being particularly unhappy about not being able to reach agreement. 'I didn't want us to be seen as pushovers that season, in the light of our development as the newest county. We wanted to compete in matches, but not to make it easy for the opposition. I didn't want us to be seen as spoilsports, but we were two bowlers short.'

So Lara batted on and on. Graveney had to wander around the dressing room all day, embarrassed ('if looks could kill') and young David Cox (30-5-163-0) experienced the steepest of learning curves. But Cook says he wasn't fazed by the experience. 'He was a cheeky chappy, with a Cockney humour, who'd been on the Lord's groundstaff. He'd won a few second-eleven games for us and deserved his chance. He took the day's experience well; he was happy to be there.'

Graveney was impressed by Cox on that final day. 'I wish I'd had his flowing action, I'd have been a better bowler. He got neck ache, watching the ball disappear, but he never gave up. He needed more protection from an experienced spinner, but the experience didn't scar him. I tried consoling him during the lunch and tea intervals, but he remained chirpy. What counted against him was the ridiculously short boundary on one side. Mis-hits were going for six. A nightmare for a young spinner.'

John Morris agrees. 'When I got to the ground on the first morning, I thought the boundary towards the Extra Cover Bar was ridiculously short. Bowling from the pavilion end to a left-hander of Lara's class, with his ability to hook and pull, meant you were on a hiding to nothing.'

So it proved. But before Lara rewrote the record books, he scratched around on the second day and enjoyed several strokes of good fortune. The West Indian pace bowler Anderson Cummins had bowled enough overs at Lara in domestic cricket to believe he had spotted a weakness. He thought Lara stepped across his stumps early on, just a fraction too much, and would be vulnerable to a leg-stump yorker. He had dismissed him that way playing for Barbados.

Brian Lara, on his way to 501

Cummins' first ball to Lara was deliberately short, hoping he would have a go at the bouncer. He did, and it spliced up in the air between bowler and Morris at mid-on, agonisingly short of both. When he had got shakily to 12, Cummins tried the leg-stump yorker. It worked, and Lara was bowled behind his legs. But Peter Wight, umpiring at Cummins' end, had spotted a no ball. 'Durham's players were delighted,' he recalled, 'until they turned around and saw me with my arm up. Then, soon after, he was dropped by the wicket-keeper. I remember thinking that might be expensive. He then murdered the bowling. It was a privilege to see batting like that.'

Chris Scott's dropped catch behind the wicket when Lara was on 18 was on the monumental side of expensive. He remembers it with painful clarity. 'It was a regulation edge off Simon Brown, and it went straight in and out. I'd have caught it 99 times out of 100, even though it was very windy that day. A few overs earlier, I'd taken a good catch diving forward to get Dominic Ostler. Simon tended to wobble the ball around after it had pitched and the wind didn't help

– but no excuses. I've always been a bit of a cricket badger, who looked up to great players, and I wonder if I played the man not the ball for that nick. I froze, because of the stature of the batsman, and it just went in and out. Was I looking to throw the ball up too soon because we'd got such a great player so cheaply?'

Then Scott wrote his name into the lexicon of immortal cricket quotes as his mistake dawned on him. 'My first comment was "Oh, no!", followed by an expletive. At the end of the over, as we walked to the other end, I said to Wayne Larkins, who was alongside me at slip, "I bet he gets a hundred now." I thought no more of it until a couple of weeks later. Simon Hughes, who was commenting on a Sunday League game on TV, revealed what I had said, and the quote was all over the place after that. I regret that, especially when someone drops a catch these days and my quote gets dragged up on TV or radio.

'I really felt for Simon Brown that day, because he was bowling superbly that season and could have got into the England team if he'd achieved the rare feat of dismissing the great Lara so cheaply. He was the best

After the catch goes down: (left to right) Phil Bainbridge, Chris Scott and Wayne Larkins

bowler in the country around then but had to wait another two years for his England chance.'

At least the rain on the third day eased Scott's pain. 'I'd had a bad time on the Friday night after Lara got his hundred but, when it poured on the third day, I consoled myself that he wouldn't get masses more because there would probably be a declaration game. But when we only had four fit bowlers and were just playing for points, it dawned on me it was going to be a long day!'

Lara's attention to detail and hard work are often overlooked when dissecting his glorious strokeplay. At tea on the second day, after being reprieved twice, he was so dissatisfied with his batting that he headed for the nets and for throw-downs with his friend Keith Piper, looking for that elusive timing. After tea, he was outscored by Roger Twose and, although he reached 111* off 143 balls by the close, he was still uncertain in his touch.

On the Monday morning, Tim Munton drove into the ground around 8.30 and noticed with interest that Lara was already in the nets, working assiduously with Bob Woolmer. 'He had a set of stumps positioned at silly mid-off. He was worried about slicing the ball and therefore hitting the stumps. So he set himself to avoid hitting those stumps and that helped him bring his bat down straighter. On that second night, even though he'd got an unbeaten hundred, he felt he was slicing too much to third man. Not only was he an unbelievable talent, but he worked hard when he wasn't happy about his batting.'

By lunchtime, Lara's timing had returned and he plundered 174 runs in the morning session. But he still wasn't entirely convinced he was at his best. He faced more throwdowns with Piper on the outfield before having a significant conversation with Woolmer, Reeve and Munton.

Lara, on 285*, asked Woolmer what was the highest first-class record – and Woolmer, of all people, had been on the ground at Karachi in 1958/9 when Hanif Mohammad scored 499. 'My father was working over there, and I flew over for holidays from my prep school. Dad dropped me off at the ground where Hanif was closing in on the record, and he then went off to work. I didn't remember much about it. There was a big crowd, a matting wicket, a very rough outfield and a bloke getting run out. That bloke was Hanif, going for his 500th run, off the last ball of the day.'

Warwickshire v Durham, Edgbaston, 2, 3, 4 & 6 June 1994

Match drawn

Umpires: T.E. Jesty & P.B. Wight

Durham

W. Larkins	c Penney b Munton	13
M. Saxelby	b Small	19
J.E. Morris	c Lara b Smith P	204
S. Hutton	b Davis	61
P. Bainbridge *	c Reeve b Smith N	67
J.I. Longley	lbw b Smith N	24
C.W. Scott +	lbw b Small	13
A.C. Cummins	lbw b Twose	62
D.A. Graveney	not out	65
D.M. Cox		
S.J.E. Brown		
	b 2, lb 17, w 3, nb 6	28
	(for 8 wkts, dec)	**556**

1/35, 2/39, 3/225, 4/365, 5/393, 6/420, 7/422, 8/556

Small	22	8	80	2
Munton	28	4	103	1
Reeve	5	2	12	0
Smith PA	15	5	51	1
Davis	36	12	105	1
Smith NMK	32	6	97	2
Twose	9.5	1	42	1
Lara	11	1	47	0

Warwickshire

D.P. Ostler	c Scott b Cummins	8
R.G. Twose	c Cox b Brown	51
B.C. Lara	not out	501
T.L. Penney	c Hutton b Bainbridge	44
P.A. Smith	lbw b Cummins	12
K.J. Piper +	not out	116
D.A. Reeve *		
N.M.K. Smith		
R.P. Davis		
G.C. Small		
T.A. Munton		
	b 28, lb 22, w 2, nb 26	78
	(for 4 wkts, dec)	**810**

1/8, 2/123, 3/437, 4/488

Cummins	28	1	158	2
Brown	27	1	164	1
Bainbridge	33	4	169	1
Graveney	7	1	34	0
Cox	30	5	163	0
Larkins	5	0	39	0
Morris	5.5	1	33	0

So, if there was one person above all others in English cricket in 1994 who knew the highest individual first-class score, it was Bob Woolmer. He asked Lara, 'Why? You're not going for that?' Lara asked if Reeve was thinking of declaring. Reeve, conscious of the need to get the over-rate up for the season to avoid a fine, said a declaration was in his mind. Lara said he wanted to go for the record and walked away. Woolmer, a keen student of cricket history, told Reeve to let him have a crack at the record. 'I said, "Let's see how it goes." He was so single-minded that day.'

Woolmer felt there was now an inevitability about Lara establishing a new record. To be fair to Durham, no one wilted in the field, the bowlers kept running up and trying their darndest on a pitch that was now very flat, meat and drink to a player such as Lara. Trevor Penney, who made just 44 in a stand of 314, simply did what he was told by Lara. 'I ran when he told me to run, and for how many. He just told me to relax and enjoy it, we barely talked about the cricket in between overs. He had this amazing ability to switch off, then re-focus.'

At tea, Lara needed another 82 for the record, and his team-mates were more nervous than him. Neil Smith, next man in, recalls: 'I had pad rash! An astonishing feat was in prospect, and I kept telling myself, "Give Brian the strike, run when he says so, don't hog the strike." I was in a proper state.'

Mercifully for Smith, he was not needed. Keith Piper, Lara's trusted aide when he needed throw-downs earlier in the match, was still there, motoring to an unfussy century. Piper was to render Lara an invaluable service as the finger of history beckoned.

Lara was unaware that, if there was no prospect of an outright result in a championship match, then stumps would be pulled up half an hour early. In this instance, 5.30pm rather than six o'clock. Time was now against the little master, and Piper knew it.

John Morris began what was to prove the final over, with three dot balls. The fourth, a bouncer, clanged Lara on the helmet. 'He had three swats at it before it reached him,' recalls Morris. 'I'm the only bowler in first-class cricket to ping someone on 497* with a bouncer. What a claim to fame!'

By now, Piper had had enough. He realised that Lara didn't know the regulations. There were only two balls left, and three runs were needed. 'I went down the pitch to see if Brian knew what I knew. I had checked with both umpires and told him there were only two balls left. He just nodded and smashed the next ball through the covers for four.'

As the celebrations started in earnest, the commercial department went into overdrive, marching Lara across to the famous Edgbaston scoreboard for historic photographs. Hundreds of commemorative scorecards were being sold within an hour of Lara's final shot.

Hanif's brother, Mushtaq Mohammad, lived in Birmingham and tried to get to the ground in time for the historic moment, but he was held up in traffic and arrived ten minutes late.

Allan Donald was luckier. Although touring with the South Africans, Donald lived two miles away and often popped into Edgbaston. 'I watched Brian's last thirty runs with the members in the Extra Cover Bar, and it was just awesome to be watching cricket history. I loved being there with the members.'

One innings had catapulted Lara into the upper echelons of sporting superstardom. Over the next few days his agent's mobile phone went into meltdown as he cut eye-watering deals. For his part, Lara said all the right things in a chaotic press conference. 'The blow to my head was a surprise, but being told I needed three runs off two balls made me very nervous. I don't think I'm a great cricketer yet. I've still got a lot of cricket ahead of me, and I need to be more consistent.'

Well, there's nothing more consistent in recent decades than 1,176 runs from 1,175 balls in his first seven first-class innings for Warwickshire at an average of 235, nor an aggregate of 2,689 from 24 innings so far in 1994. Nor becoming the first batsman since Don Bradman in the 1930s to hold both the Test and first-class records.

Perhaps the opinion of Anderson Cummins is relevant: 'I was very impressed by his stamina. I knew he had the ability, but to concentrate for that long and to keep going was amazing.'

There were so many sub-plots from this match. The unlucky wicket-keeper Chris Scott soon got his miss out of his system 'because you play every day, don't you? But the following season wasn't a great one for me, and that Lara drop may have impacted on me. It did prey on my mind later on, but I have no one

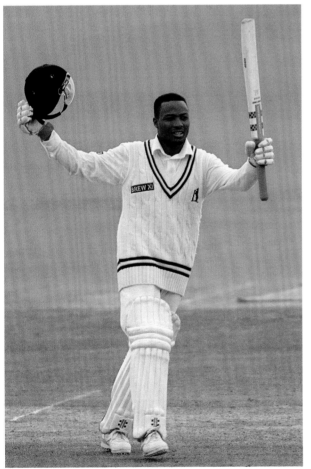

*Scenes from 501: (above) Reaching 100, (top right) with
Simon Brown and (bottom right) with Trevor Penney*

to blame but myself. I wasn't too impressed late in '94 when the Sports Personality of the Year producer asked me to come on the show on BBC TV because Brian Lara was picking up the Overseas Personality of the Year award. The producer had seen that quote from me. I declined! When it's mentioned to me these days I take it in good part the vast majority of the time, but I suppose it's defined me as a cricketer.'

John Morris remains a rarity: a batsman who scored a splendid double hundred on the first day but never gets a mention in any match reports.

David Cox had some sort of recompense next time he returned to Edgbaston, two years later, for a championship match. He took ten wickets in the game and scored 45, but Durham still lost. After topping the batting averages for Durham in 1996, he left the club two years later.

Perspective is needed over Lara's phenomenal achievement. The pitch was reported to Lord's by the umpires, as they deemed it too favourable for batting. With Durham missing two bowlers and the boundary so short on one side, it was cruel on the bowlers and fielders, with only 12 wickets falling for 1,366 in three days.

Lara seemed aware of the bias towards batsmen in this game because he didn't seem to glow with happiness afterwards. A proud sense of achievement, yes – but not euphoria. Perhaps he was just too fatigued. Perhaps he was aware that he had played far greater innings before in more testing circumstances. He certainly did so in subsequent innings for the West Indies, winning Test matches almost single-handedly against wonderful bowlers.

But you still have to score 501*. He had his luck – especially courtesy of the sharp-eyed umpire Wight – but his stamina was extraordinary and the way he battled back into form over three days to make history was admirable.

FIFTY BY FIFTY

Score	Mins	Balls	6s	4s
50	97	80	-	6
100	144	138	-	14
150	201	193	-	22
200	224	220	2	30
250	246	245	5	37
300	280	278	7	44
350	319	311	8	49
400	367	350	8	53
450	430	398	9	55
500	474	427	10	62

MILESTONES

100 First batsman to score seven 100s in eight first-class innings *(This remains a unique record)*

286 Highest score at Edgbaston, passing Peter May's 285 for England against West Indies in 1957 *(Alastair Cook, with 294 for England against India in 2011, has subsequently passed May, but Lara's 501 remains Edgbaston's only triple-century)*

306 Highest score by a Warwickshire batsman, passing 305* by Frank Foster in 1914 *(Mark Wagh has subsequently passed Foster with 315 at Lord's in 2001)*

325 Equalled Don Bradman's 1930 record of reaching 1,000 runs for the season in only seven innings

376 Passed his own 375, against England in April, as the highest score by a West Indian

386 Passed Bert Sutcliffe's 385, for Otago in 1952, as the highest score by a left-hander

425 Passed Archie MacLaren's 424, for Lancashire in 1894, as the highest score made in England

458 Scored his 347th run of the day, passing Charlie Macartney's 345 for Australia against Notts in 1921

475 Hit a record 69th boundary, passing Percy Perrin's 68 (all 4s) for Essex at Chesterfield in 1904

501 Highest first-class score, passing Hanif Mohammad's 499 for Karachi v Bhawalpur at Karachi in 1958/59

With stands of 314 with Trevor Penney and 322 with Keith Piper, he is the only batsman to have taken part in two triple-century partnership in the same innings.

His total of 1,551 runs in eight first-class innings (from his 375 at Antigua) passed the Australian Bill Ponsford's record of 1,400 runs in eight innings, for Victoria and an Australian XI, in 1927.

Lara became the holder of the record highest scores in both Test and first-class cricket. After nine years, in October 2003, he lost the Test record to Matthew Hayden's 380 for Australia but regained it with 400* against England in April 2004 – so, at the start of 2019, he has held the record for a total of 24 years. Only Don Bradman, from July 1930 to April 1933, has also held both records.

Dermot Reeve shares the limelight in front of the scoreboard and (below) the chaotic press conference. The author is to the right of Brian Lara in the pink shirt.

v Surrey, B&H Semi-Final, The Oval, 7 June

Warwickshire's supporters could have been forgiven for thinking that the sequel next day to Brian Lara's astonishing 501* would be a case of After the Lord Mayor's Show.

Instead, the players produced what was, given the circumstances, their most impressive display of the season. Knocking out a strong Surrey side unbeaten so far in one-day games was an excellent performance, but to manage it, with all the attendant hoopla over the previous 24 hours, was a tremendous effort.

Lara's contribution at The Oval was simply inspirational. Battling fatigue and the various emotions experienced in becoming a world record holder the day before, Lara batted down the order to gain some sort of physical respite. He had to be woken up to bat at number six, with the match in the balance, and he delivered. His 70 off 73 balls was simply Lara, with all the charm and finesse now almost taken for granted. But he decided the semi-final in that time at the crease, even though out on his feet.

'That innings was the hallmark of a great player,' says Gladstone Small. 'A true great rose to the occasion and tipped the balance for us.' John Morris, who bowled the historic delivery at 5.30 the night before, says Lara's 70 was far superior to 501* on a flat pitch against a limited Durham attack. 'You get the measure of a batsman when you examine what he does to win you a game. That's how the pros judge you. I can't imagine what it takes out of you to score 500, then travel down to London that night and be expected to put on a show when your team desperately needs you. That was an unbelievable performance from Brian.'

The challenges facing Lara at The Oval were daunting. His agent's determination to cash in on his world record added to his flowing personal in-tray. The after-match public attention at Edgbaston the night before was stifling enough, but all the way down to London the calls were coming through. He had to fulfil a hastily organised photo opportunity at the team hotel on the morning of the match after submitting to bleary-eyed interviews on TV and radio. Having heard the normally fluent Lara struggle to form sentences on Radio 4's Today programme at 8.30, I honestly believed he would be unable to play

two hours later. He seemed catatonic with fatigue, like one of those dancers in the American marathons of the 1930s, shuffling around for hours, desperately clinging on for money.

Stuart Nottingham, Warwickshire's physio, was concerned for Lara that morning. 'I drove him from our hotel to the ground, and he was extraordinarily tired, totally pooped. I almost had to drag him out of the hotel. No wonder he slept so much at The Oval. I felt sorry for him that day. Just 25 years of age, he had to deal with everyone wanting a piece of him now that he was a world star. It was too much at that age.'

For Lara's sake, the best scenario was to win the toss and bat on a typically true Oval pitch, with a fast outfield and hope that the openers batted long enough to allow their star number 3 some rest. Instead, Surrey won the toss, and Alec Stewart and Darren Bicknell couldn't wait to get out there.

Lara started in the slips, as usual, but couldn't concentrate and soon moved to the outfield. Gladstone Small recalls Lara's distress. 'He couldn't see the ball and, when he went out to the boundary, he couldn't pick it up, saying he was seeing stripes in his eyes. He was completely shattered.'

Lara lasted all but the last ten overs of Surrey's innings before he had to come off. We all wondered if his contribution to the game was over. At the end of the innings, he was fast asleep in the dressing room, and the players were concerned that he wouldn't be able to bat. Because he had been off for a certain amount of time, he would not be able to bat till four wickets were down. Bob Woolmer took charge: 'Don't wake him up, let him sleep.' 'That was great management,' says Small.

Lara finally emerged to join Asif Din on 120/4, with Surrey favourites, defending 267 and Tony Pigott bowling with pace and hostility. So far, Lara's limited-overs form had been patchy, but he chose this day to double his aggregate in his five previous one-day innings. Cometh the hour, cometh the man ...

Dermot Reeve joined Lara on 158/5. The game could have gone either way. But a stand of 93 in 20 overs between the genius, almost playing from memory, and the arch-improvisor decided the match, by the time Lara fell with just 17 needed.

It was a superb team victory, although Lara deservedly got the plaudits. Tight, sharp opening bowling from Munton and Small kept Surrey in check until they had the platform at 210/2, with Graham Thorpe and David Ward ready to accelerate. But Neil Smith snared them both, and the dangerous Ali Brown, in quick succession. The fielding was tigerish and inspiring. Dermot Reeve bowled cleverly, thwarting Surrey's momentum, captained with his usual imagination and anchored the victory charge with his usual aplomb.

Reeve picked up yet another Gold Award, and it would be churlish to minimise his all-round contribution. But Lara must have been a contender, given all that he had surmounted over the last 24 hours. Neil Smith agrees: 'Surrey were a top side, and we got into a position where we needed someone with authority and class to win it for us. Brian went out there virtually with matchsticks under his eyelids and did it. We all fed off his personal desire to be the very best he could.'

Paul Smith, who had stood alongside Lara on Tower Bridge early that morning as he fulfilled his commercial responsibilities, still marvels at that Oval innings. 'I'll never forget seeing Brian wrapped in towels in the dressing room. He wasn't well, mentally or physically. Only he could have played that innings; it was better than the 501*. Anyone who beats that won't have to play a semi-final the following day.'

This excellent win, and the manner in which it was accomplished, alerted at least one of the players to what was possible for the rest of the season. Neil Smith had seen enough false dawns and late season anti-climaxes at Edgbaston to avoid being over-optimistic, but the inspiration of Lara and the reaction of the rest of the squad were too obvious to discount.

'Brian's huge self-belief was starting to rub off on the rest of us. We were a strong unit anyway after winning the NatWest Trophy so impressively, and we brought that into the '94 season. But now we felt we could take on all-comers. That win over Surrey marked the first time I sensed we were onto something historic. If we could win there, with all the outside pressures crowding in on us, we would take some stopping.'

With one Lord's final banked, the road to the Treble lay ahead.

Surrey v Warwickshire, The Oval, 7 June 1994

Warwickshire won by four wickets

Umpires: D.T. Constant & B. Dudleston

Surrey

D.J. Bicknell		c & b Reeve	39
A.J. Stewart *+	c Burns	b Twose	24
G.P. Thorpe		c & b Smith N	87
D.M. Ward		b Smith N	61
A.D. Brown	c Penney	b Smith N	8
A.J. Hollioake	lbw	b Reeve	3
M.A. Butcher	c Munton	b Reeve	4
A.C.S. Pigott	*not out*		13
J. Boiling	*not out*		9
J.E. Benjamin			
C.E. Cuffy			
		lb 11, w 6, nb 2	19
55 overs		(for 7 wickets)	**267**

1/59, 2/92, 3/210, 4/232, 5/236, 6/242, 7/254

Small	11	2	38	0
Munton	11	2	36	0
Reeve	11	0	48	3
Twose	5	0	33	1
Smith NMK	8	0	54	3
Smith PA	9	0	47	0

Warwickshire

D.P. Ostler		b Pigott	44
M. Burns +	c Thorpe	b Benjamin	18
R.G. Twose	c Stewart	b Pigott	46
P.A. Smith	lbw	b Pigott	8
Asif Din	c Cuffy	b Boiling	19
B.C. Lara		b Hollioake	70
D.A. Reeve *	*not out*		46
T.L. Penney	*not out*		12
N.M.K. Smith			
G.C. Small			
T.A. Munton			
		lb 3, nb 4	7
54.1 overs		(for 6 wickets)	**270**

1/28, 2/106, 3/117, 4/120, 5/158, 6/251

Cuffy	11	0	66	0
Benjamin	11	0	41	1
Butcher	3.1	0	26	0
Pigott	11	0	43	3
Hollioake	7	0	49	1
Boiling	11	1	42	1

v Northamptonshire, Northampton, 23 – 27 June

This was the most intensively competitive championship game that Warwickshire played all summer.

It involved huge pride and great skills from both sides, an enthralling duel between Brian Lara and Curtly Ambrose, an ugly spat on the field between Lara and his captain that continued in the dressing room and ended in an exhilarating run chase by the Bears that saw them get home with just three balls to spare.

Obviously the match and its outcome meant more to the Warwickshire players, but it was also memorable for the Northants players, like their spinner Nick Cook: 'It was a high-quality game, played properly. Really intense, like a Test match. We had great crowds in every day – like a one-day semi – and we all fed off a fantastic atmosphere.'

David Ripley, Northants' wicket-keeper that day and now their head coach, still talks about the game. 'I was telling our young players about it only the other day. In these days of T20, with the IPL and other money-spinners luring away the top players from our domestic cricket, they need to know about the quality on display in the mid-1990s. There were so many world-class players then in county cricket, and England players were coming back to play for their counties. No central contracts then. They were expected to perform for their employers.

'That first day in particular against Warwickshire was different from any other I have experienced. It wasn't just another routine day of county cricket but a great one – even though we were on the wrong end of it – and we all got lifted up by the challenge and the sense of occasion.'

It certainly was a high-octane first day. Warwickshire closed on 448/9, the centrepiece another astonishing innings from Lara. His 197 featured punishment to all the bowlers except one: Curtly Ambrose. He was at his peak that summer for Northants, finishing top of the first-class averages, and he was intent on overcoming his West Indian team-mate in their duel.

Ambrose had enormous professional respect for Lara. His Northants team-mate Paul Taylor recalls getting the heads-up about Lara a couple of years earlier. 'Amby said to me, "Watch out for B.C. Lara,

he's the next great batsman," and he was spot on. That was a terrific contest between the two on that first day. I was at the other end, trying to stem the flow, while Amby was full on at him, going for just over one an over, beating the bat regularly. For me, Amby was the best in the world at that time, and he really wanted to get Lara out.'

That was something Ambrose had never managed in his duels with Lara in domestic cricket in the Caribbean. And he still failed to lower his colours, despite conceding just 12 runs in the 45 deliveries to Lara. Ripley watched the contest at close quarters. 'It was fantastic, Curtly bowling rockets, giving Lara the big stare, desperate to get him out, or at least not concede any runs. So much pride from both great cricketers, both on top of their game.'

A Pyhrric victory of sorts was claimed by Ambrose when he hit Lara on the head, splitting his helmet, but he had scored 170 by then. That blow would have ramifications later in the game but, after shrugging it off, Lara continued to blaze away. He was only dismissed by a wonderful leaping catch at long leg by Mal Loye, the ball destined for the six that would have brought Lara to his double century. Paul Taylor, the bowler who benefited from Loye's catch, wasn't gulled by this success. 'I can't exactly say I bounced him out! He'd hit your best ball for six, and you'd stand there, wondering what to bowl next. He'd place the ball deliberately two or three metres wide of the fielder. It was a privilege to bowl at Lara.'

Nick Cook agrees, although he had a cunning plan early on to frustrate Lara. But Baldrick was thwarted by Captain Blackadder, aka Allan Lamb, the skipper. 'I bowled round the wicket, very tight on his middle stump, trying to tie him down. For a few overs it worked, and I hardly went for a run. But Lamby convinced me to be more attacking, to bowl over the wicket at Lara. That only freed up his arms, and he kept driving me through the offside. So my plan was scuppered. But it probably wouldn't have worked – he played it so late, he must have seen the ball so early. He just found the gaps, without thinking about it seemingly. Quick hands, amazing bat speed from such a light bat. Timing, poise, elegance, charisma – what more do you want?'

Trevor Penney scored just 39 out of a stand of 168 with Lara and felt totally inadequate at the other end. 'Brian made me look stupid, he was so brilliant that day, especially against Ambrose. There was no Caribbean love between those two that day, it felt like war. I thought, "I'm in trouble here" as the ball kept flying past our noses. Brian loved the battle, he wouldn't shy away. Those two battled with such pride against each other.'

Just as well Lara had batted so wonderfully because he was late arriving in the morning and had to face the ire of Dennis Amiss and Dermot Reeve. By now, the captain was realising that Lara was taking little notice of his notions of team discipline, and the chief executive was nominally in control of Lara's time-keeping. Lara was a no-show for net practice and the fielding drills, and Amiss and Reeve were getting angrier.

Kirk Russell, the Northants physio, had a close view of the fractious discussions when Lara eventually turned up. 'It was very close to the start when Lara did turn up. I got turfed out of my room on the balcony so that the three of them could have a tense meeting.

Clearly Amiss and Reeve were fed up, and it was just as well that Warwickshire were batting first and the openers put on a decent stand, because Lara was in no state to bat when he arrived.

'He was asleep in their dressing room when the first wicket fell and he had to be woken up. When he walked past me on the balcony, he was bleary-eyed, half-asleep and he asked, "Which end am I batting?" Just as well he was a genius, he was sensational that day.'

He was reprieved first ball, a desperately close lbw shout from Tony Penberthy. After umpire Allan Jones ruled in his favour – to Northants' intense disappointment – Lara spent a few overs on reconnaissance, getting his feet moving, combatting the fire and bounce of Ambrose, and then played a scintillating innings.

It was to be his last meaningful involvement in the match, as the gulf between Lara and Reeve became public, with Amiss pressed into the role of peacemaker.

On the second morning, Lara complained of a headache after being struck on the head by Ambrose

Northamptonshire v Warwickshire, Northampton 23, 24, 25 & 27 June 1994

Warwickshire won by four wickets

Umpires: A.A. Jones & B. Leadbeater

Warwickshire

Batsman	Dismissal	Runs	Dismissal 2	Runs 2
A.J. Moles	c Lamb b Penberthy	32	(6) b Ambrose	10
R.G. Twose	c Ripley b Penberthy	35	b Curran	39
B.C. Lara	c Loye b Taylor	197	(7) c Lamb b Cook	2
D.P. Ostler	c Ripley b Taylor	17	(1) b Cook	87
T.L. Penney	c Ripley b Ambrose	39	(3) c sub b Ambrose	43
P.A. Smith	b Taylor	1	(4) st Ripley b Cook	4
D.A. Reeve *	c Felton b Taylor	5	(5) not out	15
K.J. Piper +	st Ripley b Cook	11	not out	7
N.M.K. Smith	c Penberthy b Curran	28		
G. Welch	not out	35		
T.A. Munton	c Lamb b Ambrose	36		
Extras	b 6, lb 14, w 1, nb 6	27	b 1, lb 11, w 1, nb 10	23
Total		**463**	(for 6 wkts)	**230**

1/71, 2/86, 3/124, 4/292, 5/303, 6/319, 7/348, 8/365, 9/395, 10/463
1/107, 2/168, 3/190, 4/191, 5/208, 6/213

Northamptonshire

Batsman	Dismissal	Runs	Dismissal 2	Runs 2
R.J. Warren	lbw b Munton	10	(9) not out	94
N.A. Felton	c Reeve b Munton	5	c Penney b Smith P	23
R.J. Bailey	c Piper b Welch	54	c Piper b Munton	2
A.J. Lamb *	c Penney b Welch	81	b Smith N	22
M.B. Loye	c Reeve b Welch	3	c Penney b Welch	113
K.M. Curran	b Smith P	23	c Piper b Smith N	56
A.L. Penberthy	c Piper b Munton	21	c Penney b Munton	19
D. Ripley +	lbw b Munton	4	(1) c Piper b Munton	16
C.E.L. Ambrose	lbw b Reeve	2	(11) b Munton	0
N.G.B. Cook	c Piper b Munton	8	(8) c Reeve b Smith P	1
J.P. Taylor	not out	4	(10) c Reeve b Munton	26
Extras	b 9, lb 4, w 5, nb 34	52	b 7, lb 11, w 1, nb 32	51
Total		**267**		**423**

1/11, 2/32, 3/169, 4/181, 5/194, 6/240, 7/252, 8/255, 9/257, 10/267
1/43, 2/43, 3/48, 4/83, 5/205, 6/249, 7/256, 8/341, 9/423, 10/423

Bowler	O	M	R	W	O	M	R	W
Ambrose	27.4	10	49	2	13	1	56	2
Taylor	32	4	139	4	3	0	20	0
Curran	18	4	53	1	6	0	52	1
Penberthy	19	2	105	2	6	0	39	0
Cook	13	3	69	1	9.3	2	51	3
Bailey	6	0	28	0				

Bowler	O	M	R	W	O	M	R	W
Munton	25.1	4	53	5	41.4	12	79	5
Reeve	20	8	29	1	17	8	24	0
Welch	12	1	58	3	26	8	81	1
Smith PA	14	2	53	1	30	8	90	2
Smith NMK	12	3	33	0	51	18	118	2
Twose	9	0	28	0	10	5	13	0

the day before. According to Reeve, he was grumpy in the field when Northants duly batted. He says Lara advised him to take off Munton after getting two early wickets, but Reeve countered that he liked eight-overs spells and that he was a captain's dream. Lara snapped back, 'He's a bad captain's dream.'

Lara then aimed a volley at umpire Allan Jones from the slips when Jones at square leg ruled a nick from Rob Bailey hadn't carried to the keeper. Jones said, 'I saw the ball bounce – not out,' to which Lara replied, 'You must have ****ing good eyesight then!' Jones, an experienced hand as an umpire, snapped back, 'There was nothing wrong with my eyesight when I gave you not out first ball yesterday – you concentrate on your batting, and I'll do the umpiring.'

Reeve says he tried to reason with Lara, but his whole body language was dismissive and disrespectful of Jones. A few overs later, an edge off Bailey did carry to Keith Piper and, as the fielders celebrated, Lara shouted over to Jones, 'Well, that one carried by three feet!'

As the fielders gathered around, Reeve says he simply said, 'Brian – don't', but Lara then unleashed a torrent of abuse at him. He is adamant that Lara told him to '**** off!' seven times, in front of his team-mates.

Time for full disclosure. I collaborated with Reeve in his autobiography and, 18 months after the Northampton flashpoint, he still had a very clear recollection of what happened next, and the precise dialogue. Dominic Ostler, Keith Piper and Graeme Welch, all standing close by as the new batsman walked to the middle, have confirmed the veracity of Reeve's account to me.

Reeve says he instantly realised it was now a vital moment for him, that his leadership was on the line as Lara challenged him. 'I said firmly, "Brian, you're turning into a prima donna." My exact words, no swearing and not loudly. The rest of the team melted away in embarrassment, leaving the captain to deal with a superstar out of control.'

At the end of the over, in which he had abused his captain and the umpire, he pointed to his knee, shouted to Allan Jones 'sore knee' and walked off the field. He was to remain in the dressing room for the next two days of the match. Reeve read Lara's account in his book with interest. 'He says he went off because he was feeling dizzy, that the spat was just a minor incident. He said there was no intention to abuse the umpire or dispute the decision to his face, that it was the kind of incident which happens occasionally in cricket and is forgotten by the time the next interval comes around. That was nonsense.

'That was the worst example of player indiscipline I have experienced in my career. I had never heard a team-mate speak like that to another, never mind a captain being on the receiving end. It led to the worst week of my cricketing life, as Warwickshire handled Brian Lara with kid gloves and made me realise I lacked support at the club.'

Reeve believes he was made to feel expendable over the next week, that in the short term Lara's well-being was more important to the club than the captain's. He was incensed that Lara initially opted out of the Sunday League match at Northampton, then changed his mind under keen persuasion from Dennis Amiss. Lara's absence would have alerted the media because it was a televised match, and Amiss had to work overtime on Lara, who was still complaining of headaches and a sore knee. Having told Trevor Penney he was playing, Reeve then had to relegate him to twelfth man to accommodate a reluctant Lara.

Over the next few days, Reeve had meetings with the cricket management and senior players. He says he was left with the feeling that he just had to grin and bear it. He felt isolated, even more so when Amiss told him that Lara was demanding an apology for calling him 'a prima donna'. He was dismayed. 'I said he was turning into a prima donna, which is not the same thing. Dennis made it clear that Lara should get his own way, even though he and the senior players would try to deal with it.

'At that point, I felt Brian Lara was bigger than Warwickshire CCC. With my form below par, Brian was undeniably more productive than me, and they could allow me to fade away, with Tim Munton taking over the captaincy. Hanging over my head was a major consideration – the benefit system. That's always been one of the ways in which a county keeps a player sweet, as you wait to be granted one, keeping your nose clean. I was due a benefit and I knew that, if I refused to play ball over the Lara situation, I might miss out.'

Reeve swallowed his pride and phoned Lara, who eventually said he was sorry the incident had happened. He then added the tart rider, 'But you never wanted me here in the first place', a reference to Phil Simmons and Manoj Prabhakar being at the top of the club's list at the end of the previous season. In the end, Lara agreed that he and Reeve had to make the best of the situation.

'According to Lara's book, this was the worst fortnight of his life. I wonder how he would have felt in my position. I was isolated, out of form as a player, getting no support on a serious disciplinary matter, and having to swallow my pride because I needed a benefit.'

Although some of the first-team players would have been relaxed about Reeve not playing, others were more vocal in their support. On the third day of the Northants match, the follow-on was enforced, and the Warwickshire bowlers toiled manfully to take seven second-innings wickets on a flat pitch and in uncomfortable heat. Lara spent that day in the dressing room, feeling unwell. At lunch and tea, he asked the score. Roger Twose, not a docile, conformist character and very much in the Reeve camp over the incident, replied, 'Why don't you get up and have a look at the scoreboard?'

Tim Munton, in the vanguard of the pursuit of victory with ten wickets in the match from 67 valiant overs, feels Lara could have handled the situation better. 'It's a shame that, as we look back on such a great year, it's tainted by the relationship between Dermot and Brian. But twenty blokes living in each other's pockets for six months is always going to have its flashpoints. Looking back, of course we all could have done things differently to make it more harmonious. But our success is testament to the deep bond and respect we all had for each other most of the time. A lot of players from other teams ask how did we maintain that spirit – great spirit comes from shared goals and being successful. Factions become major issues when you're not winning. The fact that we were successful helped us block out the negative stuff and move on. That Northampton match epitomised how good we were at concentrating on the essentials, where it really mattered. Whilst I suspect Christmas cards don't pass between Australia and Trinidad, ultimately Dermot and Brian deserve credit for putting the flash

point of Northampton behind them for the common good of the team for the rest of the season.'

Munton's durability made a huge impression on a young player making his championship debut. Graeme Welch bowled first change, snaring Rob Bailey and Allan Lamb for his first two victims, and added 68 useful runs for the last wicket with Munton – it was the stuff of dreams for the 22-year-old. 'I couldn't believe my luck. What an insight into the game at that level. I'm standing at short leg, listening to Lara and Reeve having a pop at each other, then ducking out of the way of Ambrose's bouncers. Tim copped a full toss from him that he inside edged onto his thigh. It gave him the biggest, blackest bruise, from groin to knee, that I have ever seen. Yet he still got into line to Ambrose. Tim set a great example to me. These blokes were legends to me, yet they all made me feel so relaxed. It was an incredible experience.'

Despite being on the back foot for almost the whole match, Northants wouldn't buckle. Loye batted more than seven hours, and the batsmen really had to be winkled out on the final afternoon.

The target was 228 in 38 overs, against an attack boasting three Test bowlers and that fierce competitor, Kevin Curran. With their own justified designs on the title, Northants would not bend the knee without a monumental effort in the field.

Dominic Ostler batted fearlessly to set up the charge, smashing 87 off 80 balls, having been promoted from four to opener. By now, Ostler was a vital member of the batting line-up. Flexible, able to open or bat in the middle order, he was growing in assurance, biffing powerfully off the front foot and subtly using the reverse sweep. He set a magnificent example when Warwickshire chased their target after tea. 'I loved the challenge of opening against Ambrose. I hit him for a massive six, hooking over square leg off the meat of the bat. As I stood there, savouring how far the ball had disappeared, he loomed over me and said, "If you do that again, I'll kill you." That's how much he and his team-mates wanted to avoid defeat. And that's why it was such a great win for us.'

So much had happened on and off the field over those four dramatic, draining days. That tremendous victory maintained Warwickshire's buoyancy as July loomed. If they kept winning, the Lara/Reeve imbroglio could be shunted into the sidings.

v Lancashire, Edgbaston, 30 June – 4 July

Trevor Penney was never the sort to talk up his contributions. The ultimate, selfless team man, Penney preferred to talk about the deeds of his team-mates rather than his exceptional fielding and under-rated batting. So when Penney says his hundred in this match was his best innings for the club, the stage is his.

With Brian Lara missing through a knee injury, it was time for the other established batsmen to fill the gap against a powerful Lancashire bowling attack. Penney did just that, hitting 111 off just 130 balls. On a rock-hard pitch, green at both ends, the great Wasim Akram was a formidable force, and Penney stood firm.

'It was always great facing Wasim because he was out to intimidate you and either get you out or knock you out. He was very verbal and aggressive. I preferred that type of bowling rather than the medium-paced dibbly dobblers, with the wicket-keeper standing up. I was very proud to help win this one for the team. A crucial victory over a top side.'

Penney had a kestrel's eye and wristy, improvisational style. He didn't always look secure against fast bowling, but he had his own method of playing and wouldn't be intimidated, despite his charming, modest personality. Tim Munton felt it was a crucial innings in Penney's development. 'He had been pigeon-holed as a batsman who was a brilliant finisher in one-day games, coming in at six or seven, running swiftly, playing some unorthodox shots with those hockey player's hands, but this hundred defined him as a true championship batsman in the middle order. He really showed his mettle in a tough situation.'

Jason Ratcliffe, who added 136 with Penney for the fourth wicket, felt the hundred was a tremendous innings. 'Trevor didn't always look easy on the eye, but he had stacks of bottle. He had quick wrists and feet and ran so fast between the wickets that he kept rotating the strike. He had 30 on the board before you knew it. It was a fast wicket, and Wasim was seriously quick.'

It was also a major test for Ratcliffe, batting at number five against one of the championship's best attacks. Although missing out on an opening slot at

the start of the season, he diligently scored a stack of runs in the seconds (1,219 runs that summer at an average of 55.40), and kept hoping for a recall. It came when he was playing at Swansea for the second XI. 'I got the call on the first morning to say that Lara was out with a sore knee, so I dashed up to Edgbaston. It was a psychological test for all of us, trying to fill the gap left by Brian, and Lancashire were a heavyweight team. I just wanted to play and was really pleased with my 69. Mind you, Brian would have got 169!'

Graeme Welch, playing in only his second championship match, gained further experience of the mental demands of county cricket. On the first day, he bounced Wasim first ball, hitting him on the hand, then the next ball he bowled him middle stump for nought. He gave Wasim a verbal send-off as his team-mates gathered round him. 'One of the lads said, "You're a brave man, giving Wasim the verbals. Wait till you bat against him. Do you know how quick he is?" I did soon enough!'

When Welch came into bat at number seven, he soon grasped what lay ahead. 'In front of me there was only Wasim and the umpire. Everyone else was behind the bat.'

Wasim's first ball, a bouncer, clanged Welch on the grille, by his left cheek. He never saw it. The helmet was cracked inwards, and he needed a replacement. 'Roger Twose sent his out, but it was about three sizes too big and it kept slipping into my eyeline. I could barely see a thing. And I was due to face Wasim Akram, who had the pin with me!'

Wasim decided to go round the wicket to Welch, who by then knew he was in for a torrid exploration of his technique and nerve. Second-eleven cricket had not prepared the young man for a challenge like this. 'Next ball, Wasim bowls me one that's short and wide, so I had a flash at it. I got just a feather on it, to be caught behind. At tea Dickie Davis, who was the non-striker, said, "Why did you walk? The umpire wasn't going to give you out." I said, "It seemed like a good idea!" My Dad still has that dented grille as a reminder of Wasim and, when I look at it, I think I had a lucky escape.'

After Wasim and Glenn Chapple blew away the Warwickshire tail, a slender lead of 15 didn't bode well for the Bears, especially as they had to bat last on a pitch that was turning and bouncing on the third day. Perfect for Neil Smith, who improved on his career-best figures for the second home game in a row.

A target of 180 on a tricky wicket was hardly a formality but, after Andy Moles and Roger Twose blunted Wasim's initial, hostile burst, the Bears cantered to victory just before the forecasted rain materialised. Twose's masterly innings again underlined the growing maturity of the other batsmen that papered over the cracks left by Lara's absence. No one could replace a genius, but it was encouraging to see others take responsibility.

That was an important factor for Tim Munton, who was hugely encouraged by the win. Before the match, in a meeting with Dermot Reeve, Dennis Amiss and Bob Woolmer, he had to stick to his guns over team selection. 'Dermot was already out with a groin problem, Brian was highly doubtful, and it was suggested we rest a few more players for the Lancashire game. The reasoning was that we had a great chance of winning all three one-day competitions, with the championship not on the priority list. I disagreed. I felt we could win the title, because we were now on a roll and confidence was soaring.

'Eventually I got my way, and that was a fork in the road for me. I didn't know how many games I would be captaining, but I felt I had to have the sides I wanted. No key players should be rested, unless they were unfit. In my psyche that Lancashire game was such a big one. It gave me so much confidence that I could lead the team and that we could kick on if we were without important players. After that match, selecting the strongest possible team for championship games was never an issue.'

And if Messrs Reeve, Amiss and Woolmer needed any further persuasion after this match about Warwickshire's title credentials, a glance at the table would have been reassuring. Three wins in a row, five victories out of eight, still unbeaten and they were now fourth in the table. At the halfway mark, Warwickshire were building momentum. The inevitable injuries didn't appear to be slowing their progress.

Warwickshire v Lancashire, Edgbaston 30 June, 1, 2 & 4 July 1994

Warwickshire won by six wickets

Umpires: V.A. Holder & M.J. Kitchen

Lancashire

G.D. Lloyd	b Small	7	c Piper b Small		0
S.P. Titchard	lbw b Munton	3	b Smith		28
J.P. Crawley	c Davis b Welch	141	b Munton		54
N.H. Fairbrother	c Piper b Munton	76	b Smith		12
N.J. Speak	c Penney b Welch	32	c Penney b Smith		6
M. Watkinson *	st Piper b Smith	40	lbw b Smith		17
Wasim Akram	b Welch	0	c Ratcliffe b Smith		22
P.J. Martin	b Davis	17	lbw b Smith		0
W.K. Hegg +	c Ostler b Davis	0	c Ostler b Munton		2
G. Yates	c Piper b Small	33	b Smith		19
G. Chapple	*not out*	19	*not out*		5
	lb 8, nb 16	24	b 9, lb 6, w 4, nb 10		29
		392			**194**

1/4, 2/28, 3/192, 4/274, 5/287, 6/293, 7/334, 8/338, 9/342, 10/392
1/0, 2/100, 3/108, 4/114, 5/137, 6/150, 7/150, 8/161, 9/187, 10/194

Small	15.5	3	45	2	5	3	7	1
Munton	17	3	52	2	26	7	62	2
Welch	15	3	72	3	10	2	44	0
Twose	12	2	32	0	4	0	16	0
Davis	30	8	99	2	1	0	8	0
Smith	25	4	84	1	20	9	42	7

Warwickshire

A.J. Moles	c Crawley b Yates	87	c Hegg b Chapple		25
R.G. Twose	b Wasim	38	b Watkinson		90
D.P. Ostler	b Yates	25	c Hegg b Yates		22
T.L. Penney	c Lloyd b Wasim	111	*not out*		31
J.D. Ratcliffe	c Crawley b Chapple	69	c & b Watkinson		0
K.J. Piper +	c Fairbrother b Chapple	0	*not out*		5
G. Welch	c Hegg b Wasim	5			
N.M.K. Smith	c Lloyd b Chapple	3			
R.P. Davis	c Titchard b Wasim	9			
G.C. Small	c Hegg b Chapple	0			
T.A. Munton *	*not out*	6			
	b 10, lb 20, w 2, nb 22	54	b 5, lb 1, nb 4		10
		407	(for 4 wkts)		**183**

1/111, 2/162, 3/243, 4/379, 5/381, 6/386, 7/390, 8/394, 9/395, 10/407
1/75, 2/122, 3/171, 4/171

Wasim Akram	36.4	10	82	4	16	5	39	0
Martin	22	5	57	0	5	1	21	0
Chapple	22	5	52	4	8	1	33	1
Watkinson	25	5	88	0	19.2	5	58	2
Yates	24	3	98	2	2	0	26	1

Results: 2 June to 4 July

County Championship

June 2,3,4,6 Edgbaston Durham **Match drawn**
Durham 556-8 dec (Morris 204) Warwickshire 810-4 dec (Lara 501*, Piper 116*)

June 16,17,18,20 Edgbaston Kent **Won by 76 runs**
Warwickshire 417 (Twose 142, Ostler 94) & 288-6 dec (Ostler 87) Kent 359 (Hooper 136) & 270 (Smith N 7-133)

June 23,24,25,27 Northampton Northamptonshire **Won by four wickets**
Warwickshire 463 (Lara 197) & 230-6 (Ostler 87) Northamptonshire 267 (Munton 5-53) & 423 (Munton 5-79)

June 30, July 1,2,4 Edgbaston Lancashire **Won by six wickets**
Lancashire 392 (Crawley 141) & 194 (Smith N 7-42) Warwickshire 407 (Penney 111, Moles 87, Ratcliffe 69) & 183-4 (Twose 90)

AXA Equity & Law League

June 5 Edgbaston Durham **Won by 84 runs**
Warwickshire 236-8 *(40 overs)* (Ostler 83) Durham 152 *(39.2 overs)* (Smith N 3-27)

June 19 Edgbaston Kent **Won by six wickets**
Kent 210-7 *(40 overs)* (Ward 63, Smith N 3-34) Warwickshire 211-4 *(38.1 overs)* (Asif Din 86*, Lara 63)

June 26 Northampton Northamptonshire **Won by 114 runs**
Warwickshire 218-6 *(40 overs)* (Ostler 78) Northamptonshire 104 *(33.2 overs)* (Smith N 4-19, Davis 3-19)

July 3 Edgbaston Lancashire **Lost by 93 runs**
Lancashire 204-7 *(40 overs)* Warwickshire 111 *(29.4 overs)* (Yates 4-34)

Benson & Hedges Cup

June 7 *(Semi-Final)* The Oval Surrey **Won by four wickets**
Surrey 267-7 *(55 overs)* (Reeve 3-48, Smith N 3-54) Warwickshire 270-6 *(54.1 overs)* (Lara 70, Twose 46, Ostler 44)

NatWest Bank Trophy

June 21,22 *(1st Round)* Edgbaston Bedfordshire **Won by 197 runs**
Warwickshire 361-8 *(60 overs)* (Twose 110, Ostler 81) Bedfordshire 164 *(56.3 overs)* (Robinson 67)

County Championship

	P	W	L	D	Bt	Bl	Pts
Surrey	9	6	2	1	22	30	148
Leicestershire	8	5	2	1	24	27	131
Nottinghamshire	9	5	1	3	20	28	128
Warwickshire	8	5	-	3	22	25	127
Essex	8	4	2	2	16	30	110
Durham	9	3	5	1	23	29	100
Middlesex	8	3	-	5	21	26	95
Sussex	8	3	1	4	18	25	91
Lancashire	8	3	3	2	13	28	89
Somerset	8	3	4	1	19	20	87
Gloucestershire	8	2	3	3	12	29	81
Northamptonshire	9	2	3	4	12	21	65
Worcestershire	8	1	3	4	23	26	65
Kent	8	1	4	3	18	26	60
Derbyshire	8	1	5	2	16	24	56
Glamorgan	8	1	3	4	14	22	44
Hampshire	8	-	4	4	14	22	44
Yorkshire	8	-	3	5	17	27	44

AXA Equity & Law League

	P	W	L	T	NR	Pts
Lancashire	8	6	2	-	-	24
Warwickshire	7	6	1	-	-	24
Yorkshire	8	5	2	-	1	22
Worcestershire	7	5	1	-	1	22
Nottinghamshire	9	4	3	-	2	20
Surrey	8	4	2	-	2	20
Glamorgan	7	4	2	-	1	18
Durham	8	3	2	1	2	18
Leicestershire	7	4	3	-	-	16
Kent	8	4	4	-	-	16
Derbyshire	7	3	3	-	1	14
Hampshire	7	3	4	-	-	12
Somerset	7	3	4	-	-	12
Sussex	8	2	5	-	1	10
Northamptonshire	8	1	5	1	1	8
Middlesex	8	2	6	-	-	8
Essex	7	1	6	-	1	6
Gloucestershire	7	-	6	-	1	2

v Worcestershire, B&H Final, Lord's, 9 July

How often does a Lord's final resemble a soufflé that failed to rise? That was certainly the case here, as Warwickshire cantered home with almost ten overs to spare.

It had been one of the more eagerly anticipated finals of recent years. Local rivals who knocked enough sparks off each other in their games to ensure no quarter would be given. Steve Rhodes, Richard Illingworth and Neal Radford stood comparison with Keith Piper, Dermot Reeve and Roger Twose when hyper-aggression on the field was assessed, while Tom Moody and Graeme Hick were in Brian Lara's class as match-winners.

There was every reason to believe this one would be a classic, given good weather. With Lara a colossus that summer, neutrals also wanted a Lord's ticket: no wonder it was a 29,000 sell-out.

But Worcestershire didn't do themselves justice. Professionals in sport hate the word 'choke', as if it suggests a lack of mettle, but there's no doubt this

Crucial wickets in the morning
Top : Keith Piper catches Tim Curtis off (right) Gladstone Small
Bottom: (left) Trevor Penney after running out Tom Moody, (right) Paul Smith after trapping Graeme Hick lbw

talented, experienced group of players failed to deliver on this big occasion. And their opponents, yet to win the B&H Cup after just one losing final in 22 years, needed no second bidding to keep the collective boot on Worcestershire's windpipe.

Perhaps the die was cast the day before, when the Worcestershire players had a peek at the pitch. The captain, Tim Curtis, remembers his dismay. 'When they peeled back the covers, we couldn't believe the surface was so green and damp. You expect that in September, for the NatWest Final, when there's dew around and it's not so warm, but not in midsummer. Looking back it was case of win the toss, win the game.'

And Curtis lost it. The day eventually blossomed into a lovely, warm midsummer afternoon, but it was hazy in the morning and the pitch hadn't dried out. The ball swung, and Worcestershire batted tentatively, as if expecting the worst. The plan was for the openers to blunt the new ball craft of Gladstone Small and Tim Munton, protecting the heavy artillery of Hick and Moody as the wicket eased.

But Small and Munton gave a masterclass in how to bowl in helpful conditions. They bowled the first 17 overs off the reel, Small protecting his troublesome groin strain by bowling outright his allotted 11 overs. They gave the batsmen nothing to hit and, by the time 11 overs had gone, both openers were out.

At one stage Hick scored 11 runs off 46 deliveries; it was that tough. Paul Smith, the man for the big occasion, nailed him lbw, and all the bowlers chipped in handily, maintaining the pressure. That told on Moody eventually. He had laboured long and hard before chancing his arm to keep the strike. He chose to run to Trevor Penney. End of story. A direct hit. Run out. Déjà vu.

Twose and Ostler started jauntily, and the result was never in doubt after they put on 91, despite Lara failing again in a one-day game, a surprising feature of his 'annus mirabilis'. It didn't matter. Twose encapsulated Warwickshire's collective self-confidence by pulling out the reverse sweep to Richard Illingworth's first delivery. They liked that up on the Warwickshire balcony. Illingworth was one of the Worcestershire players they particularly enjoyed winding up, because of his short fuse and Yorkshire truculence. They never gave the spinner much peace when he bowled or batted against them.

Warwickshire v Worcestershire, Lord's, 9 July 1994

Warwickshire won by six wickets

Umpires: H.D. Bird & K.E. Palmer

Worcestershire

T.S. Curtis *	c Piper	b Small	13
A.C.H. Seymour		b Munton	3
G.A. Hick	lbw	b Smith P	27
T.M. Moody	run out		47
G.R. Haynes	c Piper	b Smith N	22
D.A. Leatherdale	c Ostler	b Smith P	4
S.J. Rhodes +	lbw	b Twose	0
S.R. Lampitt	c Penney	b Smith P	1
R.K. Illingworth	lbw	b Reeve	18
N.V. Radford	*not out*		23
P.J. Newport	*not out*		1
	lb 2, w 5, nb 4		11
55 overs	(for 9 wickets)		**170**

1/10, 2/28, 3/55, 4/100, 5/124, 6/124, 7/125, 8/126, 9/168

Small	11	4	26	1
Munton	11	3	29	1
Smith PA	11	1	34	3
Reeve	9	1	38	1
Smith NMK	5	0	16	1
Twose	8	1	25	1

Warwickshire

D.P. Ostler	run out		55
R.G. Twose	run out		37
B.C. Lara	c Hick	b Newport	8
P.A. Smith	*not out*		42
Asif Din	c Rhodes	b Moody	15
D.A. Reeve *	*not out*		9
T.L. Penney			
K.J. Piper +			
N.M.K. Smith			
G.C. Small			
T.A. Munton			
	lb 1, w 5		6
44.2 overs	(for 4 wickets)		**172**

1/91, 2/98, 3/103, 4/147

Moody	11	2	31	1
Newport	8	0	29	1
Lampitt	9.2	1	38	0
Illingworth	6	0	22	0
Radford	8	0	39	0
Hick	2	0	12	0

With Paul Smith rattling along at a run a ball, the result was a formality after that impressive opening stand. Reeve was there at the end, relishing yet another successful one-day final for him, his fourth winner's medal at Lord's in eight years. With everyone revolving around his excellent leadership on the field, it seemed an eternity ago that he had been considering his future at the club.

Yet it was only ten days earlier – and Lara's gesture in the Lord's dressing room before play started suggested peace had broken out between the two.

Lara asked permission of Bob Woolmer to address the squad. He said his behaviour recently had not been fair on the players and the captain. He apologised, then shook hands with all the squad, including Reeve. As he gave Reeve an awkward hug, the captain glanced over to see his staunch ally Roger Twose wiping away a tear. It was an emotional few minutes, and Reeve was touched. 'I was surprised and moved by that gesture and by what he said. It was certainly a great way to get the boys together as a unit before the game.'

Bob Woolmer thought Lara's timing was perfect. 'He said he'd got some things wrong, that he'd been under pressure, please forgive me. He said it was just a little wobble, that he was fully committed to the team. I thought that was brilliant, and it proved a catalyst for the rest of the season. He mended fences.'

Onwards and upwards then for the Bears. They had been distinctly unfancied for the B&H by the bookies in April. Now they were making solid progress in the other three competitions. Fatigue and injuries would be a concern, but winning kept such worries at bay.

Celebrating the first trophy of the summer

v Surrey, Guildford, 14 – 18 July

Another important statement here from Warwickshire. Their fourth successive championship victory, this one against the team sitting top of the table.

Surrey were not yet the force of the next decade, when they scooped three championships and six one-day trophies, but they paraded some fine, established players at Guildford as well as developing talent such as Graham Thorpe and Adam Hollioake. And they were to remain top of the table till the end of July.

Injuries were beginning to bite into Warwickshire, with Dermot Reeve and Gladstone Small absent against Surrey. Yet this handsome victory was achieved without a significant contribution from Brian Lara. Indeed, crucial impetus came from two young and inexperienced players.

This was only the third championship match played by Graeme Welch and the debut of Dougie Brown, the enthusiastic, willing Scottish all-rounder, whose progress in the professional game had been delayed by his successful pursuit of a degree in physical education, then teaching. But at 24 the fire burned bright in Brown to prove himself in county cricket.

'I was chomping at the bit, couldn't wait to get started. I'd had a good season in the seconds – runs and wickets – and the injuries gave me my chance at Guildford. We were coming to the business end of the season, and every game was now vital.'

He was nervous, of course, but he had a laugh at Dickie Davis's expense on the way down the day before. 'We stopped at Warwick Services to fill up Dickie's sponsored car, and he filled it up with diesel, rather than petrol. Cost him a couple of hundred quid and leg-pulling all the way to Guildford from his wife Sam and me. It took my mind off the next day.'

Davis was doubly unlucky 24 hours later. The wicket was green, unlike a normal Guildford surface that usually started flat and then turned. So Brown was picked ahead of Davis, and he ended up opening the bowling in each innings.

But it was with the bat that Brown shone on his debut. Batting at number ten – surely one of the best number tens to have turned out for the Bears – he walked in at 131/8, with the vocal Surrey strut in excelsis. He joined Welch and promptly decided to give some of the aggression back to Surrey. 'Welchy and I had grown up together at Edgbaston, and we knew each other's game so well. We wanted to change the momentum of the game, and we matched each other, shot for shot. We knew we'd be backed by the positive dressing room. It was great fun. We gave ourselves something to bowl at.'

110 runs for the ninth wicket: Dougie Brown (left) and Graeme Welch

Welch saw that stand of 110 as a contest within the bigger contest. 'We were basically competing for one place in the side so we were also matching up against each other as well as playing for the team. Dougie was intensely competitive, but I wasn't going to step back and let him dominate. He had a better batting technique than me, even though I batted two places higher than him that day. There was a big crowd in, a lot of needle on the field between two aggressive sides, and Dougie and I thrived on it all.'

To stay in the game, Warwickshire needed to bowl out Surrey cheaply. They did so, courtesy of an unlikely source. Paul Smith, having picked up left-elbow and right-hand injuries while batting, was not fit to bowl. Apart from Munton and the tyros Brown and Welch, there was no seam or swing bowler on hand – apart from Roger Twose. In his five previous seasons of county cricket, Twose had picked up a five-wicket return in an innings just once.

It's not damning a fine cricketer to describe Twose's bowling as 'bustling' and 'optimistic'. He always felt he could get wickets with his military medium pace, but the scorecard often doused that admirable zeal. But Guildford proved his apogee as a swing bowler – precisely because he could indeed swing the ball.

Alec Stewart gives a clue to this match-winning 13 overs from Twose. 'My experience of Guildford was that it usually swung there, probably because of the amount of trees around the ground. Martin Bicknell, a very fine swing bowler, had a fine record there. Darren Stevens has often got wickets there for Kent. So it was set up for Twose, provided he got his line right.'

He did. Impressively. When five of the top six were snared by Twose, the only one not surprised was the irrepressible bowler. Roger Twose didn't do introspection. Anything was possible in his eyes.

So a lead of over 100 was precious for Warwickshire. With two days and a couple of sessions left, they now needed to bat for a long period, building up a massive lead, waiting for the pitch to deteriorate.

Who was the ideal batsman to book in for the long haul, accumulating patiently, relishing his painstaking role to blunt the bowling? It was a situation made for Andy Moles.

Alec Stewart admired the way Moles accumulated his double hundred. 'In my eyes Moler was the unluckiest not to play for England in the 1990s. He had an excellent opening batsman's technique and an unflappable temperament. The way he batted us out of the game here was textbook, just what a captain wants.'

Warwickshire v Surrey, Guildford, 14, 15, 16 & 18 July 1994

Warwickshire won by 256 runs

Umpires: K.E. Palmer & N.T. Plews

Warwickshire

A.J. Moles	c Ward b Benjamin	5	*not out*		203
R.G. Twose	lbw b Benjamin	5	(5) c Ward b Smith		31
B.C. Lara	c Thorpe b Cuffy	2	c & b Pigott		44
D.P. Ostler	b Cuffy	0	(2) c & b Benjamin		11
T.L. Penney	lbw b Hollioake	8	(4) lbw b Hollioake		1
P.A. Smith	lbw b Benjamin	34			
K.J. Piper +	c Kersey b Cuffy	16	(9) lbw b Benjamin		0
G. Welch	lbw b Pigott	59	(6) c Hollioake b Smith		0
N.M.K. Smith	b Hollioake	15	(7) b Benjamin		57
D.R. Brown	c Kersey b Pigott	54	(8) c Ward b Pigott		12
T.A. Munton *	*not out*	0	(10) c Kersey b Hollioake		4
	b 1, lb 10, w 5, nb 32	48	b 4, lb 10, nb 22		36
		246	(for 9 wkts, dec)		**399**

1/14, 2/21, 3/25, 4/25, 5/52, 6/86, 7/108, 8/131, 9/241, 10/246
1/29, 2/117, 3/118, 4/190, 5/190, 6/321, 7/381, 8/385, 9/399

Cuffy	17	3	74	3	24	6	63	0
Benjamin	18	3	79	3	32	10	70	3
Pigott	13.2	7	21	2	32	9	92	2
Hollioake	13	3	29	2	29.2	6	84	2
Smith	6	2	32	0	24	7	76	2

In the second innings NMK Smith retired hurt at 296 and resumed at 321.

Surrey

D.J. Bicknell	b Munton	0	c Piper b Welch	27
A.J. Stewart *	c Piper b Twose	56	lbw b Munton	1
G.P. Thorpe	c Piper b Twose	38	lbw b Smith N	43
D.M. Ward	c Ostler b Twose	17	lbw b Smith N	4
A.D. Brown	lbw b Twose	0	b Munton	29
A.J. Hollioake	lbw b Twose	2	lbw b Munton	6
A.C.S. Pigott	lbw b Munton	8	(9) b Munton	40
A.W. Smith	lbw b Munton	4	(7) lbw b Munton	45
G.J. Kersey +	*not out*	3	(8) c Welch b Smith N	2
J.E. Benjamin	lbw b Twose	0	st Piper b Smith N	31
C.E. Cuffy	b Munton	0	*not out*	2
	b 2, lb 5, nb 8	15	b 3, lb 11, nb 2	16
		143		**246**

1/0, 2/107, 3/112, 4/112, 5/116, 6/129, 7/140, 8/141, 9/142, 10/143
1/3, 2/68, 3/72, 4/86, 5/100, 6/127, 7/140, 8/203, 9/222, 10/246

Munton	18.5	5	41	4	28	6	96	5
Brown	4	1	22	0	6	1	17	0
Welch	7	0	39	0	9	3	16	1
Smith NMK	7	4	6	0	33.4	13	71	4
Twose	13	3	28	6	9	3	22	0
Lara					2	0	10	0

Moles batted 141.2 overs and more than nine hours for his unbeaten double hundred, loving every minute of the attritional battle. 'It was now a low, slow wicket, and it was obvious I had to bat time. After all my frustrations of being out through illness and injuries, it was doubly sweet. It was a short ground square of the wickets and they bowled very straight at me, so I just had to accumulate and get the ball through the field when I had a rare loose delivery. Throughout my career, my usual game plan was letting the aggressive batsmen play around me, while I blunted the bowling. That was the Guildford innings in a nutshell.

'I remember when Tim Munton came in as last man, with me needing about ten or twelve to get my double hundred. Time wasn't the issue, so I knew I'd be allowed by my captain to get there if I could. I told my mate, "Just get a big forward lunge on it and block every ball" and he did just that. The Surrey boys kept on at me that Tim would let me down, but he didn't. Every time he blocked one, he'd smile at them. I couldn't have had a better partner at that stage.'

Then Munton set to work in his more familiar role as spearhead of the attack. Facing 503 to win, Surrey never had a chance as the ball kept low at times (five lbws in their second innings) and it also turned for Neil Smith. Munton struck an early, vital blow, nailing Stewart lbw ('with the nip-backer. I was chuffed, the plan worked. That was one of my favourite wickets that season'), and he finished with nine wickets in the match.

Typically, Munton prefers to focus on the performances at Guildford of Moles, Brown and Welch. 'I was so pleased for Moler. A true Bear, he had fought so hard to get his chance a decade earlier, and he was still so proud and committed. He'd remind players that the collective cause was paramount and carry out his role as one of the best English players of fast bowling of his generation.

'Dougie and Graeme showed great promise and drive in that game. They are two of the most gifted young players to come through in my time at Edgbaston. They played with real flair, encouraged by the confident atmosphere around them.'

Welch views Guildford as a key part of the development of himself and Brown. 'We stuck our hands up to be counted. The encouragement we got

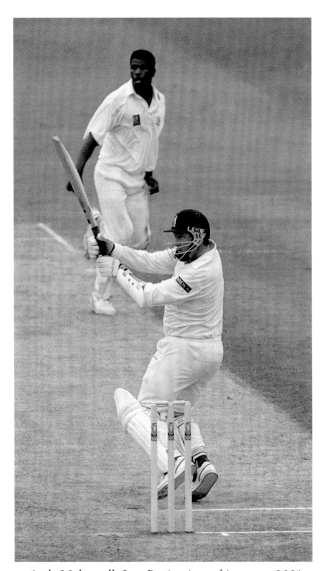

Andy Moles pulls Joey Benjamin on his way to 203*

was vital, allowing us to express ourselves. A stand of 110 on day one may not seem too much in terms of a four-day match, but it took the initiative away from Surrey after they put us in and expected to roll us over cheaply. As young players we got so much satisfaction from doing ourselves justice in such a vital game. Some saw that Surrey win as a turning point in our season.'

Guildford ended with Surrey just four points ahead of Warwickshire at the top of the table. By the start of August, they were starting to fade while the Bears roared on. Another pre-season favourite was imploding while Warwickshire's momentum seemed unstoppable.

The Sunday League charge was on as well. Victory by 13 runs over Surrey was their eighth victory out of nine. Guildford was a productive few days.

v Derbyshire, Chesterfield, 28 – 30 July

After this resounding win, Warwickshire went to the top of the table for the first time, and they stayed there for the rest of the season.

Outstanding performances from Neil Smith, Tim Munton and Keith Piper contributed handsomely, but the centrepiece of the victory was an eye-watering innings from Brian Lara.

He had been strangely unproductive of late – just 127 runs in his last five innings – but his dazzling hundred on a rapid pitch was entrancing. You just couldn't keep your eyes off Lara as he reeled off a hundred before lunch on the first day.

It wasn't a flawless innings. The Chesterfield wicket and Devon Malcolm's pace and hostility saw to that. Chesterfield had the reputation of a great cricket wicket, where the batsmen got true value for their shots on a fast outfield and bowlers who turned the ball or generated genuine pace were rewarded.

This was certainly so on the first day, when 16 wickets fell for 445 runs. It was a wonderful day's cricket, full of thrust and counter-parry. At the close, the umpires Barry Dudleston and Peter Willey said it was the best first day either had officiated in.

At the heart of it was a stirring duel between Lara and Malcolm. Malcolm had troubled Lara earlier in the year during England's Caribbean tour. At times, during spells of authentic pace, Malcolm had got Lara hopping around, getting into strange positions against the short ball, but Lara had invariably come through unscathed because Malcolm lacked hostile support at the other end – but Malcolm still felt he had Lara's number. In three weeks' time he would terrorise hapless South African batsmen with his 9/57 in the Oval Test. He was at his peak as a raw, unpredictable bowler of devastating speed.

Going for just three an over at Chesterfield, Malcolm's analysis does not do him any justice at all. He had Lara dropped at slip when on 25, a moment that had become familiar to Malcolm. 'It's amazing that around this period, Lara always got big runs after being dropped early on off my bowling. He was an astonishing batsman, but I still troubled him early on, same as in the Caribbean. He was the last batsman to give a chance to. Very frustrating. It was a great pitch for me, and I really worked up some pace.'

Dominic Cork, standing at slip, relished the contest. 'It was a very good cricket wicket, suiting both Dev and Brian. It just flew through the slips when he got an edge. Dev would regularly beat him three times an over, then Brian would hit him for four. He attacked Dev as if it was a one-day game. Those eyes wide out, coming at the bowler with that high backlift! What a contest that was. But Dev definitely troubled him. Shows what a genius Brian was to battle through to a hundred and plenty.'

Dougie Brown batted with Lara towards the end of the innings. 'It was an incredible innings. I knew all about his records, but you had to experience Brian's batting at the other end to realise just how special he was. It was ridiculous, awesome. All the guys watched every ball he batted that day. The pitch was emerald green and very fast. For mortals like me, it was very tricky to bat on. The quicker Dev bowled, the further Brian tried to hit him. At one stage, Dev had three men out on the hook, and yet Brian kept hitting it through the gaps. For variation he'd run down the pitch and hit Dev through extra cover. He just cleared the dressing room; everyone came out to watch.'

Trevor Penney shared yet another productive stand with Lara, intelligently reining himself in, giving Lara the strike, acknowledging his limitations. Without that partnership of 160, Warwickshire would have been in some strife and Penney's 41 was a valuable knock. 'Devon was seriously quick that day and, early on, he had Brian playing with both feet off the ground. He definitely disconcerted him, jumping wide of the crease and angling the ball in at him awkwardly. He was bowling at around 160kph, and I was at the other end wondering how I was going to get through this. I knew I'd struggle, but Brian just backed himself.

'Brian saw the ball earlier than others. I can see him now, the bat cocked round his earhole, yet coming down so straight. And his bat speed got him out of trouble against Devon.'

Before the enthralling first day was over, Lara had rendered his side further notable service, with some tactical advice. The key wicket for Warwickshire was clearly that of Mohammad Azharuddin, the world-class Indian batsman, who could destroy an attack almost as swiftly as Lara.

Tim Munton was nearing the end of his spell as stumps neared, and Azharuddin appeared set. Munton was minded to replace himself with Graeme Welch, just to vary things. 'As I called Welchy over, Brian ran up from slip and said, "Don't be too proud, have another over. I think you've got him." I took his advice. Next over, Azza nicked one and Keith Piper took a wonderful diving catch in front of slip's left boot. I was thrilled; it was a priceless wicket for me and the team. Brian just smiled and patted me on the back.'

Piper's brilliance behind the stumps was by now almost taken for granted, but he was stacking up some impressive statistics to back up his status as the best wicket-keeper in the land. In this game, he took eleven dismissals – a record for the county – and became the first to make seven dismissals in an innings in consecutive matches. If only he had translated his undoubted batting talent into consistent scores, he would have pressed his case for international selection.

In the last three championship games, Tim Munton had taken 29 wickets, making the ball swing as well as seam around on surfaces that were beginning to wear. Bob Cottam's coaching expertise from years back remained invaluable for the willing workhorse who was now, at 29, a thoroughbred. While England ignored his claims for a Test recall, team-mates and supporters were grateful – Munton was much more important to them in August than England.

Neil Smith, harvesting a stack of wickets in the fourth innings, helped wrap up the match before tea on the third day. The captaincy transition from Reeve to Munton appeared seamless, with Munton gladly considering any tactical advice coming his way. It was significant that Lara went out of his way to help Munton, in Reeve's absence. You are willing to draw your own conclusions.

Dominic Cork was enormously impressed by Warwickshire at Chesterfield. 'As well as having a great overseas player, they were full of top pros who worked hard, buying into what Warwickshire was all about. Munton could swing it both ways and get bounce with his height. Smith turned the ball a fair amount, with a tight line just outside the off-stump. Ostler very talented, Piper a brilliant keeper. Penney would come in and run you ragged, stealing twos down to fine leg or third man. Next thing you knew he was 20*, having only been in a few minutes! Then there were the young lads – coming into a successful, confident unit, encouraged by the senior players. They outplayed us at Chesterfield. They looked like champions elect.'

Derbyshire v Warwickshire, Chesterfield, 28, 29 & 30 July 1994

Warwickshire won by 139 runs

Umpires: B. Dudleston & P. Willey

Warwickshire

A.J. Moles	c & b Base	17	c Cork b Barnett	63
R.G. Twose	hit wkt b Malcolm	5	c Azharuddin b Base	0
B.C. Lara	c Barnett b Cork	142	lbw b Base	51
D.P. Ostler	c Base b Malcolm	6	c Rollins b Vandrau	68
T.L. Penney	lbw b Wells	41	c & b Vandrau	20
J.D. Ratcliffe	lbw b Base	8	b Barnett	3
K.J. Piper +	c & b Cork	15	c Adams b Barnett	1
G. Welch	c Barnett b Base	10	lbw b Barnett	20
N.M.K. Smith	b Base	6	c O'Gorman b Vandrau	7
D.R. Brown	c O'Gorman b Base	1	not out	3
T.A. Munton *	not out	3	c Cork b Barnett	0
	nb 26	26	b 5, lb 6, nb 12	23
		280		**259**

1/13, 2/51, 3/64, 4/224, 5/239, 6/250, 7/270, 8/270, 9/273, 10/280
1/0, 2/76, 3/190, 4/214, 5/219, 6/223, 7/233, 8/251, 9/257, 10/259

Derbyshire

K.J. Barnett *	c Ostler b Munton	16	(7) c Piper b Welch	13
D.G. Cork	c Piper b Munton	46	(1) c Piper b Smith	8
C.J. Adams	c Piper b Twose	25	(4) c Piper b Welch	41
T.J. O'Gorman	run out	12	(5) c Piper b Munton	0
M. Azharuddin	c Piper b Munton	28	(6) c Penney b Smith	36
A.S. Rollins	c Penney b Twose	1	(2) c Piper b Munton	18
M.J. Vandrau	not out	18	(9) c Piper b Smith	26
K.M. Krikken +	lbw b Munton	18	(10) not out	16
C.M. Wells	c Twose b Munton	0	(8) b Smith	24
S.J. Base	c Ostler b Munton	0	(3) st Piper b Smith	1
D.E. Malcolm	c Piper b Munton	7	b Brown	0
	lb 4, nb 23	27	b 6, lb 6, nb 7	19
		198		**202**

1/54, 2/83, 3/114, 4/126, 5/133, 6/155, 7/186, 8/188, 9/188, 10/198
1/22, 2/28, 3/34. 4/35, 5/86, 6/112, 7/126, 8/172, 9/199, 10/202

Malcolm	11	2	38	2	11	2	58	0
Cork	19.2	1	79	2	12	2	31	0
Base	17.5	2	92	5	11	2	41	2
Vandrau	5	0	59	0	24	1	87	3
Wells	4.4	2	12	1				
Barnett					12.3	2	31	5
Munton	25.2	5	52	7	22	6	57	2
Welch	21	4	83	0	20	9	49	2
Brown	6	1	26	0	3	0	11	1
Twose	14	3	31	2				
Smith	2	1	2	0	28	6	69	5
Lara					1	0	4	0

Results: 6 July to 8 August

County Championship

July 14,15,16,18   **Guildford**   **Surrey**   Won by 256 runs
Warwicks 246 (Welch 59, Brown 54) & 399-9 dec (Moles 203*, Smith N 57)   Surrey 143 (Twose 6-28, Munton 4-41) & 246 (Munton 5-96)

July 21,22,23   **Edgbaston**   **Essex**   Won by 203 runs
Warwicks 361 (Lara 70, Smith N 65, Moles 57) & 268 (Twose 92)   Essex 215 (Munton 6-89) & 211 (Knight 113, Brown 4-25, Munton 4-41)

July 28,29,30   **Chesterfield**   **Derbyshire**   Won by 139 runs
Warwickshire 280 (Lara 142, Base 5-92) & 259 (Ostler 68, Moles 63, Lara 51)   Derbyshire 198 (Munton 7-52) & 202 (Smith N 5-69)

Aug 4,5,6,8   **Worcester**   **Worcestershire**   Match drawn
Warwickshire 216 & 346-5 (Penney 84*, Moles 67, Lara 57)   Worcestershire 473-4 dec (Curtis 180, Smith N 4-141)

AXA Equity & Law League

July 12   **Edgbaston**   **Glamorgan**   Won by four wickets
Glamorgan 155 *(38.3 overs)* (Smith P 5-38, Smith N 3-28)   Warwickshire 156-6 *(38.3 overs)* (Reeve 52*)

July 17   **Guildford**   **Surrey**   Won by 13 runs
Warwickshire 249-7 *(40 overs)* (Twose 96*, Ostler 55)   Surrey 236-8 *(40 overs)* (Brown 69, Ward 63)

July 24   **Edgbaston**   **Essex**   Won by three wickets
Essex 147 *(35.4 overs)* (Smith N 3-28)   Warwickshire 148-7 *(34.2 overs)* (Smith P 45)

July 31   **Chesterfield**   **Derbyshire**   No result
Warwickshire 239-8 *(36 overs)* (Twose 74, Smith N 36, Cork 4-44)   Derbyshire did not bat

Aug 7   **Edgbaston**   **Worcestershire**   Lost by 3 runs
Worcestershire 182-8 *(38 overs)* (Haynes 76, Twose 3-36)   Warwickshire 179-8 *(38 overs)* (Smith N 47, Ostler 42, Radford 4-36)

Benson & Hedges Cup

July 9 *(Final)*   **Lord's**   **Worcestershire**   Won by six wickets
Worcestershire 170-9 *(55 overs)* (Smith P 3-34)   Warwickshire 172-4 *(44.2 overs)* (Ostler 55, Smith P 42*)

NatWest Bank Trophy

July 6,7 *(2nd Round)*   **Leicester**   **Leicestershire**   Won by 128 runs
Warwickshire 296-6 *(60 overs)* (Penney 65*, Smith P 50, Twose 40)   Leicestershire 168 *(47.3 overs)* (Boon 55, Smith N 3-28)

July 26 *(Quarter-Final)*   **Taunton**   **Somerset**   Won by eight wickets
Somerset 124 *(54.2 overs)* (Smith N 4-26)   Warwickshire 125-2 *(24.1 overs)* (Ostler 47, Moles 41*)

County Championship

	P	W	L	D	Bt	Bl	Pts
Warwickshire	12	8	-	4	30	37	195
Surrey	12	7	4	1	25	41	178
Leicestershire	11	6	4	1	34	39	169
Sussex	12	6	2	4	25	40	161
Somerset	12	6	4	2	26	36	158
Nottinghamshire	12	6	3	3	23	37	156
Essex	12	5	4	2	24	43	147
Middlesex	12	4	2	6	27	40	131
Kent	12	3	6	3	28	42	118
Gloucestershire	12	3	6	3	16	45	117
Durham	12	3	8	1	27	40	115
Northamptonshire	12	4	4	4	16	33	113
Hampshire	12	3	5	4	18	38	112
Lancashire	11	5	4	2	17	38	110
Derbyshire	12	3	7	2	21	37	106
Worcestershire	11	2	4	5	26	38	96
Yorkshire	11	2	4	5	24	36	92
Glamorgan	12	1	6	5	25	33	74

AXA Equity & Law League

	P	W	L	T	NR	Pts
Warwickshire	12	9	2	-	1	38
Worcestershire	11	8	2	-	1	34
Kent	12	8	4	-	-	32
Lancashire	11	7	3	-	1	30
Glamorgan	12	6	4	1	1	28
Derbyshire	12	6	4	-	2	28
Durham	12	5	3	1	3	28
Yorkshire	11	6	4	-	1	26
Surrey	12	5	4	-	3	26
Leicestershire	11	5	5	-	1	22
Nottinghamshire	12	4	5	-	3	22
Hampshire	12	5	7	-	-	20
Northamptonshire	12	4	6	1	1	20
Sussex	12	4	7	-	1	18
Somerset	12	4	8	-	-	16
Middlesex	12	3	8	-	1	14
Essex	12	2	8	1	1	12
Gloucestershire	12	2	9	-	1	10

v Kent, NatWest Semi-Final, Edgbaston, 9 August

This was the most pulsating, dramatic match of Warwickshire's season, and it encapsulated what their players could achieve, against the odds.

It sums up the fascination of cricket that Kent could lose when they needed just 83 to win, with 14 overs to go and eight wickets in hand – and this with the brilliant West Indian Carl Hooper, who was enjoying a superb season with Kent, at the crease. Such was his mastery it would surely be a simple exercise to knock the ball around for ones and twos and stroll to victory.

The target was whittled down to 44 needed off six overs, with five wickets in hand. Mark Ealham, a highly capable player, was at the crease with Hooper. A formality, nine times out of ten.

Never under-estimate a crowd's support, though. On a sunlit evening the Bears' supporters in the Eric Hollies Stand sensed the game could still be won, improbably. In the last hour the din was enormous as the chants of 'You Bears!' rained down on the players. To this observer, it was every bit as loud as any of England's cherished Test wins over Australia at Edgbaston in the past two decades, albeit not as prolonged. Certainly I have never heard such a noise in a domestic match at the stadium since Warwickshire turned over Worcestershire in the 1989 NatWest semi-final.

The supporters and Bears players fed off each other in those climactic stages. It helped that ten of their players that day were genuinely popular with the home fans, while the eleventh, Brian Lara, was simply idolised. Only Asif Din among current folk heroes was missing so the raucous backing was heartfelt for those players who had given so much back in the Extra Cover Bar and countless autograph signings. When you keep stopping for a cheery word and a hurried photo with those who cherish and support you, there's a strong likelihood that unconditional affection is on tap when it's tough on the field.

It certainly was tough against Kent. On a slow pitch, Warwickshire finished at least 20 runs short of a defendable target against a Kent side that was one of the most dangerous one-day sides around. Without Andy Moles' patient unbeaten hundred, the total would have been comfortably within Kent's compass. It still appeared a formality when they eased themselves serenely to 183/2.

Andy Moles reaches 100

If ever his team needed Dermot Reeve's powers of alchemy, it was now. He had punted on taking early wickets by using up the allotted overs for Gladstone Small and Tim Munton – to no real advantage. All he had left now were himself, Neil Smith, Roger Twose and Paul Smith. He gambled on the mercurial Paul Smith to make things happen. 'Dermot told me to run in and bowl as fast as I could to try unsettling them. "Let them know what you're about," was his instruction. The crowd got behind me, they were unbelievable.'

Reeve at his infuriating and determined best:

(left) stealing a cheeky single to the annoyance of Mark Ealham, (below) pushing past Carl Hooper

Reeve knew he was taking a risk with a bowler who could leak runs as well as take key wickets. 'Paul responded well to the big occasion, and he was at his best when he bowled effort balls on a slow wicket of uneven bounce. Early on, he bowled medium pace and was treated dismissively. He slunk away to the boundary, disgusted with himself, showed poor body language and didn't walk in with the bowler. But then the crowd woke up, galvanised Paul and suddenly he bowled like a demon when I brought him back – almost as quick as Allan Donald that day.'

With Smith engendering faint hopes of turning the game, it took two remarkable catches to tilt the contest Warwickshire's way. Neil Taylor, playing the Moles anchor role, went for the slog sweep and looked as if he would get away with it as the ball soared towards the mid-wicket boundary. But Dominic Ostler careered round the rope to pluck it one-handed and, for good measure, threw in a double somersault. In front of the Eric Hollies Stand. They cheered the local boy who, in his endearingly sheepish manner, responded to them as if it were just a normal catch.

Graham Cowdrey fell in equally spectacular fashion. Paul Smith dug one in short, Cowdrey went for the cut and Keith Piper leapt high to take the snick that appeared to have gone over his head. Stretching as high as he could, Piper grabbed it two-handed, landed painfully on his back, but retained the presence of mind to hold onto the ball on impact.

They were two astonishingly athletic efforts from Ostler and Piper, and they changed the course of the match. Smith's searing pace and those catches disconcerted Kent, and Reeve was bowling cleverly, preying on the batsmen's nerves with his slower ball, then some reverse swing and the occasional quicker delivery – backed up all the while by his cheeky grin to the batsmen, offering the belief that they were now the ones under pressure. As fielding captain, Reeve loved such a tight contest where nerve and self-confidence were paramount. His quirky field placings also got the batsmen thinking: why was he putting that man in such an unusual position?

Despite the brilliance of the fielding and the crowd's unstinting support, the game was still in the bag for Kent. Just seven an over needed, with five wickets in hand and Hooper at the crease. One good over from him, and the game was decided. But Brian Lara remained convinced that Hooper would buckle, and he kept telling his team-mates that at the end of the overs. Lara knew enough about Hooper's talent

Warwickshire v Kent, Edgbaston, 9 August 1994

Warwickshire won by 8 runs   *Umpires: J.H. Hampshire & B.J. Meyer*

Warwickshire

A.J. Moles	*not out*		105
D.P. Ostler	lbw	b McCague	12
B.C. Lara		c & b Ealham	29
P.A. Smith	c Hooper	b Ealham	5
R.G. Twose	c Marsh	b Headley	49
D.A. Reeve *	lbw	b Fleming	23
T.L. Penney	c Marsh	b Fleming	3
N.M.K. Smith	c McCague	b Fleming	15
G.C. Small		b McCague	1
K.J. Piper +	*not out*		6
T.A. Munton			
	lb 14, w 3		17
60 overs	(for 8 wickets)		**265**

1/24, 2/91, 3/104, 4/178, 5/220, 6/224, 7/248, 8/250

Wren	10	0	41	0
McCague	10	0	37	2
Headley	12	0	43	1
Ealham	10	0	47	2
Hooper	12	1	55	0
Fleming	6	0	28	3

Kent

T.R. Ward	c Smith N	b Smith P	80
M.R. Benson *		b Munton	6
N.R. Taylor	c Ostler	b Smith N	64
C.L. Hooper	c Smith N	b Reeve	44
G.R. Cowdrey	c Piper	b Smith P	1
M.V. Fleming	c Piper	b Munton	1
M.A. Ealham	c Small	b Reeve	7
S.A. Marsh +	st Piper	b Reeve	22
M.J. McCague	run out		1
D.W. Headley	*not out*		7
T.N. Wren	run out		0
	b 1, lb 12, w 9, nb 2		24
59.5 overs			**257**

1/12, 2/136, 3/183, 4/199, 5/200, 6/222, 7/235, 8/242, 9/250, 10/257

Small	12	3	32	0
Munton	12	3	31	2
Reeve	11	0	44	3
Smith PA	10.5	0	66	2
Smith NMK	10	0	45	1
Twose	4	0	26	0

from their days together in the West Indies side, but he also knew his brittleness when the pressure was on.

Then the decisive moment. Ealham was caught off a skier, but unaccountably he and Hooper didn't cross when the ball was in the air. That is something you learn in schools cricket; there's always a chance that the dolly will be dropped and you get a run. As a consequence Hooper didn't face one of the next 11 balls, as they bowled tightly at Steve Marsh and the fielders made some spectacular stops. Hooper was frustrated, Reeve bluffed him out, and the innings folded.

It was an improbable win, achieved in a crucible of tension and eventual delirium from the home supporters. So many sporting occasions are decided by the individuals with the strongest minds, and this was a classic example.

Dominic Ostler still remembers the noise generated by the crowd that day. 'They drove us to win by sheer willpower. Everything we tried in that last hour worked. Eleven guys wanted to make it work for everyone else, and Dermot's instinctive captaincy was brilliant.'

Neil Smith, who watched Ostler's catch off his own bowling in disbelief, believes that was one of the turning points. 'That one and Pipes' catch gave us the necessary lift. We only needed a couple of sparks to get us going. How you get out of a tight situation defines a successful side. And the crowd was our twelfth man.'

Keith Piper, modestly deflecting praise for his brilliant catch, stressed the mental strength of the players. 'We had so much faith in each other. We knew that if we pressed the right buttons, Kent would fold.'

That's the nub of the matter. As Warwickshire celebrated lustily, Kent held a prolonged inquest in their adjoining dressing room, with their coach Darryl Foster trying to work out why they invariably came second best to Warwickshire.

Matthew Fleming was convinced it was a psychological issue. 'We weren't mentally strong enough to beat them. I found that hard. Who would you rather have in your side – Hooper or Twose? On natural talent Hooper, but Twose had the mental

Dermot Reeve is carried off the field

edge in '94. You look to your top overseas player like Tendulkar or Steve Waugh to close out a game like that one, but Hooper was just too mercurial. We also had a fair amount of insular characters in our dressing room and an introspective coach. Warwickshire just had the hold over us; they had an aura about them.'

Graham Cowdrey agrees. 'If there was one side we wanted to avoid in one-day competitions around that time, it was Warwickshire. Player by player there wasn't a lot between the two teams but our overseas superstar didn't do it on the day, even though he'd played some miraculous innings for us that season. If we'd been chasing 266 anywhere else, we would have won – but not at Edgbaston. We always knew that we would struggle at Edgbaston whenever we went there. They were on a roll by then, and opposition sides were beginning to fear them before a ball was bowled. And Dermot's work in the field was fantastic. He reminded me of Keith Fletcher in the way he'd set unusual fields, and the ball would go to where he'd placed the fielder.'

Tim Munton, having taken over from Reeve as captain in the championship, was delighted to have him back as leader against Kent. 'That game was one of the best examples of how brilliantly ahead of his time he was. Dermot's strategy and control were fantastic. We should never have won that game, but Dermot helped us transfer the pressure onto Kent. Keeping Hooper off strike was decisive and those two wonderful catches. Paul Smith bowled as quickly as anyone in county cricket that day; he was like his hero Beefy Botham in the way he roughed up Kent's batsmen when they were coasting.'

If ever you needed proof that so much of professional sport is played between the ears, you can point to this match. Natural ability is taken for granted at this level, but getting yourselves out of trouble takes a different sort of aptitude. Having won against the odds in such spectacular fashion, it looked as if nothing could now stop Warwickshire cleaning up all four titles within the next month. Momentum was with them, morale after this Kent triumph stratospheric.

v Hampshire, Edgbaston, 30 August – 2 September

The first championship for Warwickshire in 22 years was sealed in the grand manner, in front of the home fans and by an innings.

There had been a wobble at the start of August, with a battling draw to stave off defeat by Worcestershire, then a thumping innings hammering at home by Nottinghamshire. Some of the players had looked a touch jaded, as niggling injuries kicked in, but the cricket management sensibly saw those below-par performances as simply bad days at the office. After all, they had gone 12 championship matches without defeat before the Nottinghamshire game. The message was clear: focus on how they had got to the top of the table at just the right stage of the season and tap into that deep well of self-confidence.

It worked. Beating Yorkshire and Sussex by eight and ten wickets respectively banished any negativity, while fatigue tends to dissipate when you are winning handsomely. An innings defeat of Hampshire to spark the celebrations constituted an impressive hat-trick of victories from 18 August to 2 September. There was no need to sweat over the final championship match at Bristol, in mid-September, when the weather is often poor (as it transpired, with play possible only on the third day).

Warwickshire marched to the title in familiar fashion. The ball turned on the first day as Hampshire were bowled out cheaply, then the batsmen rocketed along at speed, giving the bowlers time enough to bowl out Hampshire again on the final day. That formula had served Warwickshire well in '94 and, with the spinners and Tim Munton sharing the wickets, Hampshire only lingered for 51 overs in their second innings.

This was Brian Lara's last hundred in the championship and one of his most spectacular. His 191 off just 222 balls was a peerless example of his coruscating brilliance. With Roger Twose sharing a fourth century partnership with him, Lara orchestrated a scoring rate of five an over. The loss of 110 overs to rain on days two and three was safely sidelined due to the tremendous rate of scoring.

Hampshire's all-rounder Kevan James toiled manfully with his medium pacers but admitted he was meat and drink to Lara in this mood. 'I just got fed up with his bat appearing about a foot wide. I had a moral victory when he got an inside edge down to fine leg, and I swore at the world in general – not at Brian – as if I'd been unlucky. Brian came up to me and said gently, "Calm down, calm down – easy," as if he knew it was his day. Others would have called me a prat for my over-reaction but, when you're playing like a god, a little moan from someone like me isn't going to bother you. I thought, "He's right, why am I getting so worked up?" It was usually a waste of time bowling at Lara in his pomp.

'That innings he made it look so easy. You couldn't take offence at his casual air. He just picked us off.'

Shaun Udal, the Hampshire off-spinner, eventually dismissed Lara, courtesy of a stunning catch, low at mid-wicket by Robin Smith, but claims little credit. 'It was a long hop that he tried to hit over the Eric Hollies Stand, and Robin took it one-handed. It wasn't part of a subtle plan! It wasn't a great deal of fun bowling at Lara. He was so fleet of foot. I'd rather bowl at Sachin Tendulkar than Lara, who'd destroy you in half an hour. Sachin was more of an accumulator, whereas Lara was a magician. The noise levels upped whenever Lara walked out to bat.'

As the pitch deteriorated into a dustbowl on the final day, there was an air of inevitability about the innings defeat. Kevan James couldn't wait to get out of the ground as the champagne corks popped. 'They were a very good side at the time, but they had an air of superiority. Piper was very vocal behind the stumps, and they were hard work. I just wanted to get in the car and piss off.'

Shaun Udal remembers watching the prolonged celebrations from the dressing-room door, wistfully wondering if he would ever experience that with Hampshire. 'But it wasn't to be. Fair play to Warwickshire. Well led by Reeve and Munton, and Neil Smith was a wily off-spinner, Piper a brilliant keeper. And there was always Lara. They gelled and impressed as a unit.'

Udal at least had one personal consolation in that game. On the final morning, he learned he had been picked for England's Ashes tour that winter, getting

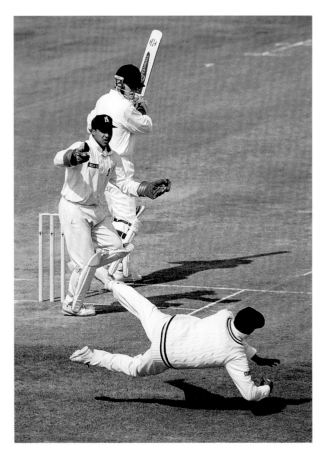

Hampshire collapse on the first day

Facing page
Top: Middleton caught Moles bowled Smith
Bottom: (left) White bowled Munton,
(right) Terry caught and bowled Davis

This page
Above: Nicholas caught Small bowled Munton
Right: Lara diving to field in the slips

the nod ahead of Neil Smith. When the Ashes and England 'A' squads were announced during the Hampshire match, only Keith Piper was selected from the team of the season. That just made the championship success even sweeter in the eyes of the Bears players and supporters.

As the players posed for celebratory photos, mingling with the fans, Reeve graciously included Munton in the official pictures of the pennant's presentation, insisting also that he should share the inevitable media interviews. That was only right and proper. Munton had won eight games out of nine as championship captain as well as leading by example with his 81 first-class wickets, a personal best. Only the Kent spinner Min Patel bowled more overs in the championship than the yeoman Munton. He would never undervalue this captaincy lark, but it certainly hadn't affected his form.

So the Grand Slam was definitely on now. Two banked, top of the Sunday League and the NatWest Final tomorrow. For Munton, after a couple of glasses of bubbly, the trek down the motorway at rush hour lay ahead. But he enjoyed one satisfying treat on the way down. 'A fish and chip supper! Perfect after such a draining day that turned out just the way I wanted. I had time to think through the season as I munched away.

'How times have changed. We wouldn't now be playing a Lord's final off the back of a fourth day in the championship, over a hundred miles from Lord's. But that's how it was, and you just got on with it. But what a pleasure, going to a final after winning the championship the day before. Why interrupt success? We'd had enough down times as experienced pros, we just wanted to have more exciting days. None of us complained about the tight schedule. You don't when you're going well, do you?'

A strong Worcestershire side, still smarting from defeat in the Benson & Hedges Final, lay ahead on the morrow. Worthy adversaries in the quest for a third trophy. The main worry was an uncertain weather forecast. They were right to be concerned on that Friday night when they arrived in North London.

Warwickshire v Hampshire, Edgbaston, 30 & 31 August, 1 & 2 September 1994

Warwickshire won by an innings & 95 runs

Umpires: K.J. Lyons & R. Palmer

Hampshire

T.C. Middleton	c Moles b Smith	18	c Moles b Munton	2
V.P. Terry	c & b Davis	71	c Piper b Munton	36
G.W. White	b Munton	30	b Smith	18
R.A. Smith	c Twose b Davis	5	c Munton b Davis	34
M.C.J. Nicholas *	c Small b Munton	2	*not out*	36
K.D. James	c Smith b Welch	25	c Lara b Davis	0
A.N. Aymes +	c Lara b Munton	0	c Penney b Davis	0
S.D. Udal	c Moles b Davis	64	b Smith	1
R.J. Maru	c Ostler b Small	32	c Piper b Smith	6
C.A. Connor	c Moles b Munton	21	lbw b Smith	14
J.N.B. Bovill	*not out*	0	lbw b Smith	4
	lb 8, nb 2	10	*b 5, lb 7*	12
		278		**163**

1/74, 2/129, 3/133, 4/136, 5/136, 6/139, 7/208, 8/240, 9/277, 10/278
1/27, 2/60, 3/76, 4/120, 5/120, 6/120, 7/121, 8/129, 9/149, 10/163

Small	20.2	7	49	1	6	4	2	0
Munton	23	5	44	4	14	5	34	2
Twose	5	1	19	0				
Welch	16	6	45	1				
Smith	18	5	36	1	19.2	4	65	5
Davis	26	7	77	3	11	1	50	3

Warwickshire

A.J. Moles	c Ames b Connor	24
R.G. Twose	st Aymes b Udal	137
B.C. Lara	c Smith b Udal	191
D.P. Ostler	c Nicholas b Bovill	25
T.L. Penney	b Bovill	20
G. Welch	c Aymes b Connor	43
K.J. Piper +	lbw b Bovill	16
N.M.K. Smith	*not out*	29
R.P. Davis	c Connor b Udal	17
G.C. Small	c Udal b Connor	2
T.A. Munton *	b Connor	7
	b 1, lb 10, nb 14	25
		536

1/54, 2/349, 3/384, 4/403, 5/434, 6/474, 7/484, 8/519, 9/521, 10/536

Connor	31	3	124	4
Bovill	27	4	99	3
James	19	1	86	0
Udal	28	1	142	3
Maru	14	0	74	0

164

Brian Lara steps out of the pavilion to play his last championship innings of the summer

	Brian Lara in the County Championship							
1	Glamorgan	147	10	Northamptonshire *(1)*	197	18	Worcestershire *(1)*	5
2	Leicestershire *(1)*	106	11	Northamptonshire *(2)*	2	19	Worcestershire *(2)*	57
3	Leicestershire *(2)*	120*	12	Surrey *(1)*	2	20	Nottinghamshire *(1)*	15
4	Somerset	136	13	Surrey *(2)*	44	21	Nottinghamshire *(2)*	0
5	Middlesex *(1)*	26	14	Essex *(1)*	70	22	Yorkshire *(1)*	21
6	Middlesex *(2)*	140	15	Essex *(2)*	9	23	Yorkshire *(2)*	17
7	Durham	501*	16	Derbyshire *(1)*	142	24	Sussex	17
8	Kent *(1)*	19	17	Derbyshire *(2)*	51	25	Hampshire	191
9	Kent *(2)*	31						

Warwickshire hold the county championship trophy for the first time in their history – their previous title was won in 1972, the year before the cup was presented by the Lord's Taverners

v Worcestershire, NatWest Final, Lord's, 3 – 4 September

In the end the Grand Slam was not to be. Sport is not an exact science, and we'll never know how influential the toss of a coin proved to be as Warwickshire's hopes of the quadruple were scuppered on two successive damp mornings at Lord's.

Typical NatWest Final conditions, unless NW8 was in the grip of a heatwave in September. And Worcestershire's victory was the ninth time in a row – and the 18th out of the last 21 – that the trophy was won by the side batting second.

Exactly a year earlier, on a blissfully sunny morning the Sussex total of 321/6 was 98 more than Warwickshire managed as they defended their trophy. Instead of the bowlers being nullified on a flat pitch, Warwickshire had to fight tooth and nail a year later, just to get to a respectable total. Then their bowlers were simply blown away by the daunting power of Graeme Hick and Tom Moody as the wicket eased.

When a player of Brian Lara's ability takes 26 balls to get off the mark and then labours more than 40 overs for his 81, you get the picture. Moody's niggardly opening spell and Phil Newport's skilful swing bowling made them look like world-beaters in conditions they utilised superbly. Getting to 88 off 29 overs, with Lara still there on 36 and Twose 20 before the rain at 12.25 ended play for the day, constituted a decent effort in the circumstances.

Not even Lara could work the oracle on the second morning, another damp one, the conditions again bowler-friendly. Lara's innings was his highest in one-day cricket that season, a strangely muted contribution given his mastery in championship games, but he battled nobly before holing out to the safe hands of Graeme Hick at deep square leg.

Hick played a key role thereafter in a tremendous stand of 198 off just 212 balls with Moody as the sun beat down and set on the Bears' Grand Slam aspirations. Not even the inspirational Reeve, working through his tactical box of tricks, could conjure up a comeback on the lines of the Kent semi-final, and the result was a formality with an hour left.

The scorecard will focus on that Hick/Moody stand but one of just 29 by Damian D'Oliveira and Tim Curtis was highly relevant. That occupied the first 14 overs, when batting was still a hazardous exercise against Tim Munton and Gladstone Small. Munton in particular was as testing as Newport the previous morning, but Curtis and D'Oliveira held firm, to set up 35 overs of mayhem from Hick and Moody.

The captain Curtis modestly downplays that opening stand, but he knew what was necessary. The previous afternoon the Worcestershire players were on their coach, on the way down to London from Manchester after beating Lancashire in a championship match (Hick and Moody warming up for Lord's with a stand of 265). Over a game of cards, Curtis joked, 'Don't be surprised, if we bat first, to see me running down the pitch, trying to smash the first ball for four.' His team-mates joshed with Curtis, knowing that such bravado was foreign to such an adhesive, cussed opener.

Curtis was simply being fatalistic about the perils facing opening batsmen in a Lord's final, when the ball is moving around menacingly on a moist pitch in overcast conditions. Two months earlier, that was exactly the challenge facing him in the Benson & Hedges Final, after Warwickshire had won the toss. Curtis had laboured for 11 overs for his 13, against high-class, probing bowling by Small and Munton, so he was well aware of the lottery of the toss on a September morning at Lord's, with rain around.

'The openers' lot in a September final in the first innings is to hang around, try to locate the ball and then watch the big guns smack it around later. That's what Dolly and I managed to do, and Tom and Hicky were duly grateful. Sometimes that strategy works; others you're not so lucky.'

Curtis knew how vital it was to win the toss, and Moody's leg-pulling after victory in the semi-final was still in his mind. Moody had inspired Worcestershire to an astonishing victory at The Oval over Surrey, sharing an unbroken stand of 309 for a breathless win by just seven runs. This after losing the toss and being put in by Surrey.

In the showers afterwards, Moody said to his captain: 'TC, you're hopeless at winning the toss. It's going to be crucial in the final. I'm going to do it for you.'

Moody realised that wouldn't be possible, but they agreed a strategy, as Curtis recalls: 'Don't ask me why

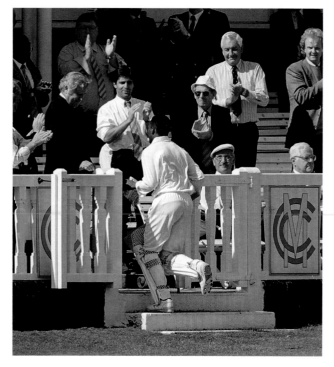

Top left: Warwickshire supporters
Top right: The scoreboard at the end of a wet first day
Above: Brian Lara out for 81
Right: Tim Munton facing on 222 for nine

but, when there was a slope on a ground, I always called heads. We all know about the famous Lord's slope, don't we? Tom knew Dermot Reeve from playing cricket with him out in Western Australia, and he forecast that Dermot would hold the coin with the tail up and he'd throw it high. Warwickshire were in the home dressing room at Lord's, so their captain was in charge of tossing the coin.

'So Dermot shows me the coin, with the tail up, and indeed he does throw it high. It starts rolling from the Pavilion End to the Nursery End and keeps on rolling. I'd called heads. The coin finally tottered and came to a halt. Heads. And that's why we won the game. Win the toss, win the cup.'

Perhaps an over-simplification from Curtis, but it was a vital first blow for Worcestershire. They had a point to prove here. They were aware that Warwickshire were garnering all the attention in pursuit of the Grand Slam, but the neighbours were quietly going about some impressive one-day business in '94. Runners-up in the Benson & Hedges Cup, they had pressed Warwickshire hard for the Sunday League. At one stage they were level, with Worcestershire enjoying the advantage of a game in hand. But they lost two of their last three Sunday games as Warwickshire broke clear of the pack.

'So winning the NatWest capped a fine one-day season for us,' recalls Curtis. 'No one ever talks about that when they focus on Warwickshire's great year. We weren't far off doing the treble.'

So no residual sympathy from Worcestershire, and Tim Munton happily accepts that. 'There was no angst from us about losing the toss and the result being influenced by that. It was just one of those things. Any county pro accepts it is often a lottery at a September Lord's final. And Hick and Moody were a formidable combo, whatever the conditions.

'So we weren't going to get all four trophies. But we'd already got two in the bag. Everyone in our dressing room recognised it was the most special period in our lives. We knew losing at Lord's wasn't going to derail our pursuit of a third trophy.'

Munton was right to maintain perspective and not bemoan ill-fortune. This was only the fifth defeat in 40 games in what was already a momentous season. Just two Sunday League matches left, in the hope of making it a historic summer.

Warwickshire v Worcestershire, Lord's, 3 & 4 September 1994

Worcestershire won by eight wickets

Umpires: N.T. Plews & D.R. Shepherd

Warwickshire

A.J. Moles	c Rhodes	b Newport	8
D.P. Ostler	c Lampitt	b Newport	4
B.C. Lara	c Hick	b Haynes	81
P.A. Smith	c Haynes	b Moody	13
R.G. Twose	c Leatherdale	b Newport	22
T.L. Penney	lbw	b Radford	18
D.A. Reeve *	c Rhodes	b Newport	13
N.M.K. Smith	c Illingworth	b Lampitt	20
K.J. Piper +	*not out*		16
G.C. Small	run out		5
T.A. Munton	*not out*		0
	b 1, lb 8, w 10, nb 4		23
60 overs	(for 9 wickets)		**223**

1/8, 2/17, 3/50, 4/90, 5/150, 6/171, 7/188, 8/215, 9/222

Moody	12	4	17	1
Newport	12	2	38	4
Radford	12	1	45	1
Lampitt	11	1	45	1
Illingworth	6	0	35	0
Haynes	7	0	34	1

Worcestershire

T.S. Curtis *		b Reeve	11
D.B. D'Oliveira	c Lara	b Munton	12
G.A. Hick	*not out*		93
T.M. Moody	*not out*		88
G.R. Haynes			
D.A. Leatherdale			
S.J. Rhodes +			
S.R. Lampitt			
P.J. Newport			
R.K. Illingworth			
N.V. Radford			
	lb 6, w 11, nb 6		23
49.1 overs	(for 2 wickets)		**227**

1/29, 2/29

Small	12	2	40	0
Munton	12	3	23	1
Reeve	6	1	30	1
Smith PA	7	1	54	0
Twose	5	0	36	0
Smith NMK	7	0	34	0
Penney	0.1	0	4	0

v Gloucestershire, AXA League, Bristol, 18 September

It was a long fortnight for the Warwickshire players after the Lord's disappointment. Bristol loomed large in their thoughts, aware that Gloucestershire could scupper their hopes of landing the treble. And the weather, uncertain at the best of times in mid-September, could easily ruin all permutations.

If the September days dragged for the players, what about those twenty supporters who stood to scoop £100,000 if the Bears landed the treble? Chickens justifiably weren't being counted by anyone associated with the club.

There had been a worrying wobble on Sundays in August when Warwickshire lost two games out of three in the run-in. Defeat by Yorkshire by 54 runs was a thrashing and had to be consigned to one-off status, but losing by three runs to Worcestershire was infuriating.

Needing 183 in 38 overs, and bolstered by a first-wicket stand of 105 in just 14 overs from Dominic Ostler and Neil Smith, this ought to have been a doddle. But Lara, of all people, got bogged down, struggling with his timing. All the later batsmen, including Dermot Reeve, batted unimaginatively against Richard Illingworth's spin, conceding just two runs in five overs.

In the dressing room an infuriated Reeve let rip at the team for a pallid effort that was at variance with Warwickshire's usual vibrancy. Lara snapped back at him, tempers flared, voices were raised, and Bob Woolmer had to restore calm.

'I had my first-ever general go at the side,' recalls Reeve, 'saying we were too complacent after such a great start. I was sick at the manner of our defeat and just wanted to talk it out. I admitted that I batted badly. But Brian didn't appreciate such honest, open discussion, a feature of the Warwickshire dressing room in recent years.'

Reeve was clearly disturbed at the prospect of losing momentum in the Sunday format but, in the penultimate game, a comfortable win over Hampshire on a revised run-rate restored some calm and order. Worcestershire's faltering challenge for the title had simplified matters: win at Bristol in 12 days' time and the treble was secured.

That delay didn't sit well with someone of Reeve's restless energy. He was content that Lara was given leave of absence from the final championship match in Bristol, allowing him time away, as long as he was fresh and raring to go for the Sunday decider, to be played after day three of the championship game.

Trevor Penney and Dermot Reeve batting during their crucial fifth-wicket partnership

Dermot Reeve is sweeping slow left-armer Mark Davies for six

Reeve would not be enquiring of Lara's whereabouts in the world at Christmas time for an exchange of Yuletide greetings, so he was happy that he was out of the way for a few days.

To the dismay of Reeve, Lara arrived late for the customary warm-ups and nets on that Sunday lunchtime in Bristol. Dennis Amiss was deputed to chivvy Lara along for the imminent start, as the captain fumed, trying to focus his preparation for such an important game. His only consolation was this would be the last time Lara would be indulged over his time-keeping this season. And Allan Donald would be back in 1995.

Yet we saw the impressive side of Lara within a few minutes of the game starting. In the blink of an eye Warwickshire found themselves 3/3. Then Trevor Penney was dropped second ball at midwicket by Courtney Walsh – luckily, not the sharpest fielder in the Gloucestershire eleven. Surely there would have been no way back, at 3/4? As Gladstone Small said afterwards, 'Four or five years earlier, we'd have struggled to get to 120 and we'd have lost.'

But Lara was admirable in restoring calm and set out to blunt the threat of Walsh, his West Indian team-mate and notable fast bowler. He told Penney,

'Forget it – pretend we're opening the batting. We don't need to score much for the next ten overs or so. Just stay in.' It may not have been the largest stand those two compiled in such a productive collaboration in '94, but it was highly significant. They added a precious 68 before Lara was out.

Then another vital stand of 75 by Penney and Reeve calmed Warwickshire's nerves even more. Their respective half-centuries in dank, dismal conditions were worth double in the context of the game and the Sunday League title.

Suitably inspired, Warwickshire wouldn't be denied. Reeve, backing a hunch, opened the bowling, and he, Munton and Small went for just three an over apiece in their canny, miserly stints. The spinners Smith and Davis capitalised as the Gloucestershire batsmen, behind on the asking rate of nearly five an over, flailed around unproductively. They were all out, with two overs to spare.

Victory by 46 runs was a massive margin, given the earlier travails, but the performance epitomised Warwickshire's powers of recovery from difficult positions. That had stood out a year earlier in the spectacular triumph over Sussex in the NatWest Final.

Gloucestershire v Warwickshire, Bristol, 18 September 1994

Warwickshire won by 46 runs

Umpires: K.J. Lyons & P.B. Wight

Warwickshire

D.P. Ostler	c Davies	b Williams	0
N.M.K. Smith	c Alleyne	b Smith	0
B.C. Lara	c Smith	b Alleyne	38
R.G. Twose	c Russell	b Smith	0
T.L. Penney	c Ball	b Walsh	55
D.A. Reeve *	c Alleyne	b Walsh	50
G. Welch	lbw	b Walsh	0
K.J. Piper +	c Wright	b Alleyne	6
R.P. Davis	*not out*		2
G.C. Small	*not out*		7
T.A. Munton			
	lb 11, w 6, nb 8		25
39 overs	(for 8 wickets)		**183**

1/1, 2/1, 3/3, 4/71, 5/146, 6/146, 7/165, 8/172

Williams	8	2	26	1
Smith	8	2	24	2
Walsh	7	1	24	3
Alleyne	8	0	37	2
Ball	5	0	36	0
Davies	3	0	25	0

Gloucestershire

A.J. Wright	lbw	b Munton	3
M.G.N. Windows		b Smith	47
T.H.C. Hancock	c Piper	b Small	7
M.W. Alleyne	c Piper	b Welch	7
R.I. Dawson	st Piper	b Davis	29
R.C. Russell +	lbw	b Davis	4
M.C.J. Ball	c Smith	b Small	3
C.A. Walsh *	c Twose	b Small	0
R.C. Williams	st Piper	b Reeve	9
M. Davies	*not out*		10
A.M. Smith	c Munton	b Smith	7
	lb 7, w 4		11
37 overs			**137**

1/10, 2/30, 3/43, 4/93, 5/101, 6/104, 7/104, 8/109, 9/124, 10/137

Reeve	5	0	17	1
Munton	6	3	16	1
Small	8	2	25	3
Welch	4	1	16	1
Smith	6	0	28	2
Davis	8	0	28	2

'I knew deep down we'd pull it off,' said Small afterwards in the dressing room. 'We'd come so far over a period of time, we trusted each other. And Brian was the icing on the cake, the final piece in the jigsaw.' He spoke as Small's three-year-old son Marcus was being carried around on Lara's shoulders in the dressing room in delight. Young Marcus wouldn't be fazed by Lara's time-keeping, unlike some of the grown-ups. To him, Uncle Brian was a hero and would stay that way. I suspect that would have been the view of the vast majority of Warwickshire supporters.

Reeve parked his reservations about Lara afterwards, amid intense celebrations. 'There are so many variables in cricket that to have won all four trophies on offer would've been astonishing – but three is amazing enough! I want to have a party forever!'

Tim Munton remembers the warm feeling of a job well done that night in the team hotel. 'We were planning to go out in Bristol, but we never got out of the bar – around forty of us. Players, friends, our families, just standing around chatting and drinking. It was a special occasion, just letting it all sink in.'

With the final day of the championship washed out on the morrow, that Sunday was the last occasion a great team and their outstanding coach were all gathered together. Lara would not be involved for another four years at Edgbaston, while Bob Woolmer was off to South Africa to broaden his matchless coaching horizons. Mike Procter had just been sacked as head coach by South Africa, and there was no doubt that the outstanding candidate was an Englishman living in Cape Town. Woolmer would find it impossible to turn the offer down.

At least Roger Twose had confirmed in the triumphant aftermath that he would return for one more year to Edgbaston before he too would answer the siren call of international cricket.

If anyone grabbed a photo in the Bristol dressing room of that celebrating eleven and their revered coach, it would soon be a collector's item.

It would also underline the ephemeral nature of professional sport. At a time of euphoria and historic achievement, the tectonic plates were being assembled to move the personnel along.

Celebrating the Treble at Bristol

Results: 9 August to 19 September

County Championship

Aug 11,12,13,15   **Edgbaston**   **Nottinghamshire**   **Lost by an innings & 43 runs**
Nottinghamshire 597-8 dec (Lewis 220*, Pollard 134) Warwickshire 321 (Welch 84*, Piper 57) & 233 (Twose 80)

Aug 18,19,20,22   **Scarborough**   **Yorkshire**   **Won by eight wickets**
Yorkshire 310 (Welch 4-74) & 347 (Moxon 116, Davis 6-94) Warwickshire 459 (Ostler 186, Moles 65, Welch 60) & 200-2 (Twose 86*)

Aug 25,26,27   **Hove**   **Sussex**   **Won by ten wickets**
Sussex 131 (Munton 4-22) & 127 (Munton 4-52) Warwickshire 183 (Ostler 50) & 79-0

Aug 30,31, Sept 1,2   **Edgbaston**   **Hampshire**   **Won by an innings & 95 runs**
Hampshire 278 (Munton 4-44) & 163 (Smith N 5-65) Warwickshire 536 (Lara 191, Twose 137)

Sept 15,16,17,19   **Bristol**   **Gloucestershire**   **Match drawn**
Gloucestershire 372-9 dec (Hodgson 113, Davis 6-128) Warwickshire 24-0

AXA Equity & Law League

Aug 14   **Edgbaston**   **Nottinghamshire**   **Won by 72 runs**
Warwickshire 294-6 *(40 overs)* (Lara 75, Ostler 59, Twose 44) Nottinghamshire 222-9 *(40 overs)* (Robinson 76, Smith N 3-47)

Aug 21   **Scarborough**   **Yorkshire**   **Lost by 54 runs**
Yorkshire 209-3 *(40 overs)* (Byas 55, Blakey 55*) Warwickshire 155 *(33.1 overs)* (Reeve 41)

Aug 28   **Hove**   **Sussex**   **Won by five wickets**
Sussex 157-7 *(39 overs)* (Wells 60) Warwickshire 161-5 *(35 overs)* (Ostler 84*)

Sept 6   **Edgbaston**   **Hampshire**   **Won on faster scoring rate**
Hampshire 197-4 *(40 overs)* (Smith 68) Warwickshire 147-4 *(28 0vers)* (Lara 56)

Sept 18   **Bristol**   **Gloucestershire**   **Won by 46 runs**
Warwickshire 183-8 *(39 overs)* (Penney 55, Reeve 50) Gloucestershire 137 *(37 overs)* (Small 3-25)

NatWest Bank Trophy

Aug 9 *(Semi-Final)*   **Edgbaston**   **Kent**   **Won by 8 runs**
Warwickshire 265-8 *(60 overs)* (Moles 105*, Twose 49) Kent 257 *(59.5 overs)* (Ward 80, Taylor 64, Reeve 3-44)

Sept 3,4 *(Final)*   **Lord's**   **Worcestershire**   **Lost by eight wickets**
Warwickshire 223 *(60 overs)* (Lara 81, Newport 4-38) Worcestershire 227-2 *(49.1 overs)* (Hick 93*, Moody 88*)

County Championship

	P	W	L	D	Bt	Bl	Pts
Warwickshire	17	11	1	5	41	55	272
Leicestershire	17	8	7	2	42	60	230
Nottinghamshire	17	8	5	4	39	51	218
Middlesex	17	7	3	7	43	57	212
Northamptonshire	17	8	4	5	28	53	209
Essex	17	7	5	5	32	63	207
Surrey	17	7	7	3	32	57	201
Sussex	17	7	5	5	28	60	200
Kent	17	6	7	4	44	58	198
Lancashire	17	8	6	3	32	59	194
Somerset	17	7	7	3	32	47	191
Gloucestershire	17	3	6	3	16	45	117
Yorkshire	17	4	6	7	38	57	159
Hampshire	17	4	7	6	32	55	159
Worcestershire	17	4	6	7	42	52	158
Durham	17	4	10	3	32	57	153
Derbyshire	17	4	9	4	25	54	143
Glamorgan	17	2	8	7	29	50	111

Lancashire -25 pts for sub-standard pitch
Glos & Yorks 8pts each for levelling scores in drawn games

AXA Equity & Law League

	P	W	L	T	NR	Pts
Warwickshire	17	13	3	-	1	54
Worcestershire	17	12	4	-	1	50
Kent	17	12	5	-	-	48
Lancashire	17	11	5	-	1	46
Yorkshire	17	10	6	-	1	42
Surrey	17	9	5	-	3	42
Glamorgan	17	9	6	1	1	40
Derbyshire	17	8	7	-	2	36
Durham	17	6	7	1	3	32
Leicestershire	17	7	9	-	1	30
Nottinghamshire	17	6	8	-	3	30
Hampshire	17	7	10	-	-	28
Northamptonshire	17	6	9	1	1	28
Middlesex	17	6	10	-	1	26
Sussex	17	5	11	-	1	22
Somerset	17	5	12	-	-	20
Essex	17	4	11	1	1	20
Gloucestershire	17	4	12	-	1	18

The Opposition's view

County cricketers are invariably very generous about any side that becomes serial winners. They know that it takes hard work, luck, a clear vision and outstanding ability to land trophies. In the short term a successful team can get up the collective pipe of opponents by displaying a harsh winner's attitude that can easily stray into arrogance – and Warwickshire '94 was no exception. That team contained more than enough good, solid, likeable characters, but as they continued to surprise the other counties as this historic season progressed, they developed a super-confident persona, impervious to the sceptics who believed they'd run out of steam, relying too much on Brian Lara's genius. They just didn't care how they were perceived outside Edgbaston.

A quarter of a century on and the ex-pros from other counties happily pay due homage to the record-breakers ...

David Graveney, Durham

They clearly had a fantastic team spirit. Dermot Reeve created a 'no fear' approach, a brand of positive play and sticking by it, no matter what. He reminds me of Eoin Morgan today, with England. Bob Woolmer was a great foil for Dermot. The side was a fascinating mix of the eccentric and the good guys. It worked.

Neil Fairbrother, Lancashire

I can't give enough praise to Dermot Reeve. By then I had been on England tours with him and thought he had a fantastic cricket brain. He cajoled players, got the best out of them and himself. As a one-day cricketer, he was ahead of his time in tactical nous. They were a proper team – some bloody good cricketers in that dressing room who played above themselves. Highly talented, but didn't get the credit they deserved at the time.

Dominic Cork, Derbyshire

I liked them, they were a solid, tough side. You could tell they felt they could beat anyone. They were like Surrey, but without the strut. More likeable. They worked hard for each other. Forget about Lara for a moment – they had so many others, like Ostler, Penney and Twose, who just got on with it, getting

runs when most needed. They weren't appreciated at the time, because they weren't fashionable, with no current England players. But the senior pros showed the youngsters how it's done. They bought into being a Bear – 'You Bears, you Bears!' – you heard it all the time when playing Warwickshire. Good on them.

Steve Watkin, Glamorgan

Apart from Lara, they had no real superstars, but they were greater than the sum of their parts. They were innovative, they kept at you. I enjoyed them, they were almost all sociable guys off the field. On it, they really knew what they were doing.

Chris Scott, Durham

They seemed to swarm all over you, so full of energy. There seemed no hierarchy in their dressing room, despite Reeve and Woolmer clearly being in charge. But they all had an input, enjoying themselves.

Mike Gatting, Middlesex

Dermot Reeve was always looking to have a game, while many other captains were cautious. He wouldn't let things drift, he was different, thinking outside the box. They had a great self-belief and once they built up momentum, they couldn't be stopped.

Hugh Morris, Glamorgan

They exuded confidence, especially when you played them at Edgbaston. They expected to beat you. They had an excellent, varied bowling attack. Dermot was very intuitive, ahead of his time and we all looked up to Bob Woolmer, one of the original coaching gurus. Bob was the cement that bound them together, coming up with those little one percenters that got you over the line.

Graham Cowdrey, Kent

If there was one side we didn't want to play, it was Warwickshire. They were 40/0 against us before a ball was bowled. They knew they were good, but unlike Surrey – who we didn't like – they weren't in your face. They didn't railroad you, they had some really good blokes in the side, but Dermot was the X-factor who propelled them into a different league.

Paul Nixon, Leicestershire

They ticked a lot of boxes in '94. We were a pretty good side – we won the championship two years later – but they were so tough to beat. Their record that summer was fantastic, they had an aura about them. They seemed to believe they'd win a game just by playing positively.

Alec Stewart, Surrey

Their team had a massive team belief, an air of arrogance about them that we had a few years later, when we started to win a few trophies. You learn how to win, then back it up for a period of time. Dermot got a group of players to perform at their very, very best. They lacked massive names. Who was going to play for England at that time from Warwickshire? But that didn't matter, they made it all count. And Lara was the best batsman I ever played against. That's a major plus for your team.

Paul Taylor, Northamptonshire

They had so many gritty players, like Roger Twose who was good enough to be considered by England. Now every team has fantastic fielders, but Trevor Penney was way ahead of the rest in '94. And, as a batter, he turned ones into twos by his speed between the wickets. And Dermot Reeve's field placings were so different from the norm. He got you thinking.

Tim Curtis, Worcestershire

They were bumptious, cocky, full of themselves – and loud. I was once batting against them and was fed up with all the noise they were making. I remarked, 'It's like a zoo out here' ... and for the next half-hour, all I could hear were animal noises! We had the usual local rivalry thing with them, and they were a strange mix of the mercurial and the reliable, the likes of Small, Munton and Neil Smith. As captain, Dermot Reeve had that swagger, that chutzpah. He had everyone following him, they had a huge amount of self-belief.

Robert Croft, Glamorgan

It was a perfect storm for them in '94, it all came together. They had an excellent blend of youth and experience, a superstar batsman, all bases covered with their bowling and a terrific tactician in their captain. Dermot split opinion because of his personality, but he was a maverick, perfect at the time for Warwickshire. He gave them an edge and he didn't mind getting up opponents' noses.

John Emburey, Middlesex

Dermot Reeve was the most innovative captain around at that time, while Bob Woolmer was far and away the best coach in the world. The players really responded to Bob's passion for the game and Dermot's quirkiness. They were a well-balanced side and, apart from Lara, the key was Tim Munton. He learned how to swing the ball and was just so reliable.

Matthew Fleming, Kent

Warwickshire had the psychological hold over us at that time. Reeve was just annoying – but he was the catalyst, dynamic, restless and innovative. They were soon respected on the county circuit for being so far ahead of the rest of us.

Geoff Cook, Director of Cricket, Durham

They only had one devastating player but they were the perfect example of group confidence, stemming from the fact they had Lara. They had no respect for opposition egos, they were a stimulated, ambitious team. Reeve worked on putting opposition backs up, he was a huge bluffer, outrageously confident. That was brilliant for the younger players. I never thought they would be so successful that year, though. Lara brought them an extra dimension.

Mark Nicholas, Hampshire

They came to be widely admired, but at the time no one could believe it was happening. The charming, avuncular Woolmer worked so well alongside the spiky, irreverent Reeve. When you played them, you were aware that they'd come at you from so many different angles. None of them had to fit into a particular bracket, they were just encouraged to be themselves. Dermot liked non-conformity and banished insecurity. When you've got a truly great player like Lara, you shouldn't be worried, but the others were smart enough just to play around him. You start to believe anything's possible.

End-of-season averages

						County Championship					
	M	*I*	*NO*	*Runs*	*HS*	*Ave*	*100*	*50*	*ct*	*st*
B.C. Lara	15	25	2	2,066	501*	89.82	9	3	11	
R.G. Twose	17	30	5	1,395	277*	55.80	3	6	8	
A.J. Moles	11	20	3	863	203*	50.76	1	5	5	
D.P. Ostler	17	28	2	1,012	186	38.92	1	6	14	
T.L. Penney	15	23	3	774	111	38.70	1	1	14	
G. Welch	11	15	3	446	84*	37.16	-	4	5	
Asif Din	3	4	1	107	42*	35.66	-	-	1	
D.R. Brown	3	6	2	113	54	28.25	-	1	-	
N.M.K. Smith	17	21	4	435	65	25.58	-	2	3	
K.J. Piper	17	24	4	454	116*	22.70	1	1	61	5
P.A. Smith	11	16	2	313	65	22.35	-	1	2	
J.D. Ratcliffe	2	4	-	80	69	20.00	-	1	1	
R.P. Davis	11	9	2	131	35*	18.71	-	-	15	
D.A. Reeve	8	9	1	109	33	13.62	-	-	18	
T.A. Munton	17	17	7	106	36	10.60	-	-	4	
G.C. Small	11	10	1	78	23	8.66	-	-	2	

Also batted: M.A.V. Bell *(1 match)* 4* (1 ct)

	O	*M*	*R*	*W*	*BB*	*Ave*	*5wi*	*10wm*
T.A. Munton	693.4	177	1,745	81	7-52	21.54	6	2
D.R. Brown	35	5	118	5	4-25	23.60	-	
G.C. Small	339	79	946	36	5-46	26.27	1	
R.P. Davis	337	99	984	31	6-94	31.74	2	
P.A. Smith	182	40	594	18	3-24	33.00	-	
N.M.K. Smith	581	141	1,690	49	7-42	34.48	4	
R.G. Twose	185.5	38	535	15	6-28	35.66	1	
M.A.V. Bell	31	5	108	3	3-89	36.00	-	
D.A. Reeve	138	44	299	8	2-31	37.37	-	
G. Welch	263	63	949	22	4-74	43.13	-	

Also bowled: B.C. Lara 21-1-112-0, Asif Din 2-0-9-0, D.P. Ostler 1.1-0-13-0

Played 17 – Won 11 Lost 1 Drawn 5

Warwickshire scored 9,221 runs for the loss of 219 wickets
at an average of 42.10 runs per wicket

Their opponents scored 8,437 runs for the loss of 272 wickets
at an average of 31.01 runs per wicket

Their run rate of 61.11 per 100 balls was the highest in the championship

One-day competitions

	M	I	NO	Runs	HS	Ave	100	50	ct	st
A.J. Moles	5	5	2	205	105*	68.33	1	-	2	
T.L. Penney	23	20	12	396	65*	49.50	-	2	9	
D.A. Reeve	24	23	7	563	65*	35.18	-	3	3	
R.G. Twose	25	23	3	701	110	35.05	1	2	9	
D.P. Ostler	25	25	1	803	84*	33.45	-	7	8	
B.C. Lara	22	22	-	634	81	28.81	-	5	9	
Asif Din	16	16	3	341	86*	26.23	-	2	2	
P.A. Smith	21	21	1	412	50	20.60	-	1	5	
K.J. Piper	16	10	7	60	16*	20.00	-	-	20	6
N.M.K. Smith	25	19	3	268	56	16.75	-	1	10	
G. Welch	8	5	1	57	26	14.25	-	-	3	
M. Burns	9	8	-	86	37	10.75	-	-	14	4
G.C. Small	20	6	3	26	7*	8.66	-	-	3	
R.P. Davis	8	3	1	12	5	6.00	-	-	3	
T.A. Munton	25	3	3	16	15*		-	-	5	

Also batted: D.R. Brown *(1 match)* 1, M.A.V. Bell *(2 matches)* did not bat

	O	M	R	W	BB	Ave	4wi	rpo
M.A.V. Bell	19	1	53	7	5-19	7.57	1	2.78
N.M.K. Smith	175.3	13	692	43	4-19	16.09	2	3.94
R.P. Davis	48.2	2	195	11	3-19	17.72	-	4.03
P.A. Smith	122.1	7	614	27	5-38	22.74	1	5.02
D.A. Reeve	170.3	20	595	23	3-44	25.86	-	3.48
T.A. Munton	204	33	731	28	3-27	26.10	-	3.58
G. Welch	53	5	204	7	2-30	29.14	-	3.84
R.G. Twose	73.4	2	368	12	3-36	30.66	-	4.99
G.C. Small	150.2	23	569	18	3-25	31.61	1	3.78

Also bowled: T.L. Penney 1.4-0-12-1, Asif Din 8-0-33-0

Played 25 – Won 20 Lost 4 No Result 1

(+ victory in the B&H bowl-out)

Warwickshire scored 5,039 runs for the loss of 157 wickets off 1029.3 overs
at an average of 32.09 runs per wicket and 4.89 runs per over

Their opponents scored 4,203 runs for the loss of 202 wickets off 1023.2 overs
at an average of 20.80 runs per wicket and 4.10 runs per wicket

Dermot Reeve and Tim Munton with the three trophies

Afterwards

It was no fluke

There were still a few refuseniks in the game who maintained that Warwickshire's 'annus mirabilis' was a fluke, that 'Larashire' would implode in 1995 now that his genius was no longer on tap.

That didn't bother Warwickshire as they continued their triumphal progress around the county circuit, repeating the formula that served them so well in 1994.

They won two more trophies in 1995, dominating the championship and riding their luck to win a thrilling NatWest Final. But luck was against them in the AXA Equity & Law League on Sundays, when a wash-out in the penultimate match after being in a winning position meant they lost out on the title on run rate. This after winning ten successive Sunday matches, recovering from a bad start to the season.

Swings and roundabouts. It may be that Derbyshire would have recovered from 81/5 off 25 overs before the Edgbaston rains came that September Sunday, but Warwickshire weren't complaining about such vagaries. Beating the eventual champions Kent by five wickets in their own backyard the following Sunday was immensely satisfying. The Bears were always happy to put Kent in their place in the mid-90s.

Garnering six trophies in 24 months was more than enough for Warwickshire to be hailed as the best team in the land. And the manner of their defence of the championship brooked no arguments, surely.

The margin of 32 points was impressive enough, but they created history by winning so many matches. The tally of 14 wins in 17 championship matches was a new record in percentage terms in county cricket history. Agreed, 1995 was an exceptionally hot, dry summer so the weather was on Warwickshire's side.

Some counties grumbled about the Edgbaston wickets favouring the bowlers too much in '95, even though only Middlesex picked up more batting bonus points and six Warwickshire batsmen averaged over 40 in the championship. And half of their 14 championship victories were away from home.

County Championship 1995

	P	W	L	D	Bt	Bl	Pts
Warwickshire	17	14	2	1	49	64	337
Middlesex	17	12	2	3	51	62	305
Northamptonshire	17	12	2	3	41	57	290
Lancashire	17	10	4	3	48	61	269
Essex	17	8	9	0	42	58	228
Gloucestershire	17	8	4	5	45	50	223
Leicestershire	17	7	8	2	41	61	214
Yorkshire	17	7	8	2	39	55	206
Somerset	17	7	5	5	40	49	201
Worcestershire	17	6	7	4	29	57	182
Nottinghamshire	17	5	9	3	41	54	175
Surrey	17	5	8	4	34	55	169
Hampshire	17	5	8	4	32	56	168
Derbyshire	17	4	10	3	39	64	167
Sussex	17	4	7	6	37	51	152
Glamorgan	17	3	8	6	40	57	145
Durham	17	4	13	0	20	53	137
Kent	17	3	10	4	40	44	132

Highest proportion of wins

Warwickshire	1995	14/17	82.3%
Surrey	1955	23/28	82.1%
Surrey	1892	13/16	81.2%
Surrey	1894	13/16	81.2%
Yorkshire	1923	25/32	78.1%
Kent	1914	19/25	78.0%

Most trophies

IN ONE SEASON

Three including championship
Warwickshire   1994

Three not including championship
Gloucestershire   2000

IN TWO SEASONS

Five including two championships
Warwickshire   1994-95

Five not including championship
Gloucestershire   1999-2000

IN THREE SEASONS

Six including two championships
Warwickshire   1993-95

Five including two championships
Essex   1984-86
Kent   1976-78
(one championship jointly won)

Five not including championship
Gloucestershire   1999-2001

The margins of victory, both home and away, marked Warwickshire out as an outstanding all-round side. After losing by just seven runs to Northants at the start of August in one of the greatest championship games of living memory, Warwickshire's run-in to the title was a juggernaut. Of their last six games four were won by ten wickets and the other two by an innings. Momentum and the ability to bowl out sides twice remain useful allies when there is a title to be won in August and September.

For Dermot Reeve, it was a happier summer than '94. He never had a moment's problem with Allan Donald, who had replaced Brian Lara as the club's overseas player – and how lucky were they to have two such wonderful players at Edgbaston in successive seasons. Reeve admired Donald for his professionalism and example he set to the team, and finishing top of the national averages with 88 wickets at 15 in just 14 championship games endeared him even more to his captain.

Reeve was delighted with his own championship efforts after injuries and poor form blighted his '94 season. He averaged 34 with the bat and 17 with the ball, missing only two championship games. And his nerveless batting, canny bowling and instinctive leadership were decisive in winning the NatWest Trophy. 'I do admit, though, that I was plumb lbw to Anil Kumble early on, but Dickie Bird reprieved me. We weren't at our best that day, but we hung on in there. That was very satisfying.

'If I had to pick one trophy that pleased me most of all, it would be retaining the championship in '95. That was a fantastic achievement. It's pointless comparing other sides from different eras, but it was great to repeat the performances of '94. We had to face criticism that we won the title because the Edgbaston wickets favoured our seam attack. But Gladstone Small and Tim Munton had a few injuries, and the only time that they and Allan Donald were together in harness was for one championship game – and that was drawn.'

Reeve was amused that some county professionals still didn't rate his side all that highly in the winter of 1995/6 when he toured with England's one-day side. 'I used to enjoy winding up some of the lads who still couldn't fathom out why we had been so successful. Darren Gough and Mark Ilott were particularly stubborn. Darren used to say, "You're not the best team," and so the debate would begin in the team bus. I'd point out the facts and they'd keep saying, "Lancashire are the best team, they've got the best players." I didn't need any invitation to stick up for my players, especially with so many Lancashire guys on the trip who would be listening as we debated the issue.'

In the end, Gough would compromise by saying that Warwickshire did not have the best players but that they played best together as a team. Reeve was quite happy with that grudging admission from Gough and told him, 'You and the other lads are very welcome to come down to Edgbaston and polish our trophies. If you're very good, we'll let you lift them up!'

Once again Warwickshire dominated the county landscape with just one world-class player, backed up by fine, solid professionals – overcoming the loss through injuries of Small, Munton, Paul Smith and Andy Moles for long periods – and the familiar brilliance in fielding. Nick Knight, signed from Essex, not only brought solidity at the top of the order, but his all-round fielding ability improved an already superb unit. It was the mixture as before.

Phil Neale, replacing Bob Woolmer as Director of Coaching, was smart enough not to tinker with the winning formula. Having just turned 40, he knew several of the Bears' squad from experiences out in the middle and, as captain of Worcestershire at a time when high-profile players helped him lift five trophies in five seasons, he was hardly an ingenu in a tough world. Neale observed, kept his own counsel unless necessary and ran the ship with a light hand on the tiller.

Neil Smith was impressed by Neale's calm manner in his first season after Woolmer. 'I'm a great believer that, however well things are going, you need to freshen things up sometimes. It was quite refreshing to hear a new voice and a new perspective. Phil came into a very difficult position, in a way, because how could he improve on a treble? The temptation for any new boss is to come in and stamp his authority on things, but he just tried to keep up the momentum and the way we were already playing. You have to say it was a smooth transition because it didn't seem to blight us in any way. The two seasons just seemed to roll into one, because the winter flew by. People wanted to be around you, and there were dinners, presentations and awards. Then all of a sudden we were into '95 and picking up where we left off.'

Allan Donald deep into September 1995 and still giving his all

It helps, though, when you have a match-winner like Allan Donald returning to the dressing room after a summer away on international duty. Not that he was a regular absentee from Edgbaston in '94. Living near the ground, he often popped in to see the players and staff when the South African tour schedule allowed. The Brummie from Bloemfontein had been a highly popular and valuable fixture at the club since 1987, and the love affair was reciprocated.

Donald's team-mates at Warwickshire still talk of him with a mixture of awe, respect and affection. He had the perfect combination of total commitment, world-class ability and dedication to the club. On top of that, he treated all Bears' supporters with an open friendliness and courtesy. His 13 years at Edgbaston mark him out as the club's greatest overseas player – and that is no slight on, among others, cricketers of the calibre of Martin Donnelly, Rohan Kanhai, Alvin Kallicharran, Lance Gibbs, Brian Lara and Jeetan Patel. That is august company, but Donald is surely 'primus inter pares'.

As recently as September 2018, the reverence among supporters for Donald was captured in just one vignette. He was at Edgbaston with the Kent side, for whom he was coaching that summer, and he took a walk around the boundary edge to get back to the pavilion from the indoor nets. It took him an eternity. The fans scuttled down the steps to shake his hand, pose for selfies and, in the nicest possible way, pester him for just a minute of his time. Donald dealt with all entreaties and backslapping with his customary good grace and relaxed humour. The word 'legend' is over-used in sport, but Donald qualifies for that when assessing his contribution to Warwickshire CCC.

He was at his superlative best in 1995, taking a wicket every six overs in the championship, bowling consistently fast, inspiring the team. He had a point to prove, in his quiet, steely way. In February 1995 Dermot Reeve received a call in Australia from Dennis Amiss, informing him that Brian Lara would be returning as the overseas player in 1996. Not Donald. Reeve was dismayed, for personal and professional reasons. He knew how devastated Donald would be. He also suspected the decision was influenced by commercial considerations, that the world's best batsman was deemed a bigger marketing draw than Donald.

Reeve had to swallow the bitter pill, after being told it was his job as captain to motivate Donald in the '95 season – as if that would be necessary. The lure of a benefit year was dangling in front of Reeve as he tussled with his own options. He decided to rely on Donald for at least one more memorable season. He wasn't disappointed. 'AD was so focused in the 1995 season that I just needed to wind him up. Allan was hungry for success with us. He was determined to show they were making the wrong cricketing decision and when he forecast to me he would take 100 championship wickets, I was delighted, because he was not given to boasts. If he hadn't missed three games because of a broken bone in his foot, he surely would have got the hundred. I've seen some great overseas players in county cricket, but I can't believe there's been a better professional and a greater team man than Allan Donald.'

Donald returns the compliment. 'Dermot always knew what he was doing as captain. We'd follow him anywhere. At that time, I'd think "No one's going to beat us" whenever I walked into our dressing room.'

Neil Smith sums up Donald perfectly. 'A captain's dream. His contribution at Warwickshire was incomparable. Day in, day out, year in, year out, he was phenomenal. His attitude and desire to be the best drove us on. Allan came back with something to prove, and he led that side. Brian led with the bat the year before, and now Allan gave oppositions a different problem.'

Donald modestly says, 'The Bears are very much part of my DNA, even though I was born 6,000 miles away. I learned so much from so many great people at Edgbaston. They gave me the tools to be a coach myself. I was very lucky. I still feel very emotional every time I go back to Edgbaston. Wherever I am in the world I follow the Bears religiously, and I always send messages of good luck at the start of each season. It will never leave my heart because of what the club means to me, the people that I played with and the people who had come and gone before.'

For Donald, the 1995 season was the zenith of his Warwickshire career. He was at his peak and, for all he knew, it could have been his last season as a Bear.

'It was an awesome performance from everybody because it was a fantastic championship in 1995. It was definitely the best I could ever recall. It was a hot summer, it hardly rained, and all the skills that define cricket were needed if you were to come out on top. You had to fight in every game.'

It was a terrific environment for younger players making their way in the game. Ashley Giles and Wasim Khan were close friends, sharing the same dreams, and they made significant strides as cricketers in the '95 season. Giles was backed by Reeve to supplant Dickie Davis as first-choice left arm spinner, and he recalls a conversation in the car with Reeve on their way down to Canterbury. 'I'd had an ok year – got my first five-for – and yet Dermot told me that next season I would take 60 wickets and score 500 runs. I thought he was talking nonsense. That game, against Kent, he decided I would open the bowling on the third morning because there was some rough on the pitch and they had a few left-handers. I took the first three wickets, and my confidence just grew. Next season I took 55 wickets and scored 555 runs and was capped. Two years later, I made my Test debut.

'Dermot made sure that the young lads weren't treated as second-class citizens within the side. All players were made to feel equal. I've never forgotten that. Dermot was a brilliant motivator and man-manager.'

Wasim Khan was equally reassured. In his first season in the championship, after serving a four-year apprenticeship in the seconds, he scored 181 against Hampshire, averaged 46 in the championship and looked a great prospect. A local lad, he couldn't believe the experience.

'The senior players were so welcoming. On my first away trips, I'd be thinking that I'd better be good and be in bed at a certain time, but if you didn't go out with the boys for a drink there was an issue. I remember getting back to the hotels in the early hours of the morning. The boys were popping the Ibruprofen to get them through the day. They loved a few beers. They played hard on the field and off it all season long, but they were model professionals.

'I remember the party in Canterbury the night we won the championship. Ash and I were sharing a room, and we were thinking as we walked back to our hotel, "Can we really believe what's happened to us this year?" We had travelled the journey together, much of it in my Peugeot 309. I remember lying in bed that night, thinking, "I can't believe I've won a championship medal." Viv Richards, Mike Procter,

Clive Lloyd, Malcolm Marshall, Wasim Akram – these guys never did it. It was an absolutely incredible thrill, the best five months of my life.'

At last the England selectors acknowledged that Warwickshire's deeds over the past two seasons deserved belated recognition, with six players being picked for tours in the 1995/96 winter. With Donald off with South Africa and Roger Twose at last qualified for New Zealand, that brought the tally to eight, compared to just two – Brian Lara and Keith Piper – the previous winter.

But there was a feeling at times in that '95 season that other clubs were catching up Warwickshire in their approach and tactical flexibility. Dermot Reeve noticed that more and more opposition batsmen were going for the reverse sweep and the paddle. Northants, in particular, played Warwickshire's spinners brilliantly in one of their matches, and Mal Loye, one of their batsmen, told Reeve afterwards that they had a team meeting the previous summer, after the Bears had beaten them in a Sunday game. Their coach, Bob Carter, had suggested his batsmen should now embrace more unorthodox methods against the spinners.

'All through that '95 season,' recalls Reeve, 'players from other counties were coming up to me, saying they would like to play at Edgbaston, which was a nice compliment. It was flattering to see more county sides premeditating against spin in 1995, and I knew that most observant sides would eventually catch us up.'

John Emburey, coach of the England 'A' side's tour to India and Pakistan, praised the Warwickshire Way and, when Leicestershire won the championship in 1996, their captain James Whitaker made a point of picking out Reeve's team as laying down the prototype of a successful team unit that didn't boast too many genuine stars. Jack Russell echoed that when assessing the stunning one-day successes of Gloucestershire a few seasons later.

Warwickshire didn't build on those two golden years, for a variety of reasons. They made a rod for their own backs by their remarkable success over two seasons. They were there to be shot at eventually, as other teams threatened their monopoly. They would not become the Manchester United of cricket, racking up trophy after trophy, year after year.

But no one involved with Warwickshire CCC will forget The History Boys of 1994 and 1995.

Victory in the NatWest Final of 1995

top: Allan Donald celebrates after bowling Kevin Curran, and Roger Twose on his way to a crucial 68
bottom: Dominic Ostler making 45 and Dermot Reeve, with two stumps, after the winning hit

Postscript

The Sliding Doors moment for Warwickshire's two great years at the top duly arrived on Sunday 17 September 1995. Having won the championship in the grand manner the previous day, by hammering Kent, they were in no mood to be rolled over in the Sunday League.

The Bears felt that Kent were lucky to win the League after they had been thwarted by the weather the previous weekend. And there was always an edge to their games against Kent during this period.

A target of 166 in 35 overs was well within Warwickshire's compass, and they had an extra incentive midway through their reply when the game was halted in the 18th over. News had filtered through from other grounds that the Sunday title was Kent's and – reflecting that this was their first trophy since 1978 – the celebrations were prolonged and emotional on the field as well as around the Canterbury ground.

Those supreme iconoclasts Roger Twose and Dermot Reeve decided that Kent would not mark the title celebrations with a victory in this final match. Twose and Reeve would have some fun at Kent's expense. If they had to relinquish the title – unluckily in their opinion – then they would do so in style.

As Reeve walked out to bat, Graham Cowdrey stood at the crease and invited the fast bowler Martin McCague to 'knock his head off'. Reeve told him where to go in the saltiest manner and proceeded to rattle Kent's players in his usual irrepressible fashion.

The irreverent Twose needed no second bidding, and he too climbed in verbally. There was another dimension. These were Twose's last few minutes in a Warwickshire shirt. He had qualified for New Zealand and was leaving England after this game. He would not bow the knee to Kent this day. Warwickshire had meant too much to him.

As he and Reeve got closer to victory, Twose goaded the Kent players, shouting, 'Remind me, Skip – what was our bonus for winning three trophies last year?' and then an over later, 'Come on, Skip, you've been in this situation before – like when we won the NatWest cup a few days ago!'

With just 25 runs needed for victory, Reeve overheard Dean Headley asking one of the umpires to save him a stump, in the likely event of a crowd invasion. Reeve shouted to him, 'Don't worry, Deano, I'll save you a stump!' – the implication being that Reeve would be there at the end, triumphant. 'I was determined to see the job home and enjoyed handing the stump over. That night we left Kent's supporters to their celebrations and went off for our own fun, enjoying the memories of six trophies from September '93 to September '95.'

That match-winning stand between Reeve and Twose epitomised the cheekiness and chutzpah of much of their cricket at the time. Those two players were mostly responsible for Warwickshire's lack of popularity in the game, but they didn't care. Doing themselves justice for the team was more important to them, and it was appropriate that Twose's last appearance helped confirm a deeply satisfying victory, while affording him the chance to rub the opposition's noses in the dirt. He had the last laugh and relished it.

By June the following year, Reeve was also gone, prematurely retired. He and Twose – arch competitors, great encouragers – left a gaping hole. Brian Lara dipped out of the '96 season, labouring under the pressures of international cricket, and his replacement, the South African all-rounder Shaun Pollock, had a reasonable season before ankle surgery in August, but no more than that. Certainly not with the same distinction as Lara and Donald in the previous two seasons.

Donald only managed 80 championship wickets in 21 games over the rest of his Warwickshire career, as international calls and injuries hampered his noble efforts. Gladstone Small and Paul Smith gave up the struggle against chronic injuries, Andy Moles retired before the decade was out, Tim Munton moved on to Derbyshire and Dominic Ostler struggled without the inspirational coaching of Bob Woolmer. Trevor Penney became marginalised, categorised as a one-day player. Keith Piper sadly lost his way.

The heart of a marvellous side was ripped out only too quickly. Some strange cricketing decisions were made, internal politics seeped into the dressing room and that unique chemistry which fosters success foundered. It happens so often in professional sport.

Over the next eight seasons, Warwickshire won just two trophies. Not even Bob Woolmer's return could halt the slide into mediocrity, and he could not regain that alchemist's touch. Not enough Junior Bears came through to the first team, with Ian Bell and Chris Woakes and the hugely promising Henry Brookes the rare shining lights.

Four major trophies have been won by Warwickshire in the 2010s and, now they are restored to the top flight after a chastening 2017 summer, their impressive captain Jeetan Patel is dedicated to building on an encouraging revival. With so many former Bears now in key coaching roles, we shall see if the production line of young local players speeds up. Since 2009, 18 players have come through the Bears' academy system and played first-team cricket. Not enough, as Ashley Giles freely admitted when he returned to the club in 2017. The coaching staff have been charged with smoothing the tough transition from academy to first team. I believe the buzz word among modern coaches is 'pathway'.

But as long as he stays at Edgbaston, the bowling coach Graeme Welch will carry the torch for the Class of '94/95, along with that able administrator and Edgbaston doyen Keith Cook. The loss of Ashley Giles to England means Welch is the sole survivor among the coaching staff from those halcyon days. He will lose no opportunity to educate the players about those great deeds of a quarter of a century ago, and use those six trophies as an inspiration.

That was certainly Giles' intention when he returned to Edgbaston as Director of Sport in 2017. He felt strongly that not enough attention had been given to Warwickshire's illustrious history and, with the full backing of the chief executive Neil Snowball, worked hard to make the current players aware of who they were following.

In the last two years the dressing room area has been modernised to embrace the past. As the players enter the dressing room in the lobby, there are two large photos of Dermot Reeve and Tim Munton holding the three trophies from 1994 and one of the

2012 squad, celebrating their championship win. In the players' dining room, all seven championship pennants from 1911 onwards are on the wall, having been retrieved from a cupboard, then framed. As the players leave the dressing room to go onto the field of play, the last things they see above the door are the Bear and Ragged Staff symbol and a mock-up of a bear's claw with the words 'LEAVE YOUR MARK'. The taller Warwickshire players slap the mantra above them as they take the field. It's homage to Liverpool FC and the famous 'THIS IS ANFIELD' message in the tunnel, but that's a suitable source of inspiration, given their achievements.

Above the players' viewing area, there is a motto 'ONCE A BEAR, ALWAYS A BEAR', which is signed by all the players who have left the club. In 2018 it was signed by Chris Wright, Keith Barker and Jonathan Trott, while Dermot Reeve, Dennis Amiss and Allan Donald have added their names when they visited the room.

And – an interesting piece of psychology – the away team is greeted by a roll-call of Bears' achievements when they walk into their changing room. Under the words 'THIS IS EDGBASTON, HOME OF THE BEARS', the seven championships and ten one-day trophies are listed. Just a little nudge in the ribs to a sceptical opposition who may not enjoy such a rich history. Dermot Reeve and Roger Twose would love tweaking their tail this way.

Giles and Snowball were very keen that new players signed after 2017 should be up to speed on the club's playing history. They felt that respect for past illustrious achievements imbued the young novitiates with an extra incentive. So they commissioned an 18-minute film detailing the great Warwickshire players and achievements since the club was formed in 1882. The first image is that of Walter Quaife, who faced the initial ball as opener in Warwickshire's inaugural first-class match against Nottinghamshire at Trent Bridge in May 1894. Giles felt that awareness of past successes ought to be an inspiration, rather than a burden, to an aspiring young player and trawled through the Edgbaston archives to pay tribute to every significant player, from Quaife to Henry Brookes.

The club's chief executive Neil Snowball fully backed Giles' mission to make the current players more aware of Warwickshire's history. 'When we sign a player from another county or they get onto the playing staff from the Academy, they go through an induction process. They have to do a tour of the ground, taking in all the historic areas, visit the museum and watch this film. It's interesting to see the reaction from the players, senior and youngsters. Tim Ambrose, a former England player, in the professional game for nearly twenty years, was quite emotional watching it. Liam Norwell, signed from Gloucestershire in the winter, was taken aback by the depth of history and the great players of the past.

'When Ashley came back from Lancashire, I said no one has yet been able to identify precisely the Bears' identity. Over time it's like osmosis, but I wanted us to speed up that process.

'We wanted the younger player and newcomers from other counties to be aware of who came before them and the responsibility they have to inspire those who will come after them. We didn't just want to stick some random slogans and pictures on the walls; we wanted it to really mean something, to inspire performances and shape behaviours.'

Snowball feels the 'ONCE A BEAR, ALWAYS A BEAR' mantra in the viewing area is particularly relevant. 'It's not just wallpaper, it's particularly special, connecting with our rich history. On his last day as a Warwickshire player before retirement, Jonathan Trott signed it and during the same match we allowed Allan Donald to slip in from the Kent dressing room to add his name. I think he qualified!

'I know every county is special and so many have a tremendous history. But to me there's something special about the Bears. That fantastic '94 team were like cricket's rock stars, with their long hair, their self-belief, the aggressive way they played, not bothered about being popular with opponents, their readiness to mix socially with our members. And they had one of the greatest batsmen of all time and a fast bowling legend the following year. I want our new crop of players to know about the 1994 players, relish their achievements and get to know them over a beer. Be inspired by them.'

Steps have been taken to remind current players and supporters of the Class of '94, even before Snowball and Giles tapped into that memorable period. All the Aylesford Hospitality Boxes were named after each of the '94 squad, and the walls are adorned with photos of that illustrious squad. In 2017 there was long overdue recognition of Bob Woolmer in one of the Aylesford boxes, rectifying a strange omission. Now, in honour of coach and captain, the Bob Woolmer and Dermot Reeve boxes are donated on day three of any Test match to the Warwickshire Old Cricketers' Association who aim to bring back WOCCA members to Edgbaston, yarning over the old days when they never made a mistake on the field. In time, conversation invariably turns to the great deeds of 1994/95 over a beer or three. The new Director of Sport Paul Farbrace has already bought into those special years and will happily continue Giles' desire of ensuring those illustrious players will never be forgotten at Edgbaston.

The past informs the present in sport. Always does, if you care to look back with respect and curiosity.

Warwickshire's championship-winning captains

Frank Foster
1911

Tom Dollery
1951

Alan Smith
1972

Dermot Reeve
1994 & 1995

Nick Knight
2004

Jim Troughton
2012

Index

25 YEARS